Praise for John Petrelli **and** Confessions of a Hollywood Trainer...

"The best trainer in the business. He keeps me in tip top condition on tour and, more importantly, he is a positive influence in my life."

—Sebastian Maniscalco, Comedian

"Training with John has literally saved and changed my life. It's a perfect fit, no pun intended. It never gets boring, as we mix it up a lot from weights to martial arts to pure fitness stuff. He keeps it real. When you train with John you are getting real life fitness and strength, not gym fitness and strength. Sure you're going to look good, but you're going to be functional, too. You'll be ready for whatever the world can throw at you. That's why we've been working out together for over a decade. He's more than a trainer; he's family."

— Ziggy Marley, Musician

"John has a unique ability for compassion, which is the ultimate form of love. I've seen him employ this ability countless times to help others overcome personal obstacles; I've seen him use it to bring out the greatness in so many people, myself included. Since the beginning of both our working relationship and our friendship he has accepted me as a person—as a human being—and in so doing given me the space and confidence to evolve into ever-better versions of myself. I know, too, that it helped him overcome his own recent challenges. I'm sure this book will be a helping hand to many, many people. Congratulations, buddy. I wish you all the best."

—Rick Yune, Actor

"My story is a long one, as I am soon to be seventy-five. But, thanks to John Petrelli, I feel like I'm forty-five. I have worked with John for almost thirteen years—to my benefit—and he has kept me focused on improving my body (and thus my mind) in many ways. His caring but disciplined approach to training is committed to excellence."

—Michael Barker, CEO & Managing Director, Barker Pacific Group

D1270358

Praise for John Petrelli *and* Confessions of a Hollywood Trainer...

"*John is the best trainer in the world, in my mind. I've trained with many people, but not anyone that I still call a good friend. The biggest thing that makes him different is how much he truly cares about you and what your goals are. And he focuses on every area of your being to help you get there. Working in Hollywood sometimes requires molding your body to fit a certain form. I can say that with John, I've never second-guessed whether I can achieve that. You're the best, brotha.*"

—Hunter Ives, Actor

"*John Petrelli is a fantastic trainer and person. He knows how to challenge his clients and keep them motivated and working toward their fitness goals. He cares about his clients and never hesitates to go the extra mile (or five) to address specific needs and concerns. As an added bonus, he is a funny and interesting guy. On days when the last thing I want to do is work out, spending an hour with John is motivation enough to get me to the gym.*"

—Jen Pollack Bianco, Writer & Photographer

CONFESSIONS
of a
HOLLYWOOD
TRAINER

CONFESSIONS

of a

HOLLYWOOD TRAINER

The JOURNEY *That* CHANGED *My* LIFE...
and the LESSONS I'VE LEARNED
That Can CHANGE YOURS

a memoir by

JOHN PETRELLI

with

SCOTT BURR

Confessions of a Hollywood Trainer: *The Journey that Changed My Life... and the Lessons I've Learned that Can Change Yours*
A Memoir By John Petrelli With Scott Burr
Copyright © 2022 John Petrelli
www.JohnPetrelli.com

Foreword
By Sebastian Maniscalco
Copyright © 2022 Sebastian Maniscalco
www. SebastianLive.com

ISBN-13 9798353329060

Independently published through Kindle Direct Publishing
https://KDP.amazon.com

Cover photo © John Petrelli
All interior photos, unless otherwise noted, from the collection of John Petrelli.

Editing, layout, format, and cover design by Scott Burr.
Connect with Scott online at www.ScottBurrAuthor.com

FOREWORD

by Sebastian Maniscalco

It is a great pleasure to be asked to write the foreword to John Petrelli's book, *Confessions of a Hollywood Trainer*. The book you are about to read was written by the man responsible for my wife and I ever crossing paths. He often reminds me of that, and I don't know if he is proud of it or he's looking for a finder's fee.

I met John in 1998, on the set of *Days of our Lives*. I was a kid fresh out of Chicago, Illinois, who moved to Los Angeles to pursue a career in entertainment.

When I met John Petrelli, I thought I was hearing my mind talk back to me. Very rarely do you run into someone that you connect with on a cultural level as well as a spiritual one. John has not only been my trainer over the last fifteen years but more importantly, he is one of my closest friends. One of the qualities that makes John Petrelli so successful—and always will—is his ability to connect with people and motivate them in ways they never thought possible. Over the years what I have learned from John is not only how to train my body but to train my mind. His work ethic is that of a mule. I have never seen a man so motivated to succeed not only for himself, but to provide his family with a better life. He unquestionably works harder than anybody I know, and he's dedicated to providing people with a road map to a healthier way of life.

I remember one time when we were on the road in San Francisco and John got to the hotel before I did. At that time we were traveling with pre-made meals, and the chicken was so frozen that John decided to blow dry it to defrost it. When I asked him why he didn't just get a microwave to the room, he told me he wanted to save me money. Until this day, I have never seen anybody blow dry food.

Enjoy this book. I have no doubt that by the end of it you will be ready to tackle any obstacle that you might face. I love you, Johnny.

Sebastian Maniscalco
Los Angeles, California
September 16, 2022

DEDICATION
and
ACKNOWLEDGMENTS

I dedicate this book to the most important people in my life: my family.

To my mother, who has always showered us with love and affection. Who has always done more than could have ever been asked or expected. Who has always given of herself selflessly.

To my father, who always wanted the best for me, even though he didn't know exactly how to express it. Who taught me that love is more powerful than anger and fear. Who taught me to be an independent man. Who taught me how to make it on my own. Who taught me that in life you learn more from mistakes than from getting it right every time.

To my wonderful sisters Gina and Rosanne. You have inspired me to be a better student of life. Thank you for making fun of me when you saw me don my first pair of posing trunks.

To my dear wife Cheyenne. You have brought me so much joy. You stuck with me when it was just me, long before it was *us*. You had faith in me and you have brought me back to faith. You blessed us with our two amazing boys, Hunter and Rocco.

To our two boys, Hunter and Rocco. For teaching me patience and a new level of love. May you gain inspiration from my journeys. Learn how to avoid the pitfalls I've made, but understand that it's okay to make mistakes. I wish for you to grow up to be men of honor as you find your way in this world. Without you I would be a different person. I wouldn't be whole. I love you for all you have done.

To my dear friends Matt, Joe, Nick, Mark, Pete, Duff, Brandon, and Sam, for being part of my adventures and making my life so much better. To my friend Rick Yune, for the inspiration. To Ziggy, for showing me a whole different side of humanity—one that has changed my perspective and shaped my decisions. To Sebastian, for making me laugh a million times over. For taking me along on your adventures and sharing experiences with me that I would have never thought possible. To Ryron, for being the kind, thoughtful, powerful human being you are and sharing your family's art with all of us. For helping me understand how to be calm in the storm, and for inspiring me to be a better teacher. Thank you also to Richard Bresler for inspiring me with your story, and for introducing me to Scott Burr. Thank you to Eric Thomas for all the early morning inspiration. Thank you to Les Brown for being a pioneer in achievement and inspirational speech, and to David Goggins and Tony Robbins for getting in my ear on the rare occasions I didn't want to show up—and for making those occasions rare indeed.

To all my clients, too many to name. Thank you for sharing your lives with me. For giving me a chance at fulfilling my passion to help. For giving a young man a new direction in life.

And lastly: to God, for being there every time I've needed You.

INTRODUCTION

Let me start off by saying: If you picked up this book looking for my latest training tips, for the top-secret method behind the madness I use to get my clients in red-carpet-event shape, or my philosophy on training, you should probably ask for a full refund now.

I have always taken my profession as a fitness coach very seriously. That being said, early on in this writing process I decided that sharing my life's journey would make a much more compelling read—more so than my going over the difference between micro- and macronutrients, or my philosophy on synergistically melding together Mixed Martial Arts with other functional training movements. (Wow, that was a mouthful... I guess I'm trying to impress you with my command of the English language before I hit you with the shitstorm of adolescent nonsense to come).

This is not to downplay what I do. If you know anything about me then you know I wouldn't do that, because the fact of the matter is that I'm not a good trainer or a great trainer. The fact of the matter is that I am—in my humble opinion—an *excellent* trainer.

Why do I say that? Because it's true. And it's true for one very simple reason: I'm never satisfied. I am always striving for growth. I'm always learning. I know for a fact that I don't have all the answers, and as a result I am constantly working to grow and improve my knowledge, my physicality, and my spirit. I'm obsessed with it. I'm obsessed with finding ways to improve every aspect of my life and the lives of those around me, my clients especially. I will do absolutely whatever it takes to help them reach their goals. I pride myself on arriving early, every day, fully prepared, with a strategic game plan. I've done this, day in and day out, for nearly thirty years.

And it is that story—the story of those thirty years, and the crazy times that came before and set me on the path my life has followed—that you'll find in the pages to come. This is my life, laid out in simple chapter and verse and told in as truthful a manner as I can manage. All of my flaws, my failures, and my strengths are here for all to see. You may like or dislike what I've written here, but I will sleep better at night knowing that honesty has been my guide.

So with that in mind, fair warning: not everything you're going to read in this book is politically correct. Not everything is sunshine and rainbows. I have not always been the good guy. Oh, and I curse a lot. I mean, a whole lot. I don't do it for shock value. What's written here is either the shit (See? Started already) that was coming out of my mouth when a particular event was happening, or it's what my twisted mind now believes I was probably saying at the time, or it just felt right when I was putting it down on paper. If I offend you: Sorry, but I'm not sorry. I can't afford to be. Growth comes from knowledge, and knowledge comes from truth, and—unfortunately or fortunately; good, bad, or indifferent—the truth doesn't care about your feelings. Yes, I swear. Yes, I've been violent. Yes, I've seen and done and experienced things that might seem unimaginable to you. I've coached some of the biggest names in the entertainment industry, and accompanied them on some incredible adventures… but I've also faced down death at the end of a gun barrel, and in the freezing waters of the north Pacific. I've lain paralyzed in a hospital bed, wondering if I would ever walk again. I've followed my foolish pride into situations that could have easily landed me in prison or the morgue. I've made mistakes. And that, more than anything else, is what I hope to impart to you in the coming pages: that we are all human and humans make mistakes, but what matters in the end is what we learn from those mistakes. I've worked diligently to understand why I made the mistakes I made in my youth, and have worked and am still working hard to grow into a better person with the benefit of that understanding. It is my humble hope that the story of the mistakes I've made and the lessons I've learned from them will, in some small way, afford you the same opportunity for insight and growth in your own life.

It is important for you to know that I've done my absolute best to retell these stories as accurately as possible. That being said, in some instances many years have passed since the event in question occurred, and I apologize in advance to anyone who was there and who remembers things differently. Also, in a couple of instances, I've combined details from events that were variations on the same theme. I've also changed some names to protect individuals' identities or to protect me from getting sued... or getting my ass kicked. Also, though much of this book is written in the past tense, I've written certain passages in the first person present tense. These were some of the most intense and impactful moments of my entire life, and I wanted us to go through them together.

All that being said, I genuinely hope you enjoy what I've written here. I hope you laugh at some of the crazy experiences I've had. I hope, humbly, to stir something inside of you, to motivate and maybe even inspire you. As with every single one of the countless clients I've worked with over the past three decades, I want you to live your life to the fullest. I want you to be healthy and happy, to love and be loved, to help and care for others, to live your dreams. All of this I wish for you. I look forward to reading the story of your life's journey one day very soon.

PART I

GROWING UP

FAMILY

For better or for worse, your family is where you come from. It's the soil from which you grow and, if you're lucky, it's the wellspring to which you can return when you're in need of support and rest. If you're lucky it's a source of strength, and bolsters you with the knowledge that you always have a home to which you can return. As I write this, I am overwhelmed with a sense of how the foundation my family created for me has shaped me into the man I've become—for better or for worse.

My mother was born in a rural part of Naples, Italy, to a family of modest means. She lived through WWII, at one point literally hiding from Nazi soldiers in an underground bomb shelter with her two older brothers and sister. When she was five her own mother encountered severe complications while giving birth, and unfortunately both my grandmother and the child passed away during the delivery. From the next room my mother listened to her mother screaming in pain as the doctor tried to deliver the baby in their home. As you can imagine, losing her own mother at such a young age impacted my mother's life tremendously, and I think it's safe to say that it played a big part in her lavishing love and affection on her own children. She knew what it was to lose a parent—to suddenly have no more time to say all the things you never got to say—and she wasn't going to miss any opportunity with her own kids. Growing up, I never had any doubt: my mother *loved* me.

My mother's older sister, Marie, came to America when she was in her twenties, and took up residence in New York City. My mother, seeking a better life and the opportunities afforded by the "Land of Promise," followed her. It was in New York that she met my father, while visiting a mutual friend for dinner. She was in her twenties and my father was forty-six, just finishing up his military career at the time. They dated for two years before they were married, in 1968, in Long Island. It was there that my sisters, Gina and Rosanne, and I were born.

When I was about four years old my parents moved us from Long Island to a small town called Frankfort, a few hundred miles Upstate. My mother's sister lived there, and my mother wanted to be closer to her family and to get us away from city life. By then my father had retired from the military, but he'd immediately gone back to work both as a volunteer firefighter for the town of Malverne and as a teller at Roosevelt Raceway in Westbury. Both Malverne and Westbury are on Long Island, and after we moved Upstate we would go for long stretches without seeing him while he put in three-month stints at the raceway. It was just my mom and us kids and, accordingly, she did it all.

My mother stands at just five feet tall, but she packs a ton of personality in her diminutive frame. Actually, that's putting it mildly. The truth is she's a stick of dynamite, a force to be reckoned with. When I was a kid I watched her play soccer against grown men in our neighborhood—and whip their asses. I watched her dig huge boulders out of our backyard to make room for a garden. When I got older she took me hunting and fishing. We had absolutely no clue what we were doing—we mostly sat out in the woods freezing our asses off—but she did it anyway, because she knew it would make me happy. That's just who she is.

For all of this, though, my mom's real gift is people: putting them at ease, making them laugh, making them feel like family. Talk to anyone who's ever spent any amount of time with her, and they'll tell you: here is a woman who is absolutely bursting with love and joy. It'll come as no surprise, then, when I tell you that back when we were growing up our house was where all the neighborhood kids hung out. The kitchen was always filled with my friends and my sisters' friends from the neighborhood. My mom was always making something for someone to eat, and the door to her kitchen was always open... even when we weren't around. Years later, long after I'd moved away, I'd often call home to find that my friends—even in my absence—were over at the house for dinner.

These days my mother's time is still filled with people: whether it's the people at church, her friends, or her grandkids, my mom is always showering those around her with her light and love. She's still always feeding people with her amazing cooking. As I write this, I realize how different my childhood would have been—how different *I* would be—without her. She raised me and my sisters with love, care, and the best of intentions—even though those good intentions sometimes became a comedy of errors—and, as you'll read in the coming pages, I returned the favor by putting her and my father through a good deal of shit while I was growing up. Nowadays, when I do my best to be a good person every day, it is with her and her goodness in mind. I love you, Mama.

I honestly don't know much about my father's childhood. He never really opened up about his past, and—given the little I do know—it's not hard to understand why. For one thing, his own father—who I never met—secretly had a second family on the side. As they say in Italian, he had a *goomah*. From this second family my father had a half-brother, of whom he almost never spoke. From the little my dad did say, I know his half-brother had a drug problem, and spent much of his life in and out of jail. I heard he passed away a few years ago. Before that, he'd been living in a New York City hostel.

My father served in the military for twenty-six years, ultimately retiring as a lieutenant colonel in the US Army. He saw combat in three wars: WWII, the Korean War, and Vietnam. I wish I knew more about these experiences, but my father simply didn't speak of them. I do remember that at least once a year he'd come down with a severe fever and spend about a week in bed sick as a dog—a side effect, he said, of his having contracted malaria while serving in Vietnam. I also have vivid memories of him screaming in his sleep as he relived some horrific wartime experience. PTSD wasn't something people talked about back then, and after so much combat experience I can only imagine what my dad suffered through in silence. As a kid, I never thought about it: I never considered the fact that he was trying to process, or at least contain, what he'd endured in the only way he knew how. As a kid it was the silence itself—how distant and cold and closed-off he seemed —that registered. If my mother was the living embodiment of warmth and love, my father seemed her polar opposite: aloof, stoic, and exceedingly sparing with his praise.

My father's military experience shaped our relationship in other ways as well: namely in that, when he wasn't ignoring me, he raised me like he was putting me through basic training. It was different for my sisters. Because I was a boy, I was held to a higher standard. I had more chores. Mistakes were punished. I couldn't ask questions. If I did, I was often made to feel stupid for asking. His word was final. I was Private First Class John Petrelli, perpetually newly-enlisted, never graduating to the next rank.

I know, I know: cry me a river, right? I'm fully aware of the fact that many, many people had and have it much, much worse than I did. I'm not here to minimize their (or your) experience, or hold up my own as some defining benchmark of childhood hardship. My objective here is simply to be truthful, to acknowledge what I understand now and didn't understand then in the hope and belief that there is something valuable to be gained from the telling.

As an adult, I've come to terms with our relationship. I understand my father better now than I ever could have then. I can understand how, between the resentment he must have felt toward his own father, his combat experience, and a childhood defined by the hardships and uncertainties of the Great Depression, emotions like love and affection must have seemed like dangerous weaknesses: vulnerabilities to be guarded and callused over. I can understand what his motivations must have been for pushing me the way he did: that he was trying to prepare me for a world that he'd often found to be harsh, brutal, and without patience or mercy. Still, the fact that I can understand all of this now does nothing to alter the fact that I didn't understand it then. It does nothing to alter the fact that for a long time my life was defined by those aspects of our dynamic that hurt the most: defined by my subconscious determination to get my father's attention and love and my own frustration and anger at my endless inability to accomplish this nearly impossible task; defined by a crippling doubt, an insidious fear and uncertainty, a creeping conviction that I just couldn't do anything right. It does nothing to alter the fact that, eventually, this fear and anger turned me into something else, something dangerous and violent, something I had to cross the country to escape.

Still, for all of this, when I consider the path my life has taken, and especially when I consider all that my parents went through, I feel very blessed that I had the childhood I had. My mother is one of the most loving people I've ever met and my father, for all his faults, was a great provider and a man of honor. I don't agree with all of his methods, but they did help shape me into the man I am today. Among other things, they filled me with a tremendous amount of resilience and determination. I thank you for that, Father.

CHILDHOOD

When we first moved to Frankfort, we lived in a small, two-bedroom apartment situated right downtown, on Main Street. It was a great spot, but as my sisters and I got older it was just too small for the five of us. Luckily, my parents were able to build a great house a short distance away, in an amazing neighborhood. For me and my sisters, it was idyllic. We didn't have to all share one bedroom anymore, there was a yard and woods for us to run and play in, and all around us in houses up and down the street and on the streets adjoining ours there were kids our age.

It was a special time. I knew every one of my neighbors, and they all knew me. My friends and I would play from sunup until the streetlights came on and our mothers called us home for dinner. We ran around in the woods and played every sport. We breathed fresh air and got our hands dirty. Every day was a new adventure. As I sit here and write this I think about my own kids, and about what it is to grow up in this modern, digital age. Nowadays it's so easy to get everything you want from behind a keyboard or a screen. You don't have to talk to anyone face-to-face, don't have to go outside your comfort zone. Back in the day, childhood was full of opportunities to step outside and challenge yourself. Disagreements on the baseball or football field ramped up to hurt feelings and physical confrontations. We learned to stand up for ourselves, broker our own peace, shake hands, and be friends again by the end of the day. Things didn't always go our way in these disputes, but we learned and we grew and we moved on. Even knocking on a friend's door to see if he could come out to play took bravery. You had to talk to his parents, had to speak up and explain yourself and what you wanted. Nowadays we all have access to any and everything we want almost instantly, we can communicate so impersonally, and I worry about what important lessons and formative experiences my kids are missing out on because of it. So much of modern life seems designed to rob us of the opportunity to develop grit: to put ourselves out there, fail miserably and get our nose rubbed in it, and then pick ourselves up, brush ourselves off, and try again with the knowledge that we may end up right back on our ass a hundred more times before we see the first glimmer of progress. I may sound like an old curmudgeon railing on about how everything was better back in my day, how kids today have it too easy, but this is how I feel. I feel like having it easy, having everything at your fingertips, at your beck and call, will actually make real life harder. Can you withstand the moments where life plays rough? My wife and I have made a conscious effort to limit the amount of exposure our kids have to the instant-gratification feedback loops that social media and video games bring with them: as far as we're concerned, a child's brain is no match for a team of engineers designing their products to be as addictive as possible. We've made a conscious effort to get them and keep them engaged with the offline world, for all its bumps, bruises, and disappointments. Like it or not, life is *not* a virtual adventure. In the woods and fields and backyards of Frankfort, New York, I learned to put myself out there, to face challenges and overcome obstacles on the way to what I wanted, to pick myself up and try again: lessons that have served me well in the decades since.

I don't have the stats to back this up, but I can tell you that when I was a kid it certainly *seemed* like Frankfort was about ninety-nine percent Italian. Our telephone book was filled with Vivaquas, Francos, Randazzos, Napolitanos... Somehow, for whatever reason, generation after generation of Italian immigrants had followed their families to this small, Upstate-New-York town. However, there's a big difference between being "of Italian descent" and being fresh off the boat, and even among all those paisans our family stood out. My sisters and I might have been born and raised in the USA, but my mom is old-school old country all the way... and that came with its own unique set of quirks. You want examples? Here's one: every fall my mother would make her own tomato sauce... by the gallon. Bushel upon bushel of fresh Roma tomatoes would fill our garage: bushels which we, over the course of a single weekend, would turn into three to four hundred jars of sauce. My sisters Gina and Rosanne would cut up tomatoes, my dad would run the press, my mom would add the salt and basil... and I, naturally, would run around getting into trouble for doing something wrong.

Want more? My mom also made her own wine... though "wine" might be a generous term for what she made. I'm pretty sure the stuff fermenting in our basement back then could have fueled the Apollo missions. The burn was so bad that you had to cut it with Seven-Up just to get it down. One time, when I was a bit older, my friends and I snuck a bottle of it out the back basement door. We thought we were so cool as we headed off into the woods to get drunk... One swig later and we were relieved of any misconceptions we might have had about making a night of it. There was simply no way in hell we were going to drink this stuff. It was like bottled gasoline. Plenty of people have snuck booze out of their parents' house, and maybe you're one of them, but how many people do you know who've had to sneak it back in?

Still want more? How about this: my mom also cured her own meat. Back when I was growing up you could walk down into our basement and find hundreds of pounds of soppressata and dry sausage hanging from the ceiling. My buddy once went down and was surprised to find himself standing face-to-face with a fifteen-pound capicola. It was business as usual in the Petrelli household, but apparently it struck him as noteworthy: after that, as far as he was concerned, our family were the "Super Dagos." If you're not familiar with that term, you should probably know that it isn't a word you want to throw around where Italians are concerned—I include it here to illustrate the point. Even in a town full of Italians, we stood out.

School provided a whole other venue for me and my sisters to experience the sometimes not-so-subtle differences between our family and the other kids'. If my mom had to write a note to the school explaining that we were going on vacation, or why we were out sick, it invariably caused a good deal of confusion on the school's end. The parts written in English they understood... the parts in Italian? Not so much. Once my sister Gina reached the age of twelve, she was put in charge of all written correspondence with the school—much to the relief, I'm sure, of all faculty involved.

School also meant lunches in the cafeteria, and here my mom truly outdid herself. Most of the other kids, even my Italian friends, would show up with your basic peanut butter and jelly sandwiches. Maybe you'd see a salami sandwich on Wonder Bread. Not the Petrelli kids. I would show up in the lunchroom with eggplant parmesan, or a mortadella and provolone sandwich on freshly-made Italian bread, straight from my mother's oven. My friends would all be eating their perfectly cut PB & Js and I'd pull out a greasy loaf of hero bread stuffed with sausage and peppers. I clearly remember several days—and this is no exaggeration—where my mom would show up at lunch time with a full, piping hot tray of pizza. I would be sitting there in class, when all of a sudden I'd hear my name over the loudspeaker: "John Petrelli, please come to the principal's office." (Do schools still even have those old public address loudspeakers? Or nowadays do they just send the kids a SnapChat?) I'd trudge down that huge hall to the office, the assistant principal would look at me over his glasses and say something like, "I don't know what she made you today, but it smells delicious," and there it would be: a full-size paper grocery bag laying sideways with a metal tray of homemade pizza inside. My mom even wrapped it in kitchen towels for added insulation. It took Domino's another thirty years to come up with the insulated delivery bag. The woman was decades ahead of her time.

Needless to say, we had the market cornered on the best lunches in the whole school... though we didn't always appreciate it at the time. You know how it is with kids. We stood out, and it was embarrassing. My sisters and I would see the other kids swapping lunches and trading snacks, but no one wanted to swap lunches with us. Crazy as it sounds, for a while all I could think about was a peanut butter and jelly sandwich on Wonder Bread. I was desperate to try one, to see what I was missing. Finally, I convinced a kid to trade me half of his sandwich for half of mine. He handed over his Wonder Bread, and I handed over my crunchy-crusted Italian. This kid took one bite of my sandwich bread and—I kid you not—*his fucking gums started bleeding*. The crust was too strong for him. Apparently soft white Wonder Bread made for soft weak gums. He took his half back before I could even take a bite.

It wasn't just the lunches that stood out: even the way we carried them to school raised eyebrows. All the other kids had cool lunch pails with characters from *Scooby Doo* and *Star Wars*... meanwhile my sisters and I brought our lunches in brown paper grocery bags. Maybe you're wondering what the big deal is—maybe you've "brown bagged" it plenty of times yourself—and if that's what you're thinking, I ask you to consider the following question: What do you think happens to a brown paper grocery bag that's stuffed with eggplant parmesan, mortadella and provolone, hot peppers, or some other form of homemade Italian goodness, and left to sit in an elementary school locker for half a day? You guessed it: by the time lunch rolled around the olive oil and juices from whatever was inside would have soaked through the bag leaving big, dark stains. I can only imagine what the other kids thought, the first time they saw us walking in. Here they were with their carefully wax-paper-wrapped sandwich triangles... and here we were, the Petrelli kids, hauling in what looked like the lunchtime equivalent of the Saint Valentine's Day Massacre.

Finally, we couldn't take it anymore. Naturally we wouldn't dare bring the issue up to our father, so we had a sit-down with our mom.

"Mom," we explained, "all the other kids have these cool lunch pails, and we've got grocery bags."

My mom felt bad. She understood our plight... or, at the very least, she understood that we weren't happy. She wanted to make it right. God bless her heart: a week later she surprised us with brand new lunch boxes. She was so excited to present them to us. She sat us down at the kitchen table, brought out a big Montgomery Ward bag, reached inside, and set them before us: three extra-large, black, metal, oval-top lunch pails.

Our jaws dropped. These things were *huge*. They were big enough to fit a full meal *and* a full-size thermos inside the dome cover. They were the same kind of lunch pail you'd see heavy equipment operators using on construction sites. These were not lunch pails for children. I could barely lift mine.

My sister started crying. My mom was so confused. She'd tried her best: she didn't understand how her efforts had come up short. We explained how the other kids all had *Scooby Doo* and *Garfield*... the construction worker edition, while an improvement over the greasy grocery bags we'd been using, didn't exactly fit the bill. Undaunted, my mom came up with a solution: when we got home from school the next day she had three glue sticks, a pair of scissors, and the Sears catalog ready. If the lunch pails she'd found didn't work as they were, then we'd make them work—with pictures cut out from the Sears catalog and pasted on.

Let me tell you: in terms of what you carry into a grade school lunchroom in Upstate New York in the 1970s, the only thing worse than an extralarge, black, metal lunch pail is an extra-large, black, metal lunch pail pasted with pictures you've cut out from the Sears catalog. My mom had told us to find pictures of things we liked, so when I arrived at school the next day my lunch pail was covered in jagged cutouts of a BB gun, a kid wearing sneakers, a basketball, matchbox cars... all with chunky white paste oozing out the sides. The other kids were ruthless; even some of the teachers were taken aback. Nobody had ever seen anything like it. I was mortified. My sisters didn't fare much better. Without intending to, my mom had taught us a valuable lesson: sometimes appreciating what you've got is all just a matter of realizing that things could always be worse. Within a week we were back to carrying our lunches in greasy grocery bags—and happy to do it.

THE BALIO FARM

When I was in sixth grade, the trajectory of my whole life changed. My sister Gina was taking horseback riding lessons, and one day I had to go with my mother to pick her up. I don't remember why I had to come, or what I wanted to be doing instead; what I do remember is being introduced to the owners of that horse farm, Cosmo and Angie Balio, who treated me like family from the moment they met me. They soon became the grandparents my sisters and I never had.

My father didn't get married until he was forty-eight, and his parents had already passed away by the time I was born. My mother's father had stayed in Italy, and he also passed away when I was very young. Cosmo and Angie filled that void. Couple that with the fact that their farm—with its bass ponds, trout streams, and hundreds of acres of woods—was like heaven on earth to a sixth-grade boy, and it wasn't too long before their farm became the only place I wanted to be. I was constantly begging my parents to take me there. After a while they started simply dropping me off on summer mornings and picking me up again at night. The whole day in between would be filled with adventure.

Looking back on it now, I see that it was during my time on the Balios' farm that I developed the resilience and determination that would serve me later in life. As I've said, pleasing my father was no easy task, and this steady diet of disapproval was slowly convincing me that, if I couldn't do anything right, then there was no reason to even try in the first place. On the Balios' farm, however, I always felt like my persistence *could* pay off, no matter how long the road, and—even in my lowest moments—that sense of resolve never fully left me. Thinking back now on the things I did there, it's clear to me just how powerful this sense was. For example: I started bowhunting around the age of twelve, and didn't harvest a single deer until I was an adult in my mid-twenties. If I hadn't believed somewhere deep down that one day all of my effort and patience would be rewarded, I would have quit early on. Want another example? My buddy Eric and I once spent an entire summer break fishing, and we only managed to catch *one fish*. That poor fish didn't meet its end on a hook, either: after a long, hot day without a single bite we decided to go swimming, and an extremely unlucky rainbow trout fell prey to the massive impact of my buddy's cannonball.

If persistence is simply the willingness to put in work—a lot of work—for the sake of a far-off reward, then the Balios' farm was the perfect place for young John Petrelli to study the practice in depth. Hunting and fishing took patience and effort, but I also earned my hunting and fishing privileges by mucking horse stalls, baling hay, and doing any and every other odd job the Balios asked of me. In the winters, before heading out into the woods after deer, I would go into the barn and shovel frozen horseshit. If you've never done it, let me tell you: shoveling frozen horseshit is a true treat. You start by heating the stall with a portable propane heater—if you don't do this, there's no way to break the frozen turds free from the frozen ground underneath. You then chip away at the turd-berg with the tip of a pointed shovel until you've cleaved off chunks small enough to move. It's a messy process that sends small bits of horseshit flying everywhere, and somehow— no matter how careful you are—at least one piece *will* land on your face. In fact, on one extremely lucky day, a chunk of frozen turd flew right into my mouth. Still, not even flying shards of frozen horseshit were enough to keep me from going hunting. Nowadays the thought of it almost makes me gag; back then, though, I felt like it was a small price to pay.

When cold weather finally gave way to spring and the beautiful Upstate

New York summers, it was time to move out of the stalls and into the fields for the prime job of baling hay. If you've never had the privilege, let me tell you: you're in high cotton if you're baling hay. On the farm the combine would hit the field at daybreak and make quick work of the standing hay. Then the tractor with a hay baler attachment would go through gathering up the cut hay, forming it into bales, binding the bales with twine, and launching them into the trailer. Back before I was old enough to run any of the equipment, my first job was to ride along in the trailer and arrange the newly-bundled bales into neat rows and stacks. The baler set the pace and you had to work quickly, as there was always another bale being launched your way. Start loafing on the job and you were liable to catch a bale in the back of the head. Once the trailer was loaded with a couple hundred bales we hauled it to the barn and unloaded the bales into the loft... and then we'd head back out for the next round. We would repeat this process over and over until sundown, sweating in the muggy Upstate summer heat for five bucks an hour. Easily one of the hardest jobs I've ever done... but also one of the most rewarding. There's no feeling in the world like the one you get staring at a once empty hayloft now stuffed to the rafters, feeling the ache in your back and arms and knowing that *you did that.*

Growing up, you're still learning who you are. New experiences and new challenges are still revealing you to yourself in often unexpected ways. These revelations shape your sense of self, and build the identity you carry out into the world. In my time on the Balios' farm, I learned the things about myself that would form the foundation I returned to when all else failed: when the person I'd become was primed and ready to ruin not only my life but also any chance I had of making a better one. I learned that I had something powerful inside me that simply wouldn't let me quit, and that when I tapped into it I was capable of more than I'd ever imagined. I learned that I could push myself harder, could endure more, could negotiate and overcome any obstacle that stood between me and my goal. As you'll soon see, in the years that followed my challenge would lie in channelling that will and energy into something positive.

JUNIOR HIGH, SOCCER, AND TAEKWONDO

I was decently athletic growing up. I wasn't a standout—I'd say I was average at most sports—except when it came to soccer. In a word, when it came to soccer, I was *excellent*. I was easily the best player on the field and —given the caliber of our team—that was saying something. During my sixth grade season we shut out every team we played and won first place in our league. Our coach had a great strategy: he had me play goalie for the first half of the game, where I would shut down every shot attempt from the other team. Then, in the second half, he'd slide me to center forward. At that point I was the freshest player on the field, not having run in the first part of the game, and I could pretty much score at will.

It felt great to win, and even better to be good at something that I enjoyed: the only problem was that soccer didn't get the attention the other sports did. In our area it was basically the bastard child of sports. It wasn't just ignored—it was actively discouraged. At one point my baseball coach told me point blank that if I played soccer I would ride the bench in baseball—crazy to think of that happening in today's world. Still, it wasn't like any of that was going to stop me. I loved playing, even if nobody else gave a shit. If you'd asked me then, I think I probably would have told you that I was going to keep playing soccer as long as I could, through the end of high school and beyond. But junior high is a time of change, and soon the natural way of things would alter my feelings toward the sport, in ways I could not have anticipated.

What does that mean? It means that I showed up to the first day of seventh grade to discover that, over summer break, all of my classmates had turned into giants. Boys in my class had shot up several inches, and some of them were even sporting thin mustaches and hair on their legs. I'd always been smaller than a lot of the other kids, but this was another level. Now they all towered over me. I was still a standout in soccer—I was small but I was fast and I absolutely refused to quit—but my performance in sports like baseball and basketball—the sports that actually mattered in our town—suffered. I just couldn't compete physically with kids already growing into early adulthood. To make matters worse, because of my small size relative to the other kids, my mom now expressly forbid me from playing football. Football was the coolest of sports. All the Pop Warner football players had beautiful maroon-colored jackets with their names on the back. In soccer, all we had were *teeshirts*. No names on the backs, no nothing. And football had cheerleaders. Cheerleaders in their short skirts and tight tops, doing splits and screaming the football players' names from the sideline... Soccer didn't have cheerleaders. Shit, we didn't even have *spectators*. No one came to our games, not even the parents of the kids who were playing. In all the years I played I don't think my parents even came to a single game. By this time my mom and dad had opened a combination grocery store and pizzeria, so my mom was always busy working the oven and running the cash register, and my dad... well, you can guess how interested he was. All I knew was that whenever I took the soccer field he was somewhere else—probably off at a Pop Warner football game with everyone else.

I wish I had a video of me playing soccer back then. That season we'd picked up a really good full-time goalie, a kid from the eighth grade, so I got to play forward all the time, and I was a scoring machine. We ended up winning our division, and I led the league in goals. Still, despite our winning record and my personal goal tally, I actually had no idea how good I was. I lacked self-confidence, lacked the kind of healthy pride I could and should have felt for my on-field successes. The fact that nobody watched us

Left to right: My mom, my sister Gina, me, and my sister Rosanne at my mom's grocery store. Check out that bowl cut.

play was actually fine with me. I didn't want the attention. The day after we won the league, I remember the principal coming on the loudspeaker during the morning announcements to congratulate us. He concluded by saying, "I'd also like to congratulate John Petrelli for scoring three goals in the winning game, and leading the league in scoring this year." I remember sinking down in my chair as everyone looked at me. I remember wishing I could just disappear.

Aside from my mother banning me from playing football, the sudden and dramatic difference in size between me and my classmates brought other problems as well. I became an easy target for bullies. To be fair, I'm sure my big mouth didn't help the situation. There were many days that year when I was beat up or chased home.

As you can imagine, at the time all this bullying felt lousy. Looking back on it now, though, I'm almost grateful for it. It led me to something that would become a huge source of positivity throughout my life: martial arts. A couple of my friends had started taking classes at a local Taekwondo school, and after months of insults and ass kickings I wanted to learn to fight more than anything. I begged my parents to let me start taking classes, and even promised to pay part of the tuition with my paper route money. After much begging, they finally agreed.

I really took to the training. At first I had no sense of how good or bad I was—all I knew was that I had some scores to settle. Soon, though, it became clear that I had a natural talent for the practice. After about six months of training I received my first promotion, to yellow belt, which allowed me to spar for the first time. Sparring at this school—like at most if not all Taekwondo schools—meant point sparring: no contact to the face, light contact to the body, and any significant strike to the target areas of the body would result in a stoppage by the referee to note and tally the point. I walked into my first class not exactly sure what to expect... and proceeded to beat everybody they put in front of me. It was a high unlike anything I'd ever experienced. I was a star in soccer, but any victory on the field was a team victory. This was all me. I immediately wanted more. Luckily the school was holding their annual tournament the next weekend. I signed up, and that Saturday my friend's parents drove the two of us and another friend who also trained over to the tournament; when they dropped me off at home again that night I was carrying the first place trophy. With only one sparring class under my belt I'd gone undefeated, 7-0, and won my division. That trophy is still collecting dust somewhere in my mom's basement, along with the VHS tape of my fights that my friend's parents were kind enough to record.

Understand: the point isn't that I was some great fighter, Upstate New York's answer to Bruce Lee. I certainly wasn't. I was one of the best in my school, but that's not saying much. The point is that, after nearly a year of almost constant bullying and a lifetime of being told by my father that I didn't measure up, excelling in Taekwondo meant a lot to me. Up to that point soccer was the only thing I was really any good at... and nobody gave a shit about soccer. Taekwondo wasn't football, but—in my mind at least—it had some of the "cool" factor that soccer lacked. These days, with a hefty number of street fights behind me (more on that later) and having trained in a variety of martial arts styles, including Gracie Jiu-Jitsu, I can see this training for what it was. We weren't badass ninjas: we were kids playing a stylized game of tag in dipped-foam gear. Still, I wouldn't trade those experiences for the world. They gave me a reason to hold my head a little bit higher at a time in my life when reasons to hold my head up were in woefully short supply.

HIGH SCHOOL, BASKETBALL, AND EDDIE BIANCHI'S IRON REFUGE

My parents had sent my older sister, Gina, to a Catholic high school located about twenty minutes from our house, and it was understood that, when the time came, my younger sister, Rosanne, and I would follow in her footsteps. I don't remember thinking too much about it at the time—my father's word was law—but looking back it doesn't make much sense. We weren't any more Catholic than any of the other families in our neighborhood, or a lot of the kids in my regular school. In fact, almost all of my friends were raised Catholic. I have to assume it was because my parents thought we'd get a better education—though in my case, the point would prove to be moot.

When it came to soccer, eighth grade had been more of the same: even though I stood at barely five-foot-nothing with cleats on, I led the whole league in scoring. That tenacity I'd discovered on the Balios' farm was in full effect: I ran harder, fought harder for the ball, and continued pushing when the other players got tired. Still, when it came time to go out for my new school's soccer team, I decided to sit it out. Part of this was a lack of discipline combined with good ol'-fashioned teenage laziness—the team started practicing before school started, over summer break, and I didn't want to give up part of my vacation—but the real core of it was ego-related: I was set to meet a whole crop of new classmates, and I didn't want to be known as a dorky soccer player right off the bat. Going to a new high school meant that I had an opportunity to reinvent myself, and I wasn't about to pass it up. So, even though I loved playing soccer, I gave it up. My ego really was that fragile.

Of course, the truth was that there was only so much I could reinvent. I'd given up soccer but, old school or new school, I was still one of the smallest kids in my class. I hadn't gone through puberty by the time freshman year began, and I walked through the doors standing four-foot-eleven and weighing in at less than a hundred pounds. Top that off with the fact that my mom still cut my hair—into what I think is still called a "bowl cut"—and you can just picture what a chick magnet I was.

Despite my small stature, the only sport I tried out for my freshman year was—you ready for this?—basketball. Fucking *basketball*. You probably won't be surprised to learn that I didn't make the cut. It was easy enough for me to write this failure off—it was easy enough for me to tell myself that my height was the problem, that it was out of my hands—but the truth is that I also wasn't prepared. I hadn't put in the work required to develop the skills that would have helped me overcome my physical limitations and deficits. At that time, I didn't want to see this; at the time it was easier for me to blame things that were out of my control—luck, genetics, whatever—than it was to own up to the part I played in my own lack of success. By the time sophomore year rolled around, I was no better: once again I opted out of soccer, and once again I failed to make the cut in basketball—and in every other sport I went out for. John Petrelli, the former soccer standout, was on a serious slide athletically. On top of that, my grades were horrible. I was barely passing most of my classes.

Looking back on it now, I believe my grades suffered due to a severe lack of effort and focus. Simply put, that tenacity I'd discovered on the Balios' farm and that I'd previously practiced on the soccer field was now nowhere to be found. And, looking back, I can see why: that tenacity and drive had nowhere to point itself. I had no goal I was after, no future success I could picture that I was aiming for. Also, although I've never been officially diagnosed, I'm pretty sure I have some form of dyslexia. I flip numbers and letters around all the time. My spelling is still so bad that spellcheck often has no fucking clue what I'm trying to say. Not that that explains my grades: in the years since I've certainly buckled down and made the grade despite the quirks of my particular learning style. The simple fact is that the victim mindset I'd used to excuse my failures at basketball tryouts now informed the way I thought about nearly everything in my life. Whether it was sports or academics, my failures were always due to factors outside my control. Some of this was good ol' fashion teenage immaturity—making excuses and blaming everyone but myself—but looking back I can see how this also had a lot to do with my relationship with my father. All of my mistakes and insufficiencies, my bad grades and athletic failures, presented further opportunities for my father to express in no uncertain terms just how stupid he thought I was. They all presented him with new opportunities to convey his disappointment, and these messages—combined with my own feelings about my athletic and academic failures—were steadily convincing me that I was just no good: that I truly couldn't do anything right.

Then, the summer before my junior year, something crazy happened. I started to grow. All of a sudden, seemingly out of nowhere, none of my clothes fit anymore. I must have grown nine inches in three months. And this growth spurt couldn't have come at a better time: despite the battering my sense of self-worth had taken and my mounting frustration I'd decided— I was determined—that this year *I was finally going to make the basketball team*. I trained all summer long. I'd seen an ad in the back of a magazine for what the manufacturer called "The Sky Walker Kit": for $29.99 you too could learn the secret method for training your body to jump higher. The seller guaranteed that their system would increase your vertical jump by four inches. It seemed like just the thing to give me the edge I was lacking, so I gave the money to my parents and they wrote me a check. I mailed in the order form, and every day I waited eagerly for the mail to come. A couple of weeks later, the package finally arrived; I tore it open like it was Christmas morning. Inside was a short pamphlet outlining a program of about ten exercises I was to perform every day. I immediately went to work. I remember the instructions had me make a piece of equipment using a rope and cut-up pieces of garden hose—a kind of rudimentary isometric trainer. So there I was, every day, all summer, out in the driveway doing isometric exercises with a rope and garden hose. My sisters had an absolute field day cracking jokes at me. I can only imagine what the neighbors thought. I didn't care, though. I had finally regained my focus. I had a clear goal at which I could channel my inner drive.

The program also required me to jump and try to touch something that was just out of my reach. I jumped all the time. First with my right foot, then with my left foot, then with both feet, then with my right foot, then with my left foot… you get the picture. I became a jumping fool… which is exactly what my father called me. I can clearly remember trying to jump and touch the ceiling at various places around our house and my father looking up from whatever he was doing to say, "Hey look, it's the jumping fool." His words hurt, as they always did, but I wasn't deterred: for the first time in a long time, I had my sights set on a goal. I was going to make the basketball team, and nothing was going to stop me.

After my garden hose workout and jumping routine I'd head over to the local track to run, and then it was off to the gym. At that time, all the kids in my neighborhood worked out at the same place. A local tough guy and former club boxer named Eddie Bianchi had turned the basement of his house into the best weight room around. It was crude, with asbestos on the ceiling, rusty metal weights, and a dirt floor, but to us it was perfect. It had grit.

Eddie was a collector for some low-level mob guys, and when they all got pinched he kept his mouth shut and took the rap. He was truly a sweet guy, the classic Rocky Balboa type; he had a huge heart of gold but he wasn't very well-educated, and he was easily manipulated. The mob guys took full advantage of him, and they convinced him that taking the fall for them was the right thing to do. Eddie went without saying a word, but he was so kind that when he went away he left the door to his basement unlocked so that every kid in the neighborhood could still get in and use the equipment while he was locked up.

It's hard to imagine what all of us kids would have gotten into if not for Eddie's basement gym. For myself, I know that it became an escape: a place where I could go to get away from the endless ragging I took at school and at home. For others, I'm sure it kept them out of trouble. I think Eddie understood on some level that giving us access to the gym might help us channel our energies into something positive, and help us steer clear of the path that had put him on the wrong side of the law. Whether he understood this or not, though, there's no denying that I and the others owe Eddie big time. That gym was a Godsend for so many of us. A place where you can build yourself up, find community, work out your aggressions, and do it all while inhaling a nice dose of cancerous asbestos? Well, that's a very hard thing to find.

In terms of the training we did and the equipment he had, Eddie was decades ahead of his time. He'd built weighted dog sleds with harnesses that we pulled through the backyard. He filled wheel barrels with rocks and rusty old weights and had us push them up and down the street. This was functional training before functional training was even a thing. Between my training at Eddie's, the martial arts classes I was taking several times a week, and my efforts with the Sky Walker Kit, I showed up for my junior year of high school a new man. I was about five foot nine now, and I'd finally put on a bit of muscle. Also, the Sky Walker Kit had really worked. Up to this point I could hardly jump up and touch the basketball net; now I could fly through the air and dunk a tennis ball. In fact, I was so obsessed with dunking tennis balls that I would do it until my hands bled. I still wasn't much to look at, but inside I felt like a testosterone-driven athletic monster.

Junior year meant other big changes, too. I was sixteen with a driver's license now, and my parents saw to it that I had a hot new ride to go along with it: a burnt orange 1982 Subaru five-speed hatchback. They say beggars can't be choosers, and I was thrilled to have my own ride, but I'd be lying if I told you that my teenage brain wasn't painfully aware of the fact that this thing did nothing to improve my image. Simply put, there was no way to pass the Subaru off as cool. No amount of washing or waxing could change what it was. On top of that, the Subaru had no tape deck, which meant that if I wanted some control over the tunes in my hot new ride I had to lug along a boombox full of about twenty pounds' worth of Duracell "D" batteries. Also, the thing was in pretty rough shape. Years and years of Upstate New York winters had rusted the undercarriage to the point that you could literally see the road going by underneath you through a hole in the driver's side floor. Still, I loved that car. It allowed me a degree of freedom that I had never experienced. It allowed me to drive over to the next town and visit my friends whenever I wanted, allowed me to grab my fishing pole and go explore new streams whenever I got the itch. I felt like the man: driving along, my boombox riding shotgun and blasting U2's "Where the Streets Have No Name." Out away from home and the kids at school, out on my own on the road, I felt like the future was wide open: like the world was mine for the taking, and my life could be whatever I wanted it to be.

Life, it seems, had other plans.

Through the summer I'd had my sights set on the varsity basketball team, but at some point I'd realized that I had another item lurking on my list as well. I'd been avoiding it for long enough, and now the moment had come: it was time for John Petrelli the soccer superstar to make his triumphant return.

I showed up at tryouts and easily made the team... and things went downhill from there. For one thing, the team wasn't all that great. After playing on teams that dominated the league all through middle school, I had a hard time reconciling myself to the fact that, in all likelihood, there would be no championship to offset the bitter pill of our area's general disinterest in the sport. On top of that, we had to share our practice field with the football team... and they made it clear right from the very start who the alpha sport was. At least now I knew how to fight: if push ever came to shove, I told myself, I'd have no trouble kicking some football player's ass.

If the problems had been just with the level of the team or just with the football players, I think I might have felt differently. The truth was, though, that these issues were relatively insignificant compared to the main one: the coach had me in at right forward, back in the position where I'd been a dominant force on the field, but in the two years since I'd last touched a soccer ball everyone else on the other teams had caught up to and surpassed my skill level. In game after game we were—and I was—simply outclassed. We got our asses handed to us over and over and over again. It was a shock. I'd quit soccer as the star player on an undefeated team: now I was an average player on a winless team. I'd previously been able to score nearly at will; now, despite taking plenty of shots on the goal, I didn't score once. Not a single goal. It wore me down. It sapped my enthusiasm and my resolve, and so halfway through the season I up and quit. And when I say quit, I mean I just walked away. I didn't even talk to the coach about it. One day I just stopped showing up. I'm honestly embarrassed to even talk about it now. It was a total loser move, and I knew it. Still, I managed to put it out of

37

my mind. I had other plans. I wasn't going to be a dork on a winless dorky team playing a dorky sport anymore: I was going to play on the varsity basketball team. All of the hard work I'd put in over the summer was about to pay off big time. Everyone would see how good the new and improved John Petrelli was, and I was finally going to show my pops what I could do. I was going to make the team in a sport that he felt was worthy of his attention.

The tryouts for the basketball team consisted of two days of conditioning, running plays and drills, and scrimmages. All of my close friends were already on the team, and had been playing together for the past two years. By comparison, I was a fish out of water. Still, there were a few open spots in the lineup, and I felt like I had the skills and the physical ability to take one of them.

The first day of tryouts went pretty well. Afterwards one of my friends who played center for the team told me that the head coach had actually pulled him aside and asked about me. He actually asked where I'd come from: I'd been so unimpressive in my freshman and sophomore year tryouts that he didn't remember me at all. Well, that was fine with me: as long as I had his attention now.

Back then, the coaches announced the team by posting a list of names outside the athletic office door. After the final day of tryouts, the word went around that the list was up, and we all went down to check. I felt like I'd done enough to make the team, but I was still nervous as all hell to go read the names posted on the board. I scanned the sheet. All the familiar names were there from the previous year's team... but not mine.

Hold on, I thought. My name had to be there. I must have just missed it. I scanned the sheet again and again. Each time the same harsh reality stared back at me. I was crushed. I had worked so hard and for so long, and I still hadn't made the grade. It took everything I had to hold back tears as my friends tried to console me. The truth is that I barely even heard them: my own thoughts were echoing loud in my ears. *I'm never good enough*, I thought. *Not for my father, not for my teachers, not for basketball, not even for soccer.*

Inside, my hurt and frustration and disappointment were crystalizing into anger.

At that moment the office door opened, and the head basketball coach was standing there. He beckoned to me.

"Petrelli," he said, "come on in here. I'd like to speak with you."

I went inside. All my friends walked away to give us some privacy. I was alone with the coach. Standing there before him, all of my anger and sorrow collapsed into fear. It's crazy to think about it now, but in that moment I was overcome with fear of this sixty-year-old man. Or maybe it's not so crazy. In that moment this guy held my entire self-worth in the palm of his hand: he had the absolute authority to decide whether I was or wasn't *good enough.* I took the chair he offered me and sat there in silence, awaiting his judgment.

"I know you worked hard to make the team," he began, "and I'm sorry there isn't a spot for you. That being said, I talked to the other coaches, and we decided we'd like you to try out for the JV team. Are you interested?"

The storm clouds parted, and a ray of consoling sunlight shone through. My mind latched onto it, and began to rebuild itself: it hadn't all been a waste of time. The coach had seen my efforts. There were factors outside my control, a limited number of spots, but he still wanted me to play. Several of the other kids who'd tried out didn't make the varsity squad either, but as far as I could tell I was the only one being asked to come back and try out for the JV team.

"Thank you!" I said to the coach. "Yes, of course I'm interested! I would very much like to do that. Thank you!"

I was excited the whole drive home. My orange Subaru might as well have been a Corvette. When I got home my mom was there waiting to hear if I'd made the team. I was excited to tell her what had happened. I hadn't made the varsity team, I told her, but the coach had asked me to come back and try out for the JV team. Maybe, I told her, when they saw how well I did at JV, they would pull me up to the varsity squad. And sure, maybe that last part was all a fantasy that I'd made up in my head on the ride home, but so what? The coach hadn't said it *couldn't* happen. It *could* happen. In fact, I was sure it was *going* to happen. I was going to make it happen.

My mom didn't see this consolation prize as good news, though. She'd had her hopes set on me making the team as much as I had.

"If they don't want you on da big team," she said, in her heavily Italian-accented English, "I would tell them to go to hell!"

It wasn't that she wasn't happy for me. She knew I was disappointed, and she was trying to protect me in the best way she knew how. I was all right, though: in that moment I was genuinely excited to try out for the JV team. I really believed that, if I could just get out on the court and play, the coaches would see and recognize where I really belonged.

Of course, my dad had his own take on the situation. The next morning, over breakfast, he looked up from his plate and said simply, "All that jumping around, and you still didn't make the team."

To be fair to my dad, I think he was at least halfway joking. The problem was, of course, that the punchline carried the same cargo as his criticisms: I was an idiot who couldn't do anything right. His words stung, but I did my best to put them out of my mind. JV tryouts were set to take place over the next two nights, and I was going to show him and everybody else. When the hour finally came I stepped on the court with a chip on my shoulder and played like there was no tomorrow. I scored a bunch of points, grabbed a ton of rebounds, and hustled my ass off. Even when the coaches tried to put extra pressure on me during the conditioning drills, I put my head down and performed. Several times while we were running suicides—a drill where you sprint to touch the various lines on the basketball floor—I'd finish first. Once the last player finished, the coaches would yell, "We're all going to run that again, because Petrelli didn't touch the last line." I guess they were trying to see what my attitude would be, trying to see how I would react. I was potentially going to be the only junior on this team of underclassmen, and they needed to see how I'd jell with the other kids. I kept my mouth shut and just kept running. Nothing was going to stop me from making this team. The second tryout took place the next night, and it was more of the same. I hustled, rebounded, and scored. I kept my mouth shut and I worked.

I expected that the coaches would once again post a sheet outside the office door with the season's roster, but at the end of the second tryout the coaches informed us that they would be handling things differently. Everyone who'd tried out would get a phone call on Saturday morning letting them know the results, and those who'd made the cut would have their first practice later that day.

Before I left, one of the coaches pulled me aside.

"You know," he said, "if you make the team, you're going to be playing with mostly sophomores. We'll even have one freshman on the team. Are you sure you can handle that?"

Looking back on it now, I wonder what he saw—what he knew—that I didn't. In that moment I thought I knew exactly what I wanted, and I told him so. I told him yes, that I didn't care, that I just wanted to play. No matter who else made the cut, I said, I wanted to be on the team.

I drove home exhausted from the tryouts. As I lay in bed trying to sleep, though, I kept thinking about what the coach had said. I thought about playing on a team with a freshman. I thought about how my mom had reacted when I told her that I hadn't made the varsity squad. All of a sudden, laying there, playing on the JV team didn't seem so great. I'd pictured a spot on that team as some great prize to be won, an affirmation of my value and an acknowledgement of my efforts, but laying there it didn't seem like a prize at all. Would making the JV team, or even getting bumped up from JV to varsity, really change anything? All of the doubts and fears I'd managed to push from my mind now felt like they were just beneath the surface, ready and eager to rise up and take over. I tossed and turned all night.

My parents woke me up early the next morning with the news that there was a phone call for me. I walked out into the kitchen half asleep and lifted the receiver.

"Hello?" I said.

"Congratulations," I heard the coach say, "we'd like you to play on our team."

I looked around. Everyone was there in the kitchen with me. My mom and dad and sisters were watching me expectantly, eager to hear the news. For one brief moment it felt like everything I'd worked so hard for was finally coming together: the Sky Walker Kit, the hours of running and lifting weights. Finally I was going to show everyone that I was good enough. I was going to be a superstar on JV, and before the season was over I'd get pulled up to varsity where I'd show everyone that I belonged. I was finally going to play on a team that had cheerleaders in short skirts doing cartwheels and back handsprings.

"Thank you," I told the coach, "but I've decided not to play."

For a moment there was silence on the other end of the line. Then the coach cleared his throat.

"Okay," he said. "I understand."

I thanked him again, and hung up.

TOUGH GUY

He didn't understand, though. I knew he didn't. How could he? How could he understand that I'd built this thing up fantastically in my mind, that I'd convinced myself that making the JV team would somehow fix and absolve everything inside me that was lacking, that it would prove that I was finally good enough, that I was worthy? And how could he understand that laying in bed that night after tryouts, this vision had collapsed: that I'd understood that making the JV team didn't mean anything, that it wouldn't change anything, that at best it would mean I was second rate again, the only junior on a team full of sophomores. How could he understand that what had felt like an accomplishment had soured in my mind into nothing but a towering disappointment, another item on the laundry list of situations in which I'd failed to measure up? No, he didn't understand. No one did. To be fair to them, though, neither did I. I wouldn't understand for years and years. At the time, all I knew was that no matter what I did or how hard I tried, nothing made a bit of fucking difference. All I knew was that I was angry all the time, and I couldn't think of a good reason to hold it in anymore. If I was going to fuck up anyway, then I was going to fuck up with flying colors.

I started getting into fights. A *lot* of fights. I got into fights over anything and everything. Simple nonsense, plain bullshit. I'm in class and I pull the chair out from under the girl sitting next to me, thinking it'll be funny. It's not. She's so pissed and embarrassed that she starts crying. We've been friends for three years, and now that friendship is over. Her boyfriend goes to another high school, and when he hears about what happened he wants to kick my ass. He's waiting for me the next day in the parking lot. He cracks me on the chin, but I pull his sweatshirt over his head and get the better of him. A couple of weeks later two of my buddies and I stop at a gas station on our way to a high school hockey game. I head in to pay for the gas, and when I come back out I see my buddies jawing it out with about ten guys from a rival high school. Without saying a word, I go into the trunk of my car and I pull out a baseball bat. I walk up to the group and I throw the bat down at their feet. I dare them to pick it up. I beg them to try and use it against us. I let them know they're going to have to kill me if they want to win. Luckily no one takes me up on my offer. It wouldn't have changed anything if they had. Even losing—badly—doesn't stop me. On one occasion I'm at a club in a rougher part of town. I've got absolutely no business being there, especially by myself, but that's all part of the fun. I'm playing foosball when a much bigger guy grabs the ball off the table and tells me that my time is up. I stand my ground and tell him I'm not leaving. He stares me down and then throws the foosball back on the table. I go right back to playing. I don't even see the punch coming. I don't know anything about it until it connects with the side of my head. My feet fly out from under me and my right temple violently collides with one of the foosball rod handles. The impact somehow knocks me unconscious and snaps me back up to my feet. If you've watched any MMA or boxing you've seen this phenomenon in action. I'm literally out on my feet. I take several more punches before the bouncers jump in to save me. I go to school the next day with a black eye and a huge knot on my right temple... and somehow that just adds fuel to the fire. Getting my ass kicked by a known local tough guy adds to the persona that I'm steadily creating. I'm a tough guy, a fighter, a fucking animal. Nobody can tell me nothing.

On the outside I looked confident and dangerous, but inside these confrontations filled me with fear. This fear would build to an almost unbearable level in the moments right before the fight, and the first contact, when it finally came, was like a pressure valve releasing. The adrenaline rush I felt in those moments was unlike anything else I'd ever experienced. It felt *so good*. All of the fear and frustration I felt dealing with my father, all of the anger I'd been bottling up for years and years would suddenly resolve itself in a moment of perfect, blinding release. It was like a drug, a temporary reprieve from all the shame and self-loathing I felt. And yet, as with any drug, the use itself perpetuated the need: I knew what I was doing was wrong, knew it was destructive and toxic, knew that I was becoming someone I didn't want to be. Each fight left me feeling worse than before, left me with another mark against me in the big book of my fuckups and failures. And yet: what else was there? Nothing I did was ever good enough: not with my dad, not with my teachers, not with my coaches. Being a tough guy made me somebody my friends celebrated, somebody the other kids respected, somebody the girls would talk to. Steadily, brick by brick, I was building a prison for myself which each new exploit made it harder and harder to escape.

FIREWORKS OVER UTICA

Despite my shit grades and my bad behavior, I somehow graduated from high school. Don't ask me how. I'm convinced that some of my teachers passed me just so that they wouldn't have to deal with me for another year. Now it's summer break, and my friends and I have only a handful of weeks to hang out and revel in our late-teen freedom before we all head off to our various colleges. They're all bound for greener pastures: prestigious universities, sports scholarships... then there's me. I'm scheduled to start classes in the fall at the local community college, the only school that would take me. Not that that came as any great surprise: like I said, my grades were horrible, and my SAT scores weren't any better. Back then I had a standing joke with my friends: What did I get on my SATs? I got marinara sauce on them, because I was eating a slice of pizza while I took the test. I have no idea now what my actual score was, but I do know that it was *terrible*. Clearly, I'm on a different path from my friends... though I have no idea how different my path is about to become.

After all those years of being an undersized dork I feel like I've got a lot of catching up to do, and I'm doing it. My friends and I spend that summer going to as many parties as we can. Several of the local clubs are eighteen and older, and we become regulars. My best friend and I are working as busboys at a local high-end restaurant, and all that summer cases of beer somehow find their way out the kitchen door and into the trunk of our cars. Every second we're not working we're partying, chasing girls, and fighting. The clock is ticking, and we don't want to waste a single moment.

Finally it's late August, the last week of summer, and we're all out for one last big night. A half-dozen of us guys are hanging out at a festival put on by the city of Utica called, descriptively, "Fireworks Over Utica." By evening the festival is in full swing, and the streets are mobbed. People are enjoying the event, taking in all it has to offer, having a good time. But this is also a weird time in New York: "wilding" has become a thing, and is making its ugly presence felt at the festival. For those of you who don't know or don't remember, "wilding" was a thing where groups of young, degenerate males would attack unsuspecting people for no reason at all. It wasn't about answering a provocation, it wasn't about theft: it was nothing but misguided, tragic shitbags hopped up on testosterone "expressing themselves" in outbursts of unjustifiable violence... and plenty of them are "expressing themselves" tonight at the festival. During the fireworks show alone, I see a bunch of guys get knocked out cold. I specifically remember this one local tough guy blasting this big, shaggy-looking guy, who looked like he'd come straight from a Grateful Dead concert, right in the face for just accidentally bumping into him. *Blam!* One punch to the temple, and Grateful Dead drops like a felled redwood. As soon as he hits the ground, random people start attacking him. They just jump on him like wolves. Seeing this hurts my heart, but I'm too much of a coward to go against my tough guy persona and say anything—let alone do anything—to help. I just stand there and watch.

The tension in the air is so high that it's almost nauseating, and as the night goes on it only gets worse. The local police are clearly and woefully unprepared for the massive crowd that has shown up, and any semblance of order is strained to the breaking point. People are flooding the streets with total disregard for direction, for the cops, for oncoming traffic. Then somebody throws a bottle, and the next thing you know bottles are flying left and right. Glass is shattering everywhere. People are shouting, running, jostling each other and starting fights. It's totally chaotic, boiling right up to the edge of a total breakdown into general violence. And me? I feel right at home. The anger that's always festering in the dark places in my mind is just begging to be let loose, to jump in and join the melee. And who knows? On any other night I probably would have let it happen. The thing is, though, tonight we've got other plans. We're due to crash a party in the next town over. It's our best and likely last chance to get drunk, get some ass, and break some shit before we go our separate ways, and we're not going to miss it for some bullshit mosh pit. We've got places to be.

Somehow, even with everything that's going on, we make it the few blocks back to where I'd (illegally) parked my car without incident. Actually, it's not even my car: my beloved Subaru with its rusted-through floorboards had finally bitten the dust, so tonight I'm out in my parents' car—a light blue 1987 Ford Tempo. That's right: Johnny Tough Guy, the eighteen-year-old high school graduate, can't even afford to buy his own car. The six of us pile into this chick magnet and head out of the parking lot. Just as we pull out, though, I look across the street and notice a friend of ours having a heated exchange with these two rough-looking guys. I don't even think: I pull over, slam the car into park, and jump out. My six buddies are right behind me.

"Do we have a problem here?"

We'd crossed the street in about half a second, and now we've encircled these guys like a pack of hungry hyenas. To their credit, they don't even flinch. They just stand there, staring back at us. One of them is much taller than the other, so to keep things simple I'll call them "the shorter one" and "the taller one." They both look to be in their mid-twenties, and there's a reason they look rough: later on I would find out that they'd both been released from jail just a few hours earlier.

It's clear to everyone what's coming; now it's just a question of who's going to make the first move. As it turns out, tonight it's their turn. Before I even have time to flinch, the taller one turns and cracks me with a straight left to the nose. This motherfucker literally beat me to the punch. I come right back with two hard roundhouse kicks to his lead leg. I've dropped people with less, but this guy isn't even phased. We're in for a fight.

Back then, when we got into fights, me and my friends had this sick, unspoken game of one-upmanship. If one of my friends managed to knock out some sorry sap, then the rest of us had to follow suit. Meaning that, even though each of us is totally concerned with whatever mess we're in ourselves, we're also keeping tabs on what's happening with everyone else. Of course, some of this is just good fight strategy: in a situation like that, you have to be aware of what's going on so you don't find yourself blindsided by what you don't see coming. However, it also has its limitations. In this case, we're all so preoccupied with what's going on inside the scrum that we don't notice the police car rolling up behind us.

The car screeches to a halt, and two cops hop out.

"Listen the fuck up!" one of them yells. "Everyone break it up *right now*, or you're all going to jail!"

Let me tell you: when the first words out of a cop's mouth are *listen the fuck up*, he's not playing around. We stop what we're doing and listen the fuck up.

The cop points to the light blue chick magnet, parked across the street. "Whose car is this?" he barks.

I make a quick judgment call and decide that, for the moment, the cop probably doesn't care about the fact that technically it's my parents' car. I raise my hand.

The cop turns to me.

"Right," he says. "I want all of you to get your asses back in that car and leave, or you're all going to lockup and the car gets towed."

Sir, yes sir. No need to tell us twice.

We break it up and make a beeline for the car. As we're piling back in, though, a call comes in on the cop's radio. I don't remember now what it was, but whatever it is makes the cops rush back into their patrol car, hit the sirens, and speed off into the night.

For once in my short and error-strewn life, I try to do the right thing. I put the car in gear, take my foot off the brake, and start driving away... and then—*THUD!*

It takes me a second to process what's going on: takes me a second to realize that one of the guys we'd been fighting has just hauled off and kicked in the passenger-side door panel of my parents' car. *You gotta be fucking kidding me.* I slam on the brakes, throw the car in park, and we all get back out. I walk around to find a size-twelve dent in the passenger-side door. The one who did it looks at me and sneers.

"I just kicked in your car door," he says. "What the fuck are you going to do about it?"

At that moment, as if on cue, the same cop car pulls back into the parking lot. This time the sirens are blaring. The cops jump back out, now pissed as all hell, and start towards us.

"That's it," he yells, "I told you all to clear out! Now everybody is going to spend the night in jail!"

"Officer," I say, "you don't understand." I explain the situation. We were leaving, I tell him, when this shitbag hauled off and kicked in the side of my car. Unbelievably, the cop actually listens to what I'm saying. He walks around the car and he sees a dent in my door the size and shape of a size-twelve Converse. He turns to the owner of that size-twelve Converse, who—and tally this one in the "fact is always crazier than fiction" category—looks him straight in the eye and says, "Yeah? I did it. So what?" It was like something out of a movie. No sooner are these words out of his mouth, though, than he turns and takes off running, full speed, across the parking lot.

The cops immediately forget about the rest of us, and take off after him. I turn around in time to see the shorter of the two once again squaring off with one of my friends, and—without stopping to think for even a split second—I make what turns out to be one of the most pivotal decisions of my life.

Just as this guy rears back to punch my buddy, I intervene. I push my friend out of the way, haul back, and kick this guy square in the jaw. I totally blind-side him. *Blam!* I actually remember letting out a primal scream as my shin smashes into this guy's face, like something out of a Kung Fu movie. A surge of adrenaline rushes through my body, and for one brief moment I feel amazing. For one brief moment, during and immediately after the impact, I am exceedingly proud of myself. Then I see what I've done.

The impact of my kick snaps this guy's head back. Several of his teeth go flying. The force travels through his body, lifting him off his feet. In my memory he literally goes parallel to the street before he comes crashing down. His head, now in free-fall, strikes the edge of the curb. Imagine the sound a watermelon would make if you dropped it from the top of a multi-story building, and you're close to the sound I heard that night as the back of this guy's head cracks open. The rest of him lands with a sound like meat hitting the counter at your local butcher shop. And he lays there. He doesn't move. Blood is pouring from his mouth and from the newly-formed opening in his skull. My stomach drops. I'm no longer filled with pride. Somewhere in the back of my mind the thought occurs to me that this guy may be dead, that I may have just killed someone. My friends, oblivious to everything but the spectacular knockout, come over and start slapping me on the back. They congratulate me like I've just won some prize. I can barely hear them. Their voices sound a million miles away. I feel sick inside.

The cops arrive back on the scene. They're escorting the taller one, who they've managed to handcuff. The taller one sees his brother lying on the ground, freaks the fuck out, and breaks away from the two cops. And yes, you read that right: I said *brother*. Turns out, with these two, it's not just a term of endearment: they're actual, blood-is-thicker-than-water brothers. The cops quickly catch up with the taller one and tackle him to the ground. They haul him to his feet and stuff him into the back of their cruiser. He fights them every step of the way, kicking and shouting. Then the cops come over to us. I'm still standing closest to the guy on the ground. The cop turns to me.

"What the hell happened to him?" he asks.

My best friend, Pete, steps in and answers for me. "I don't know," he says. "The guy just passed out."

All of a sudden someone is grabbing my right wrist from behind, knocking me off balance. I spin around, freeing my right arm while simultaneously throwing a left hook at whoever's grabbing me. My blind punch misses its mark, but the handcuff attached to my right wrist cracks some guy I've never seen before directly in the side of the head.

Yes, you read that right: I said *handcuff.*

It turns out that an undercover cop, dressed in civilian clothes, had been standing across the street and saw the whole thing. He'd come up behind me while I was focused on the cop's question, grabbed my wrist, and slapped a cuff on it before I even knew what was happening.

Here's a tip for all you wannabe tough guys and gals out there: cops, undercover or otherwise, do not take kindly to people throwing punches at them, especially eighteen-year-old punks like me. Nor do they take kindly to getting cracked in the side of the head with their own handcuffs. At this point I'm not sure what's going on—this guy doesn't look like a cop, after all, and he hasn't identified himself as one—but I see the handcuff dangling from my wrist and I figure that something isn't quite right. I freeze.

The undercover cop is pissed. He spins me around and slams me, face first, into the pavement. He puts his knee in my back, slaps on the other cuff, and cranks them both down as tight as they will go. Laying there on the concrete, I feel dazed. My ears are ringing from the impact. I'm trying to process everything that's happening, but it's all happening too quickly. It won't add up. I need a second to think.

The cop yanks me back to my feet. He's holding me by the elbow, pulling on my arm and making me lean forward. I find that I'm staring down at the guy, still lying on the pavement. He's still motionless, and I can see blood pooling underneath his head. That background thought I had in the moment after my kick landed rushes up through the confusion now clouding my mind to stand front and center. It speaks loudly and in no uncertain terms: *This guy may really be dead. I may really have just killed someone. I could really be charged with murder.*

Several more police cars arrive on the scene, and I'm hustled into the back of one of them. Through the window I watch the cops questioning the witnesses, but I can't hear anything through the glass. I know my friends won't rat me out, but the fact that the undercover cop saw me kick the guy makes the point moot. From the back seat of that police car I see my future rushing away from me. The party we were headed to, the end of the summer, community college and any dreams I may have ever had for what I would do after are suddenly a million miles away, across an ocean containing unknowns that I'm terrified to even consider. My stomach contracts with fear, and for a moment I wonder what will happen, what they'll do to me, if I throw up in the back of a police car. My head aches from getting slammed on the pavement, and my hands are throbbing from the cuffs cutting into my wrists.

A paddy wagon arrives on the scene. One of the cops comes and yanks me out of the patrol car and walks me past the crowd that has gathered. He throws me inside the paddy wagon and slams the door closed behind me. I make my way over to the wagon's small window. With the way the wagon is parked I can just barely see over to where everything happened, but my view is blocked by people crowding in to see. As the police push them back I get another look at the scene. The guy is *still lying motionless on the ground.* The street around his head is stained with even more blood.

A firetruck pulls up. The firemen pile out and hurry over. They start working on the guy on the ground. With the way they're all standing and kneeling I can't see much. I don't know what's happening. I keep watching, hoping to catch movement, a sign of life. I'm still waiting when the back door of the paddy wagon bursts open and the cops hustle his brother inside. They direct us to opposite ends of the van, attach our cuffs to the bench, and lock us in together. Alone in the wagon, the taller one stares me down. His look is pure hatred. His voice fills the space as he screams, "You killed my little brother, you motherfucker! I'm going to fucking destroy you, you son of a bitch! You killed my little brother!" Tears are streaming down his face.

I can't hold his gaze. I look down, look away, look out the window. I don't reply. He keeps on screaming.

Minutes pass, but they seem like hours. From where I'm sitting I can still see the scene. There's no change, no movement from the guy on the ground. The firemen are still working on him, but whatever they're doing doesn't seem to be enough. Finally an ambulance arrives. It slowly noses its way through the tightly-gathered crowd. The paramedics get down with the firemen and go to work.

"Please," I hear myself saying. "Please don't die. Come on, man. Please don't die."

I'm hardly aware of the fact that I'm saying this. I'm barely conscious of the fact that I'm talking out loud. My mind is somewhere else, grappling with the sheer seeming impossibility of it all. The whole thing is like a nightmare I can't wake up from. All I can think is that it isn't supposed to be like this. Just twenty minutes ago we were leaving. We were on our way to a party, on our way to what would be one of the best nights of the summer, one of the best nights of our lives. Twenty minutes ago I was starting college in a few days. Twenty minutes ago I had a future. How did this happen? How did it all go so wrong?

His big brother brings me back to the present.

"That's right, motherfucker," he says. "You'd better pray, because I'm going to fucking kill you. No matter what happens, I'm going to find you and I promise I'm going to kill you!"

The metal panel covering the portal to the cab of the paddy wagon screeches open.

"Hey," yells the cop in the driver's seat, "shut the fuck up back there!"

Three more cop cars arrive on the scene. A half dozen more cops pile out and start breaking up the crowd. As the people turn away I see faces I recognize: friends' parents and my parents' friends from the neighborhood—people who I've known and who've known me and my family for years. Seeing them, seeing their concern for the man on the ground and their disgust at whoever did this thing, fills me with shame. I know I can do better. I start sobbing.

One of the cops pounds on the outside of the wagon. Through the wall I hear him tell the driver that it's just going to be the two of us, and that he can head out.

I watch the firemen and paramedics still working on the younger brother as we pull away from the scene.

We arrive at the police station and they throw us in a holding cell. They attach our cuffs to metal rings anchored in the concrete wall. The older brother has stopped shouting now. We sit there on the cold metal bench in silence, waiting.

Looking back on it now, I really have no idea how long I was there. At this point my mind and body felt numb. I don't even remember the police taking my mugshot or my fingerprints. I know it must have happened, but I have no memory of it. It was like I was sleepwalking. I was lost in the thoughts swirling around in my head. What my parents would think. What my life was supposed to be, and what it would be now. The older brother's promise to track me down and kill me. And above it all, exploding against this backdrop at intervals like the fireworks against the black sky over Utica: the cold, sinking certainty that *I had killed somebody.*

Somehow, though, that's not what had happened. Somehow, someway, the younger brother survived. The paramedics or the doctors at the hospital were finally able to revive him. A police detective came and gave us the news. Suddenly, impossibly, just like that, I was free. I was processed out on R.O.R, "released on my own recognizance." I signed an agreement stating that I agreed to appear in court at a later date. I didn't even have to post bail. Before I was allowed to leave the building, though, the detective in charge had a few choice words with me. He led me into his office and sat me down. I don't remember his face, but I will never forget what he said.

"You have no idea how lucky you are," he told me. "That guy could have very easily died out there tonight. On top of that, we should be charging you with assault on a police officer."

I tried to explain, tried to tell him my side of the story, but he wasn't having it. He wasn't interested and I was too numb, too exhausted mentally and physically, too stunned and relieved, to insist.

"Just make sure you show up to court," he told me, "otherwise your luck will run out."

And that was that. I left his office, walked down the hall, and exited the police station with a handful of charges hanging over my head. Several of my friends were waiting for me outside. They started clapping and cheering when they saw me. They slapped me on the back and congratulated me like I was some kind of a hero. And I'm embarrassed to say: I played along with it. I played the hero. I didn't want to disappoint them. Johnny Tough Guy rides again. Outside I was all smiles and swagger; inside, I was just a scared little kid.

The celebration was short lived. I still had to face the music at home, and the prospect of telling my father what had happened scared me even more than my upcoming date with the judge. Moreover, I'd rather go to jail than break my mother's heart with the news that her son was a derelict criminal. And thankfully, at least on this last point, my father and I saw eye-to-eye. We kept it between us. Unless he told her later on, I'm pretty sure she's still unaware of everything that happened.

When my court date finally arrived, my father and I drove to the court-house together. We didn't say a single word the whole way. Unbeknownst to me, my father had arranged for an attorney to be there for my appearance, and we met up with him outside the courtroom doors. He wasn't alone, though. The District Attorney was also waiting for us. She pulled us all aside and made me an offer I couldn't believe, let alone refuse. It turned out that this DA had an absolute hard-on for these two brothers. They'd been in and out of jail for years for all kinds of violent crimes, and she'd had enough. She wanted to see them go down. At the moment the brothers were charged with kicking in the passenger-side door of my car, and the DA wanted me to testify in the case. In return for my testimony against them the District Attorney was willing to reduce my charges to one count of disorderly conduct. All I had to do was testify, plead guilty to the lesser charge, and the whole thing would be over.

In the state of New York, disorderly conduct is what's called a "violation." It isn't even a misdemeanor. Basically, it's not considered a crime. With a violation, there's no criminal record. You read that right: the DA was willing to reduce my charges for nearly killing someone *and* striking a police officer to a violation. *Are you fucking kidding me?* I wanted to kiss the District Attorney and the Judge. Yes, ma'am, just show me where to sign. It was the deal of the century, a gift from heaven.

In addition to the reduced charge, I had to promise the DA that I would never walk back through the courthouse doors. With my father and our attorney standing beside me, I made that promise. The Judge also made a condition: if I got into any trouble, for any reason at all, in the next twelve months, they would bring back all of my original charges. I told the Judge I understood. The Judge banged the gavel and called for the next case. We left the courtroom, went down to the treasurer's office, paid the fine and the court fees, and that was it. I was a free man.

Looking back on it now, I can't help but feel that God was watching over me that night. If that guy had died, I likely would have spent the next decades of my life in prison. It makes me very grateful, but it also makes me wonder. It makes me wonder what I did to deserve such grace, and if I've earned it in the way I've lived my life in the decades since. I hope I have. And I wonder, too, about those brothers. Crossing the street to confront them all I saw was a pair of shitbags who deserved what they had coming. But of course it takes two to tango, and two to fight. If they were shitbags then so was I, and if I wasn't then neither were they. I wonder about what their lives had been like up to the moment when our paths crossed. The detective and the DA told me that they were violent criminals who'd been in and out of jail. That sort of thing doesn't come out of nowhere. I can't say for sure, but I suspect that you wouldn't have to look too far beneath the surface to find some serious trauma in their past: alcoholism, violence, sexual or physical abuse... something. I don't know what exactly, but maybe it doesn't really matter. The point is that I'm sure they had more of an excuse to be acting out than I did, and more of a reason to be shown a little mercy by a system they'd been locked into battle with for most of their lives. I wonder who they would have been if not for those scars. Maybe, if we'd grown up in the same neighborhood, we would have been friends. Of course I can't know that for sure. What I do know is that I'm truly, truly sorry for what happened that night. I'm not sure if they're still alive today but if they are, I hope this message reaches them: I'm truly, truly sorry.

COLLEGE, ISOLATION, AND TURNING MY LIFE AROUND... SORTA

I wish I could tell you that I learned my lesson. I wish I could tell you that there was an absolute, instant change in my life, and that I was perfect from that point forward... but I can't. I wasn't. My demons wouldn't be put to bed so easily. I had a lot more work to do. In fact, my work hadn't even begun.

Many things did change, though. I stopped drinking, for one thing. I started college as scheduled and I dedicated myself to my classes, studying, and the gym. For the first time in a long time I did really well in school. My college grades were the best I'd ever had. I'd finally found something that interested me: criminal justice. Go figure. If my life hadn't turned out the way it did, I truly believe I would have been great at law enforcement.

Partly by design and partly as a natural consequence of this new focus, I started to isolate myself. I started spending more and more time working out alone. I'd put on my headphones and just *go*. In the gym I was able to tap into that same tenacity and focus I'd discovered on the Balios' farm. Rep after rep, set after set, I started to become an absolute savage.

The thing was, though, that during this time, the anger I felt actually intensified. I realize now what it was about: I felt trapped. This process of isolating myself was my attempt to break free, on some psychic level, from my surroundings: to break free from the life that surrounded and up to that point defined me. Without really understanding why, I found that I was actively distancing myself from some of my dearest childhood friends—guys I'd known all my life.

But old habits die hard. "*Testa dura*," they say in Italian: "hard head." I'd earned that label more than once before, and I'd earn it again. I burned out plenty of anger in the gym pumping iron, but there was only so much that working out could do. The well was always refilling, the anger was always there, and soon enough it was spilling out in the streets. As you'll read in the coming pages, my near-miss at Fireworks Over Utica was far from the end of it. I'm embarrassed to say that there were many, many more violent incidents to come.

Still, for all of that, this period in my life carried its own important lessons: lessons that have helped me tremendously and that I lean on to this day. It was during this time that I started to really learn about people, about motivation and work ethic, and about why some people succeed and others fail. Like most college-aged kids, my friends and I were always talking about what came next, about our dreams and aspirations, and in this environment I started to recognize that some of the people around me had big dreams but no follow through. For example: there was a whole group of us guys who worked out in the same weight room, and I was there so much that my workouts and theirs often overlapped. Like a lot of guys in that era we were all focused on getting as big as we could, and there was plenty of talk going around about competing in bodybuilding. Guys would tell each other, "I'm going to compete in this competition or that competition, this fall or in the spring." But for all of this talk, not one of them did. Not *one*. There was always some excuse. There was always some reason why they couldn't or didn't do what they'd said they were going to do.

There were other things, too. It was around this same time that I started seeing some of the local guys in the gym using steroids. I can proudly say that I never touched the stuff. I can also say that, despite all the talk that went around and all the promises made, I was the only guy out of that entire group who actually followed through and competed in bodybuilding.

Once I made up my mind to compete, I didn't think twice about it. I saw a poster in the gym advertising a competition that was coming up in six months and I said, "I'm going to compete in that show, and I'm going to win."

At that time I didn't know a whole lot about how to prepare. I didn't

59

know how to cycle my training, and I didn't know what to eat. This all happened back in the '90s, before the internet, and my whole bodybuilding education came from reading muscle magazines. I became obsessed: I read every issue of *Flex* and *Muscle and Fitness* that I could get my hands on.

I had a training partner help me prepare, but other than that I didn't have a lot of support. My family thought I'd gone a little bit nuts. At that time I was still living at home, and my two sisters and I shared the same bathroom. We all know that a bodybuilder needs mirrors, right? This bathroom was the only place in the house with mirrors big enough for me to practice my poses, and I spent hours in there perfecting my routine. I can clearly remember putting on posing trunks for the first time. I thought I looked pretty good: I'd been hitting the tanning beds for a couple of weeks, and to top it off I had slathered myself in brush-on tanning lotion. I was full-on *Jersey Shore* before *Jersey Shore* was a thing. My skin was darkened to a nice orangish brown. I must have looked completely ridiculous. Right in the middle of my posing routine, my younger sister walked in. There I was in my trunks, painted orange, flexing my flamingo-like calves. She burst out laughing.

"What the hell do you think you're doing?" she cackled. "Are you out of your mind?"

I could deal with ribbing from my sisters, but it didn't end there. A week before the competition I was back in the bathroom. My posing routine was already on point: now I was doing final prep. Tonight, that meant shaving my legs. Yes, you read that right: I was shaving my legs. You can't go onstage with hairy legs. I've got both legs lathered up in shaving cream and I'm working on my quad when all of a sudden I feel someone watching me. Razor in hand, I look up. My father is standing in the open doorway, staring at me. We make eye contact for what feels like an eternity. We don't say a word. Then my father shakes his head. This man fought in three wars. He still woke up screaming with flashbacks of the things he'd seen and done in

Me and my sisters, Gina (left) and Rosanne (right).

the South Pacific theatre. And now here's his only son in the bathroom in a red speedo, one foot up on the edge of the tub, BIC razor in hand, fully lathered up with Barbasol, shaving his legs. After a moment, he turns and walks away in disgust. He never says a word, and we never speak of it again.

The weekend of the competition my buddy Garrett and I drove an hour and a half to the venue. This was back before the days of handheld smart-phone turn-by-turn navigation, and with our map reading skills we barely made it to the show in time for weigh-ins. Somehow we found the place. Standing there waiting to step on the scale, I had my first chance to check out the competition. There were six other guys in my weight class and division, and they were not what I was expecting.

The whole drive there I'd been imagining that all of my competition were going to be these absolute monsters. I had images of competing against a bunch of young Lou Ferrignos and Arnolds. Standing there at the weigh-ins and sizing these other guys up, it quickly became apparent that the images I'd had in my head were a lot worse than the reality. It was an important lesson to learn, and one I've returned to often in the years since: it is incredibly easy to psych yourself out before you even start. Sometimes people let the boogeyman in their heads stop them from moving forward: they let it stop them from even starting in the first place. Standing there at the venue, it became clear to me that the boogeyman in my head was a lying little punk who I was right to ignore—a challenge that served as a good source of motivation and nothing else. These guys weren't anything close to the monsters I'd imagined. Standing there sizing them up, I realized I had a real shot at winning.

After prejudging, Garret and I drove to a payphone and I called home. My mom picked up and I told her how it went. She was thrilled. She told me they were going to come see me compete in the night show. I couldn't have been more excited. I asked if my dad was coming. After everything—

after all of my failures in high school and my run-in with the law—it was time for a win, and I was hoping with all my heart that he would be there to see it. There was a pause on the other end of the line. I'm not sure she replied. If she did, whatever she said wasn't a commitment. We said our goodbyes and I headed back to the venue to get ready for the main event.

Finally, it was time for the night show. I was amped. My training partner and I stood there in the wings, waiting for my turn to hit the stage, as music blared and the other competitors ran through their posing routines. A thousand thoughts were running through my head. I didn't know if my mom had managed to make it in time, or if my dad had decided to come. I remember doing a bunch of push-ups to get pumped, and my buddy verbally psyching me up as they announced my name. He gave me a big slap on the chest, and I was so amped up that for some stupid reason I gave him a wicked headbutt. Later he told me that I'd almost knocked him out, but I had no idea. I was in my own world as I walked out onto that stage.

I remember that I wasn't really nervous. I felt right at home on the stage. I was excited. The butterflies in my stomach felt amazing. Standing under those lights in front of the gathered crowd, there was nowhere else I wanted to be. And in the end, I did it. It was a close contest, but I achieved my goal. I did what I'd said I was going to do. I won the teenage division. I had finally marked a tally back in the win column. It had been a long time, and it felt so good. And it marked a new chapter in my life. Standing up on that stage, I made a decision. Quitting was over. I was done with it. It was a thing of the past. I had a new identity now. I was a winner.

My mom recorded the whole thing with a camcorder. We still have the VHS tape somewhere. On the video you can hear my mom crying as they announce my name. My father, though? My father never showed up. I don't know why. We never talked about it. We never talked about the competition at all. And honestly, even after all these years, that's something I still can't understand. I'm a father now myself, and I can't imagine not being there for my sons. I can't imagine not *wanting* to be there. Then again, I guess there's plenty my father and I never understood about each other. Chalk this up as just one more thing. Maybe he still hadn't recovered from the shock of seeing his only son shaving his legs.

GOING FOR THE STATE TITLE, AND BLACK BELT

I was flying high after my first win, and it wasn't long before I set my sights on the next competition. Teenage Mr. New York State was eight months away, and I planned on competing and winning that title. I went to work right away, training as hard as I could in preparation for the show. I started bulking up, packing on weight. I wanted to blow the rest of the competition out of the water.

The competition wasn't the only thing on my calendar, though. By now I'd been training in the martial arts for seven years, and my teacher thought it was time for me to test for my black belt. As luck would have it, the black belt test and the bodybuilding competition would take place within a week of each other.

I'd moved on from Taekwondo, at this point. Now I was training in a style called Chinese Goju. I'd started off at a school called the University of Martial Arts, under an instructor named Ron van Clief. If that name sounds familiar to you, there's a good reason: Ron faced off against the great Royce Gracie at UFC 4, losing by rear naked choke. To date Ron is still the oldest man to ever compete in the UFC, having entered the world-famous Octagon at fifty-one years of age. By the time I was due to test for my black belt the school had split, and I'd left Ron to go with the other instructor. I was one of the top students at that time, and I felt a good deal of pressure from both camps, but ultimately I made the decision I made for a variety of reasons.

The instructor I followed was affiliated with famed full-contact Karate fighter Bill "Superfoot" Wallace, and it was under his banner that I would be testing for black belt.

Even though Chinese Goju isn't perfect, especially in the context of what we all know now thanks to MMA and the UFC, it was a much more practical style of martial arts than Taekwondo, and taught me some useful techniques for standup fighting. I'd already figured out that point sparring offered little in the way of real-world, transferrable self-defense skills: my mouth had written some checks that my ass couldn't cash back when Taekwondo was all I knew, and sent me out in search of something more grounded in the reality of the street than the confines of a martial arts competition. After all, as they say: out in the street, there are no judges handing out trophies for points. Obviously Ron's loss to Royce at UFC 4 showed that Chinese Goju had some deficiencies of its own, but I would hesitate to throw the baby out with the bathwater: my training in that system carried me through more scrapes than I care to remember.

I'll spare you the specific details of all I did in the months leading up to these two big events, but suffice it to say I trained like an absolute fiend. I was beyond motivated: I was *driven*. I had a new identity to uphold, a win streak to maintain, and I did not plan on dropping the ball. I spent countless hours under the bar, countless hours on the mat. I gave it everything I had. Heading into the home stretch I was in the best shape of my life.

So here I am, nineteen years old, going to school full-time *and* working full-time catching shoplifters as a Loss Prevention Detective at Bradlees Department Store (more on that later). I'm planning on winning the biggest bodybuilding contest in New York, getting my black belt, *and* completing my two-year college degree all within the next month. I'm no saint, but I've come a long way since my arrest that night at Fireworks Over Utica. Those moments when I seemed bound for prison feel a long, long way away, and —for the moment, at least—I'm doing all I can to keep it that way.

The black belt test is up first. Despite all of the training I did leading up to it, I'm not too proud to say that that black belt test was one of the hardest things I'd ever done physically up to that point. The test took place over a full day... and maybe "test" is a misleading term. This was more like getting jumped into a gang.

That day started with an hour or more of sit-ups, push-ups, running, and every other calisthenic exercise you can think of. This was followed by Kata. If you don't know, Kata are those choreographed routines that a lot of you probably think of when you imagine someone doing martial arts: long sequences of punches and blocks and kicks that you perform solo, demonstrating all the techniques of your specific art. For my test, I had to perform every Kata I'd learned from white belt to brown belt. After that, it was self-defense against a single unarmed attacker. Then self-defense against multiple unarmed attackers. Then self-defense against a single attacker with a weapon. Then self-defense against multiple attackers with weapons. Then striking on the pads, showing power and form. Then a Kata with a "bo" staff. For nearly four hours, my instructors challenged me on every level. They barked commands, rejected my efforts, encouraged me to quit, challenged me to do more and push harder. I always did. Finally it was time for the last event of the day: sparring. For this, my instructors had made special arrangements: a few black belts from a few different affiliate schools had all come in to spar with me. Not only were they all fresh as daisies, but one of these guys had several professional kickboxing matches under his belt. I was completely exhausted from everything I'd done to prepare for the test and from the test itself; add to that the fact that I was on a restricted diet for the bodybuilding competition that was only a week away, and you start to get the picture. By the time sparring came around, I was just about spent.

Round one. We're using dipped-foam gloves designed for point sparring, but tonight we're going full contact. Within the first ten seconds of my first match I get hit with a vicious hook that dislocates my jaw. I'm unable to bite down on my mouthpiece after that, and as a consequence I start breathing through my mouth. If you know anything about the combat arts, you know that spells trouble. Still, I make it all the way through to my fourth match before I pay the price. My opponent lands a clean roundhouse kick to my head—very similar to the one I used in the street just a year earlier—that knocks me out cold. The next thing I know I'm coming to, flat on my back on the mat and staring up at the lights. I hear someone counting to ten, but I can't figure out what it means. I don't understand what's going on. They're already to "four" by the time I wake up.

Now here's another voice. It's my Sensei warning me that if I don't get up and continue I will fail the test. Somehow—don't ask me how—I make it back to my feet before "ten." My reward? I get my ass kicked for two more fights. At least I manage to keep my teeth in my head. Finally, I finished all the matches. I'm completely exhausted. Someone has to literally help me stand as I'm presented with my black belt.

There were several people in the audience that day cheering me on, but none of them were my family members. My mom had told me that she couldn't bear to watch me get beat up, and I believe her. My dad—well, my dad never said anything about it. I guess he wasn't interested. Seven years of hard work and a grueling, day-long test, and I never had that moment of celebration with them. Instead I pulled myself together in the locker room and drove myself to the ER for an x-ray of my jaw. The doctor looked the x-rays over and said, "Yep, your lower jaw is dislocated..." and then he popped it back into place. I remember going home afterwards and doing my best to eat something, but my face was so sore that it was impossible. Eventually I just gave up. I went to my room and collapsed for a short nap, and then I got up, got cleaned up, and drove myself to work. That's right: I had to work that night. If ever there was a time to take a day off and rest this was it, especially since I'd be competing for the title of Teenage Mr. New

York State in one week's time, but I'd promised my boss that I would cover for him that day. I wasn't going to let a little thing like a day-long ass-kicking slide me back into being a guy who quit, who flaked out on his commitments. I was a guy who finished what I started now, and that meant keeping my word no matter what.

For the next seven days my whole body was bruised and sore. I felt like I'd been put through a meat grinder. Still, I could deal with the discomfort. The bigger problem was eating. It was still painful to chew, and this spelled trouble for the upcoming competition. I was planning on competing in the teenage heavyweight division, which was one hundred and eighty-five pounds and above. I'd been right on the cusp, but now I could tell that I was losing weight. In the back of my mind I had an inkling that I'd probably dropped a few too many pounds, but I just couldn't bring myself to look the problem in the eye. I didn't weigh myself at all during that week. I was going to find out on the day, along with everybody else.

On the morning of the competition I drove to the venue, registered, and stepped on the scale. The number staring back at me was shocking. I'd lost ten pounds in the week leading up to the contest. I was a mere one hundred and seventy-five pounds, ten pounds under the heavyweight limit. I wouldn't be competing as a heavyweight: I'd have to drop down into the lightweight division. There were six other guys in that weight class, and I wasn't really sure how I stacked up against them. One guy in particular was incredibly ripped, and had managed to pack a bunch of muscle onto his shorter frame. I'd hazard a guess that he was using some chemical enhancements... but for the moment that didn't make any difference. The cards had been dealt, and now they had to be played.

After the weigh-ins I went off in the corner and tried to pump up, but my body was so depleted that I couldn't even do push ups without my muscles cramping. This was going to be rough.

I'll spare you the boring details; the long story short is that I ended up taking second place in the teen lightweight division. I lost to the shorter guy. For what it's worth, he went on to also win the open men's lightweight division. Not that it made the loss sting any less. This was my first loss in bodybuilding, and I didn't like it. It was also my first real exposure to the rampant use of steroids in bodybuilding competition. It wasn't just the guy who beat me: based on what I saw that day, I would guess that the vast majority of the competitors in the men's division were on steroids.

I had my heart set on winning that title, but it didn't happen for me. What did happen, though, was something that meant just as much, if not more: my whole family, my father included, showed up to watch me compete. It was the first time in a long time that my father had shown any sort of interest in me or in what I was doing. I so longed for his acceptance, and his presence at the competition gave me hope that one day I would finally earn it.

After the contest, my body was a wreck. It had been through a lot over the past couple of weeks, and now it was screaming at me to take my foot off the gas and rest. I remember going out to a restaurant with my girlfriend after the show, and being unable to eat because the roof of my mouth was covered with sores. Still, only a few days after the contest, I dove right back into training at the gym. I couldn't help it. The weight room was my refuge, the one place in my life where I could consistently clear my mind, focus my energies, and center myself. Sadly, though, it wasn't the same with Chinese Goju. With the black belt finally around my waist, I lost my motivation. Looking back now I recognize that I was just burned out, that I needed a break to recharge. Instead I tried to push through, and so brought myself to a place where I confused burnout with genuine disinterest. My training became less frequent, and it wasn't long before I stopped showing up to class altogether. I felt bad about quitting—I was a guy who didn't quit things anymore, remember?—and I definitely felt like I was letting my instructor down, but I put it out of my mind: bodybuilding was my focus now, and it needed all of my time and energy and attention if I was going to push it as far as it would go.

CALIFORNIA DREAMIN'

My focus was on bodybuilding, but my plan didn't end there. In my mind and in my heart a vision was forming, a new and exciting and auda-cious dream: I would follow in Arnold's footsteps. I would go as far as I possibly could with bodybuilding, and then I would use that platform as a launchpad into Hollywood stardom.

A lot of people dream of being rich and famous. We see celebrities on TV and in movies, see their smiling faces in magazines and on billboards, and we imagine the amazing lives they must live. Everywhere they go they're celebrated and adored. Everyone wants to be their friend; everyone wants their approval and attention. Everybody loves them. It's easy to forget—in fact, the whole phenomenon of celebrity seems designed to make us for-get—that rich and famous people are just that: people. Whether you live in a mansion in Malibu or a shack in the slums, you're the tenant of your own heart and mind, your own inner world, and no amount of fame or celebrity will fix or fill what's broken or missing inside. Having now spent the better part of my life working closely with the rich and famous, I can say all of this with more authority than most—and in the coming chapters I will tell you some stories that I hope will show you exactly what I mean. At nineteen years old, though, I was as sold on the big Hollywood illusion as anybody—maybe even more so. My father's habitual indifference to me and my inter-ests and accomplishments made me feel invisible and insignificant in his world: the only world, in my mind, that mattered. Within that constant, fame seemed to hold some magical key: if I was famous, if my face was plastered across movie screens and billboards all over the country and all over the world... Well, there would be no way in hell for him to ignore me then. If I was bigger than life then I couldn't be small, not even in his eyes.

Of course I didn't dare breathe a word of this dream to anyone. I was too embarrassed, too worried about what people would think. Looking back on it now I can see that, in all likelihood, once their initial laughter subsided they likely would have supported me. My not telling them had more to do with my own lack of self-confidence than it did with them. When I considered it practically, the dream seemed far-fetched even to me: how could I expect anyone else to take it seriously? Besides: childish dreams like that were some serious sissy shit, and I still had my reputation as a tough guy to uphold. Inside, I was starting to feel trapped.

I had finished my two years at our local community college with excellent grades. Unlike when I graduated from high school, I now had options. The smart play was for me to go on and finish my bachelor's degree, but I didn't want to commit to another college and two more years of school. California was always on my mind, but it also meant leaving behind everything I knew and understood. California was a big unknown, a giant question mark looming against the Pacific. I didn't know what to do... so I decided to do nothing. I told my parents I was going to take some time off before I started at another college. Really I was kicking the can down the road, hoping that the Universe would make the decision for me. As luck would have it, it did... but not before I more or less forced its hand.

TIME OFF

My life during that time was composed around my full-time job in loss prevention and lifting weights. I was so obsessed with training that often

"*...a testosterone-driven athletic monster.*" *Twenty-year-old John Petrelli in his drawers.*

times I would find myself alone in the gym, late at night, while my friends were out partying. I didn't mind. Going out was fine for them, but I had bigger plans for myself. Every rep got me one small but palpable step closer to my goal. Still: I wasn't a monk, and there were times during that year when my friends convinced me to come out with them. And where we went, violence followed.

I know what you're thinking. I'd escaped an assault and battery charge by the skin of my teeth, and I've promised the Judge and the DA that I will stay out of trouble as a condition of the deal. On top of that, I was now a black belt in martial arts. Martial arts is supposed to teach you honor, discipline, respect, self-control, and a black belt is supposed to represent and uphold these virtues... Why the fuck, then, was I always getting into fights? To this, and despite the muscle I was packing on and the PRs I was putting up under the bar, I can only cop to my own weakness. My environment, the guys I was hanging out with, were all exerting an influence on me that I wasn't strong enough to overcome, or confident enough to resist. At this point in my life, despite the dream of the person I wanted to be and the life I wanted to live, my peer group and who I was within it formed my whole identity. Understand: I'm not blaming them. I don't blame my friends, my parents, or the neighborhood I grew up in. There are plenty of people who grew up the way I did, in places like the place I grew up and surrounded by the type of people I was surrounded by, who didn't do what I did. My failings are my own, and I take full responsibility for them. I could have acted differently, but I didn't. I had a tough guy reputation that I thought I had to uphold, and for the moment that meant more to me than what I would have gained if I'd had the strength to just let it go.

NEW YEAR'S BASH

It's New Year's Eve, 1992, and we're hanging out in a club called "The Network" in the heart of Utica. The place is packed so tight you can't even move. It's loud and it's hot and I can't stand it. The New Year's ball has already dropped, and I'm thinking about how to start drawing the evening to a close. I'm standing near the dance floor and I'm talking to some girl, when all of a sudden some guy runs up to me. He needs something, and I can tell by the look on his face that it's urgent.

This sort of thing is what happens when you're a known local tough guy. You'll be out somewhere and some friend of a friend of a friend, somebody who you've never met but who knows you by reputation, will get themselves into trouble and come running up begging you to help him and his friends out of the jam. Half the time my friends and I would jump in and save their asses without ever even finding out who the fuck they were, or what it was all about. This is the stupid shit you do—the stupid shit I did—to uphold a reputation. In my mind I think I somehow managed to rationalize it: to convince myself that I was doing something righteous, helping out someone in need and fighting the bad guys. Deep down I knew better. Deep down I knew that this shit was truly incompatible with the path I wanted to walk in life, incompatible with the success I wanted for myself. There was a war going on between my ears, and the good guys were losing. That night at The Network, the good guys lost.

"Pete needs your help!" this guy says. "He's outside!"

At least this time the call for help isn't totally random: Pete is one of my best friends. A couple of us make a beeline for the door. As soon as I get outside I see Pete. Blood is leaking from the top of his head and running down his face.

"Who did this?" we ask.

Pete points to this big motherfucker standing a few feet away. The big motherfucker is smiling. The big motherfucker is *big*. Pete is six-foot-four, two hundred and fifty pounds. This guy is bigger.

Without hesitation we circle around this giant. I get an angle on his back and—*BLAM!*—I punch this fucker as hard as I can, right in the back of the neck. He goes down. To this day, I'm actually not sure if it was from the shot I hit him with, or from someone else hitting him at the same time. All I know is that he fell hard. As soon as he hits the ground, all holy hell breaks loose. It's like a piranha frenzy. This guy is already out cold, but now people start coming out of the woodwork to kick him square in the face. People I don't even know. It's winter and guys are all wearing big steel-toe boots. I see at least five kicks land directly to the giant's head and face. In no time at all he's a bloody mess, laying there motionless in the street. Some of his friends try to intervene, but they get laid out too.

We've got other concerns, though. It's evident that we need to take Pete to the hospital, and fast. Blood is gushing from the wound on his head. One of our friends gives us his teeshirt and I use it to wipe the blood out of Pete's eyes. Up close I get my first good look at the top of his head. His scalp is torn wide open and I can see big, jagged shards of glass embedded in his skull, glinting in the streetlight.

We load Pete into somebody's car and we rush off to the ER. The place is packed. What did we expect? It's two in the morning on New Year's Day. A bunch of other losers like us are keeping the place super busy. When the nurse gets a look at Pete's head she moves us to the front of the line. A minute later they call Pete's name and escort us into a private room. Soon the doctor comes in. He examines Pete's injury and goes to work. He takes a large needle and injects the area with some kind of pain killer, and then with a pair of forceps he starts pulling these big chunks of glass out of Pete's skull. He drops them all into a metal basin. As we stand there the basin slowly fills with a gory mixture of coagulated blood globs, glass, hair, and flesh.

While all of this is going on, Pete runs us through what happened. Turns out he was squared up to fight the big motherfucker when out of nowhere one of the big motherfucker's buddies smashed a beer bottle over Pete's head. That's when the runner rushed off to find us.

The gashes in Pete's scalp are too big for stitches, so after all the glass is removed the doctor staples Pete's head shut. He looks like something out of Frankenstein's laboratory. It's an improvement on how he looked when we walked in, but it's still pretty gnarly.

After Pete's head is stapled and bandaged, the doctor informs us that in cases like this they're required to file a police report. He leaves the room to get the paperwork, and that's all the time we need to sneak out. They have Pete's contact information from his insurance card, but we all agree that they aren't getting anything else.

I get home late and I fall into bed. I feel like I could sleep for about a month, but I don't get the chance. Early the next morning I'm woken up by a phone call. It's a police detective, and he's looking for me. He wants me to come down to the station to give a statement about what happened. I'm not the only one who gets the call. My friends and I got our stories straight on the ride home from the hospital, so we're ready. Who knocked the big guy's face in? None of us can remember. Sure, we all say, we saw a bunch of fighting, but it was nobody we knew. We weren't really paying attention: our main concern was getting our buddy to the hospital. We're all sorry that we can't be more helpful.

Ultimately Pete does have to go to court, but he's cleared of all criminal charges. The whole thing becomes just another in a long list of things we laugh about: another story of a brutal encounter that affirms our bullshit mythology about ourselves and what cool guys we are. This, despite what the police told us: that the big guy needed plastic surgery to repair his shattered nose and face. That he would never look the same; that he would carry the scars of this event for the rest of his life. Those scars, and God only knows what else. I shudder to think what kind of long-term damage a face-plant into the concrete, let alone a half-dozen kicks with steel-toe boots to your unprotected head, does to a person's brain. I shudder to think how that man's life was changed by what we did to him that night. I'm deeply ashamed, but I force those thoughts from my mind. I laugh with my friends. I go to the gym and I push weights and I tell myself that I'm strong, so that I can ignore the truth I know in my heart: against the opinions of my friends and the other obstacles standing between me and the person I want to be, I couldn't possibly be any weaker.

I AM THE BURGER KING

I feel like a ticking time bomb, like I'm on a collision course with disaster, and like my ever-mounting frustration and anger and my misguided sense of loyalty to my friends and my petty concern for my reputation all have control of the wheel. I feel like, if I don't somehow manage to get out, to break free from my surroundings—and *soon*—it's all going to come crashing in on me.

I'm so on-edge that even a trip to a fast food restaurant holds the potential for violence. And please understand, before I get into this: I am truly, truly ashamed of the way I acted in what I'm about to tell you. If you read this and feel like you're reading a story about an asshole—you're right. As I said, my goal in writing this book is not to make myself look good or minimize my own misdeeds but to be completely truthful and honest: to acknowledge what I did in the hope that something valuable can be learned from my mistakes, and from the recounting of my own process of learning from them. This incident truly and accurately portrays my fucked-up state of mind at this point in my life, and so I'm inclined to include it on its merits.

Also, and even though I look like a complete dickhead... it's maybe a little bit funny. I'll let you decide.

On this particular afternoon, my good friend David "Duff" Holmes and I are making our way back from Syracuse. Thinking back now I can't remember exactly why we went, but Syracuse was a big deal to us small-town kids, and we didn't need much of an excuse to head down. What matters to this story is the fact that, like always, as twenty-year-olds who do nothing but work out, Duff and I are hungry. So we swing by Burger King. I pull into the drive-thru and I order a grilled chicken sandwich. Duff gets two double cheeseburgers and a Coke. Burger King has a promotion going—buy one double cheeseburger and get one free—and Duff is taking advantage. We place our order at the box and the attendant asks us to pull to the side while they prepare our order. Apparently no one but me orders a grilled chicken sandwich at *Burger* King, and they don't have any pre-made. Our order is going to take a minute.

No problem. We pull over to the side, and a few minutes later a female employee comes out with Duff's Coke and our bag of food. She hands it all to me through the driver's-side window and says, "Sorry for the wait. Here's your order. Thank you for coming to Burger King!"

Rule number one, as it was so eloquently articulated by Joe Pesci in *Lethal Weapon II*: "They always fuck you at the drive-thru." You never pull away without looking in the bag first. Before this girl can take two steps back toward the building, I check the bag. Inside I see *two* little parcels, both of them wrapped in wrappers saying "double cheeseburger."

We've got a problem.

"Excuse me," I say to the employee, "my grilled chicken sandwich is missing."

This chick stops in her tracks, turns around, gives me a look and says, "My manager made your grilled chicken sandwich and put it in the bag, so I *know* it's in there."

I'm taken aback. It's more attitude than I'm expecting, more attitude than I'm looking for, especially from someone who just handed me two sandwiches when we ordered three. It's more attitude than I'm looking for from someone who's now standing between me and *food that I already paid for.*

"Well," I say, "you're standing right here. You just handed me the bag. You haven't walked two fucking paces from my car. Do you think I'm hiding a grilled chicken sandwich? I didn't eat it. It's not up my friend's ass. Why don't you walk back over here and take a look in the bag? Then you can tell me that it's in here."

Perhaps unsurprisingly, she doesn't feel comfortable walking back over to the car.

"You know what?" she says. "My manager will handle this..." and away she walks.

We sit there, waiting for the manager. We're both starving, but there's no way either of us is eating any of this food. It isn't even food anymore: now it's *evidence.* Minutes tick by, and there's no sign of the manager. We're getting impatient. The evidence is getting cold. Plus: have you ever tried to sit in a car with a bag of fast food? It's almost impossible to not open it up and eat something. Whole teams of scientists have developed special smell chemicals and compounds designed to make fast food as irresistible as possible. To a pair of hungry twenty-year-olds, those (maybe) ten minutes feel like an eternity. Finally we've had enough. We're going to handle this matter ourselves. We're going inside.

Just as we're getting out of the car, a man in his mid-forties—a Burger King manager straight out of central casting—pokes his head out of the restaurant's front door and yells at the top of his lungs, "I made your grilled chicken sandwich, I put it in the bag, now you'd better put your car in drive and get the hell out of here!"

I am not exaggerating. This is word-for-word what came out of this guy's mouth. Not, "How can I help you?" or, "I think there must be some kind of mistake." Nope. This guy belts out, "You'd better put your car in drive and get the hell out of here!" This balding, middle-aged guy, weighing all of a hundred and fifty pounds, wrapped in a Burger King uniform and topped with a paper hat and eyeglasses, is screaming at us like we're his step kids and we just spent his Tuesday night bowling money on wine coolers.

For a moment I can't even process what's happening. It occurs to me that maybe we've stumbled into the filming of one of those hidden camera shows: that at any moment producers and camera operators are going to hop out and let us in on the gag. It just doesn't make sense otherwise. Surely this guy isn't actually trying to start some shit with us. We've been in so many scraps with so many guys that are so much scarier than this Burger King manager. The idea of this guy deciding to start something, to yell at and insult us, over a grilled chicken sandwich is just ridiculous. Or at least it it would be, if—one—we weren't starving—two—we weren't still short one grilled chicken sandwich, and—three—this guy didn't need to learn *just who the fuck he was talking to.*

We exit the vehicle, cross the parking lot, and step up to the manager... who's now standing in front of the restaurant's entrance and yelling so loud that people in other cars have stopped to watch.

"I made your grilled chicken sandwich," he yells again. "I put it in the bag, now get in your car and get the fuck out of here!"

"Look," I say, in as calm a voice as I can muster, "the girl handed me the bag. I immediately looked in it. She was standing right next to us. There wasn't—"

I don't get to finish before Duff cuts me off, though. "Dude," he says to the manager, "do you think we need to steal a fucking grilled chicken sandwich? What the fuck is your problem?"

The manager comes back even stronger. He's screaming right in our faces, now. There are beads of perspiration popping out on his forehead, and veins are bulging out of the sides of his neck. For a moment I forget all about the sandwich and I start worrying that this guy is going to have a heart attack right in front of us.

"I told you," he screams, "get back in your car and get the hell out of my parking lot!"

At that, Duff throws his Coke down at the manager's feet. The cup bursts and sprays Coke all over the manager's pants and shoes.

"Now you've done it!" the manager says... and with that he turns and heads back inside.

He's not getting away from us that easily, though. We follow him. Inside he turns and confronts us again.

"Get out of my restaurant," he yells.

There have been customers going in and out of the Burger King this whole time: parents with their kids, older couples have been walking around and past us. Behind and around the manager I see faces staring at us, watching us with fear and concern like we're something dangerous, something out of control. In all fairness to them, they're not completely wrong.

Duff gets up in the manager's face. "You're going to take your ass behind that counter," he says, "and you're going to make that motherfucking grilled chicken sandwich."

Next to us in line, a woman is standing with her two little kids. She decides that this is the moment to interject. She reprimands us. "You boys," she says, "need to calm down."

I turn to her. For some reason I feel compelled to explain the situation. "Ma'am," I tell her, "you don't understand. I ordered a grilled chicken sandwich, and—"

I get cut off again, though, this time by a guy walking back from the bathroom.

"Honey," he says, "what's going on?"

Duff turns his attention to the newcomer. "I'll tell you what's going on," he says. "What's going on is it's about to get ugly in here, so maybe you should take your family to a safe place."

The newcomer doesn't need to be told twice. He grabs his wife and kids and they hightail it out the door.

The manager has seized the opportunity afforded by this exchange to make his escape, back around the counter and into the kitchen. He's on to Plan B: if yelling isn't working, maybe ignoring us will make us go away. The thing he is yet to realize is that Duff and I aren't going anywhere. I push my way to the front of the line of people waiting to order, slam the bag I'm still carrying down on the counter, and tell him, "I ordered a fucking grilled chicken sandwich, and we're not leaving until I get a FUCKING GRILLED CHICKEN SANDWICH!"

I have to hand it to Mr. Manager. He's visibly trembling at this point, but he's not backing down. He comes charging back up to the counter and he yells, "I am the assistant manager. I made that grilled chicken sandwich my-self! I put it in the bag! Now I'm warning you, for the last time, to get the hell out of here!"

With that, he turns and storms off to his office. The problem is, this poor bastard's office is literally ten yards from the counter where he was just yelling at us. On top of that, his "office" is literally a cluttered little five-by-five room *with no door*. So here he is, sitting at his tiny desk in his tiny office with no door, still in full view of two of the angriest buffoons he's probably ever seen. And what does he do? *He pretends we're not there.* He opens up a blue money bag and he starts counting coins. He's counting fucking quarters and packing them into coin rollers while we stare at him from ten yards away.

The other employees don't know what to do. They've stopped taking orders. Customers are walking out without their food. Then one of the other employees, a rather large guy working the fryer, puts in his two cents.

"You know," he says, "New York state doesn't have the death penalty anymore, so you two had better watch your step."

Duff turns on him. "Hey man," he says, "you'd better keep that fat mouth of yours shut. Otherwise, if you're feeling so damn froggy, why not hop your lard-ass over the counter and we'll see how it turns out for you."

I suppose that maybe it goes without saying that at this point I am *amped*. Adrenaline is pumping through my veins like speed. My heart is pounding, my mind is racing. I feel like I could literally kill someone. But, for the moment at least, all of this energy has nowhere to go. It has nowhere to focus or vent itself. I need to do something, but I don't know what. I look over to the entryway, and notice the payphone mounted to the wall. Without a second thought I go over to it, pick up the receiver, and dial 911.

You read that right: *I dialed fucking 911.*

Even today, looking back, I don't know what the fuck I was thinking. The only thing I can think is that on some subconscious level I knew that if I didn't do something we were going to end up on the evening news.

The operator picks up. "911, what is your emergency?"

I start telling her our story. "We were going through the drive-thru at Burger King. I ordered a grilled chicken sandwich and my buddy Duff wanted two double cheeseburgers. That's what I ordered. Now they're claiming that they made my grilled chicken sandwich and put it in the bag, but there's no grilled chicken sandwich in the bag!"

There's a long pause, and then the operator deadpans: "Sir, what seems to be the problem?"

I don't know how I can explain it any more clearly. How can she not understand what the fucking problem is? I explain it again. "The problem," I say, "is that there's no fucking grilled chicken sandwich in the motherfucking bag! Why is that so hard for everybody to understand?"

Can you even imagine what the poor woman on the other end of the line must be thinking? At least she has a story for her friends: that time some idiot called up thinking that this nonsense was an emergency. Elsewhere people are being shot, robbed, attacked... and I'm here wasting her time with this bullshit. Still, she's the epitome of professionalism as she calmly responds, "Sir, is there an emergency?"

This infuriates me. In that moment I genuinely can't understand how anyone could be so hardheaded as to not understand something so simple. "You're damn right there's an emergency!" I scream into the phone. "I just got through telling you! I went through the drive-thru, we ordered two double cheeseburgers and a grilled chicken sandwich, and—"

She cuts me off. "I understand that, sir," she says. "I'm asking you if there's an emergency."

"Yes, there's a fucking emergency!" I scream. "I just told you, we only have the two double cheeseburgers! And on top of that, they're acting like I'm fucking trying to steal a grilled chicken sandwich. Who in their right mind would steal a fucking grilled chicken sandwich? You need to send some cops down here right now to straighten this shit out, before someone gets hurt!"

That gets her attention. She responds quickly, and her tone has changed. "Sir," she says, "is anyone there injured or hurt?"

"Not yet," I tell her, "but if you don't send the cops down here immediately, a whole bunch of people are going to get hurt."

"Sir," the operator says, "you are not going to harm people over a grilled chicken sandwich."

"The fuck I'm not!" I say. "Look, I don't want to hurt anyone over a grilled chicken sandwich. I really don't. But now it's a matter of principle. I want that grilled chicken sandwich, I paid for a grilled chicken sandwich, and we aren't leaving here until we get that fucking grilled chicken sandwich!"

God only knows how long this nonsense would have kept on if not for the fact that, at that moment, out of the corner of my eye, I spot movement. Mr. Manager has emerged from his office and he's moving with definite purpose through the kitchen. He's headed straight for Duff. I drop the phone and I head over. We arrive at almost the same moment. The bag with our food is sitting on the counter between us, and Mr. Manager grabs it and rips it open. Out spill the two sandwiches. Mr. Manager picks up the first one and unwraps it to reveal a cold double cheeseburger. He unwraps the second one and Lo and fucking Behold, it's my motherfucking grilled chicken sandwich. The manager looks at us with triumph in his eyes. He points his finger at the sandwich.

"See?" he proudly yells. "I told you! I told you I made that grilled chicken sandwich!"

For a second Duff and I are literally speechless. *We never actually looked inside the wrappers.* We went by what the wrappers had written on the outside, and both of them said "double cheeseburger." It only takes a couple of seconds for us to regroup and launch our counteroffensive, though.

"Well," Duff says, "in that case, where the hell is my other double cheeseburger? We ordered a grilled chicken sandwich and *two double cheeseburgers.* And anyway, you wrapped it wrong. You wrapped the grilled chicken sandwich in a double cheeseburger wrapper, you dumb mother-fucker! I guess that's why you make seven bucks an hour!"

Mr. Manager retorts with—I shit you not—"I make seven *twenty-five* an hour!" He's already walking away as he says it. He goes over to the pile of pre-made and wrapped burgers sitting under the heat lamps, grabs two double cheeseburgers, and brings them back over to the counter. He rewraps the crumpled grilled chicken sandwich and he puts the three sandwiches neatly into a new bag. He sets the bag on the counter, slides it over to us, walks back to his office, and puts his head down on his desk.

The place is so quiet you can hear a pin drop. The only sound is the tinny warble of the 911 operator's voice still trickling out of the pay-phone. I never hung up. The receiver is still dangling from the end of the cord. Seeing it, I realize that the cops are probably on their way. I grab the food and we run out the door, hop back into my car, and peel out of the parking lot.

We're fired up, furious, yelling and cursing as we pull back onto the New York State Thruway. Eventually the absurdity of the whole situation starts to seep in through our thick skulls, and we start to laugh. We terrorized a bunch of innocent people, nearly gave this poor guy a heart attack—*we could have killed someone*—all over a shitty Burger King grilled chicken sandwich. *What the fuck were we thinking?* We laugh our asses off. To us, in that moment, it's the funniest thing that's ever happened.

And since we're running down the list of completely asinine and embarrassing things I said and did that day, I'll add one more: before my anger completely subsided, I actually called a personal injury attorney, one of the ones always running low-budget commercials on TV, to see if I could *sue Burger King*. I know: What the fuck, right? What did I have to complain about? Psychological trauma? Emotional distress? I don't know what to tell you. This was the '90s, and it felt like everybody was suing everybody over everything and getting paid. Not me, though. I knew I had no case when the lawyer, when I told him what had happened, started straight up laughing. I hung up the phone.

Duff is one of the guys I used to run around a lot with back in the day, and I'm sure he came as close to ruining his life as I did. Thankfully, though, he was able to find direction, and actually managed to turn his passion for throwing hands into a profession: he became an MMA trainer. Most notably he's worked with Matt "The Hammer" Hamill—a deaf UFC fighter who appeared on the "The Ultimate Fighter" on SpikeTV. You may remember him: Hamill had a long-running feud with future UFC middleweight champion Michael Bisping, and was even the subject of a biopic called "The

Hammer" about his struggles and eventual rise to become the first deaf wrestler to win a National Collegiate Wrestling Championship.

I've always had a lot of love for Duff, and I'm glad he's found his calling in life. We don't get a chance to talk as often as I'd like, but when we do the Burger King story usually comes up. And we still laugh about it... only now our laughter is pointed in the right direction. Driving down the New York State Thruway that afternoon, the whole thing—the manager and what he'd said, the scared employees and customers, the concerned 911 operator—had seemed hilarious, like a big joke. Now, though, it's crystal clear to the both of us that the only thing laughable in this story is us: two punkass kids who thought that acting out, causing a scene, and scaring a bunch of unsuspecting people just trying to go about their lives made us tough. As I said, I'm not proud. I think about that poor bastard with his head down on his desk, making seven twenty-five an hour to put up with shit like this from assholes like us. I think about how happy I was, in that moment, to see him lose. I knew better, had been raised better than that... and yet there I was, acting a fool. Like with the other incidents, I wish I could tell you that that was the end of it: that after that I saw the light, learned my lesson, and moved on... but I can't. I promised to be honest, and the truth is that I had more to learn—and that for me, *testa dura*, the stakes would have to go as high as they could go before I did.

BRADLEES

At that time I was still working in loss prevention at Bradlees Department Store in the Riverside Mall in Utica. Basically, it was my job to catch shoplifters—and I took my job very, very seriously. If you stole from my store, your ass was mine.

I caught plenty of people who just took stuff for the thrill of stealing, and who were basically harmless. We had kids who took merchandise on a dare: small items like gum or a pack of baseball cards. We also had plenty of people who just stole on compulsion: lawyers, businessmen, housewives, you name it. I caught people I knew from my neighborhood: friends' parents and siblings. I saw it all. As I said, most of these were basically harmless. Then there were the hardcore thieves. These were people who stole to support a heroin or a crack habit: people who *needed* whatever it was they were stealing in order to get a fix. We also had our share of professional shoplifters: people who'd been stealing for decades, and who were slick as snot. When it came to confronting these professionals and junkies, when I was on the case, things had a tendency to get violent.

Back then Bradlees had a return policy that allowed people to get a full cash refund for any item *without a receipt*. It was more or less an open invitation to scammers and thieves. I remember one incident in particular involving a guy who'd used this tactic one time too many. This cat's M.O. was taking expensive luggage off the shelf, claiming he'd purchased it on a previous visit, and cashing it in at the front desk. We'd had our eye on him for a while—we even had him on tape—and one day I finally caught him in the act. I waited until he'd collected his refund, and then I approached him and displayed my badge. Yes, I had a Bradlees Loss Prevention badge. The thief tried to push his way past me and out of the store, and in the exchange he somehow managed to break the gold necklace I wore back then. A word of warning: *never* break an Italian man's gold necklace... especially if that Italian man happens to be a weight-room junkie all hopped-up on cops-and-robbers fantasies. Nothing good can happen to you after that. At this point I have the thief's path blocked, so he decides that his best option is to turn and make a run for the other exit, on the opposite side of the store. He takes off, and I take off after him. We're charging down the aisles when all of a sudden this quiet girl who works in the ladies' department cuts him off.

She steps right out in front of him and she screams, "Where the fuck do you think you're going?" It surprises the guy so much that he does a quick, one-hundred-and-eighty-degree turn and takes off running again... only now he's headed straight for me. We've got less than ten feet between us and we're both running at full speed. At the last second before impact I step out of this guy's path and I hit him with a clothesline that takes him off his feet. My arm wraps around his neck, and I lock it straight into a rear naked choke. Now that I have my brown belt in Gracie Jiu-Jitsu I know it wasn't applied as cleanly as it might have been, but the hold does the job regardless: this guy is asleep in under ten seconds.

I want you to picture the scene. It's a normal afternoon at the Riverside Mall. People are peacefully shopping, perusing the aisles... and then all of a sudden, out of nowhere, these two guys come charging into the middle of everything. A girl steps out into the aisle and screams an obscenity at the top of her lungs, and then the two guys collide in a violent clinch that leaves one with a death grip on the other's neck. Can you even imagine? I remember looking up and seeing a mother and her young son standing directly beside us, staring at us in horror. I wonder if they felt safer, because of my intervention. I wonder if they were more or less inclined to spend their shopping dollars at Bradlees or go elsewhere, after witnessing that incident. Or at least I wonder that now. At the time I considered it a job well done. Bradlees had hired me to stop the thieves, and I was fucking doing it. I was supremely proud of myself as I literally dragged this guy's unconscious body past rows of shoppers who'd stopped to watch and back to our security office to wait for the police to arrive.

But things didn't always go my way, and one incident in particular went a long way to convincing me that my luck was quickly running out: that time was almost up for the tough guy persona I'd created for myself, and that if I didn't find some way out soon my propensity for confrontation was going to take me down along with it.

It was the dead of winter, and the mall was relatively quiet. I was working with another loss prevention agent named Ken, and a few hours into our shift we were both getting hungry. Up to that point we'd been working the CCTV camera system, watching the same guy make his way around the store for the better part of an hour. This guy's cart was already loaded to the top with clothes, and as we watched he just kept piling more on. What made us suspicious was the fact that he didn't seem to be checking the prices on anything that he pulled. It seemed strange, but as time went on our hunger got the better of us and we convinced ourselves that we were following a dead end: that this guy was either loaded or just wasting time, creating a problem for one of the salespeople to clean up later. Satisfied, we headed out into the mall for a bite to eat.

We weren't gone long—we always got our food to go to minimize our time off duty—and when we got back the same guy was now up at the front register, checking out. Instead of the pile of clothes, though, his shopping cart now contained only a single item: a large box containing—according to the packaging, at least—a clothes hamper. We knew something was up, and we sprinted back to the office and started reviewing the CCTV footage. It didn't take us long to find what we were looking for. The grainy, black-and-white footage clearly showed this guy pulling the hamper box down from the shelf, cutting it open with a boxcutter he took from his pocket, stuffing all the clothes he'd collected inside, and then taping the box closed again with a roll of packing tape he'd also brought from home. Say whatever else you want to about this guy, but you have to hand it to him: he came prepared. Our girl at the register had no idea the box was full of clothes, had no reason to check: the thing looked brand new, straight off the shelf. Nor did she have any reason to try to negotiate such a large and bulky item across the countertop reader. The box—and its hefty payload—never left the cart.

By the time Ken and I found and reviewed the footage, the guy had already paid for the hamper and left the store. Now he was making his way out of the mall, out to the parking lot and his waiting car. Ken and I rushed after him, and we found him pushing his cart down a corridor leading to one of the mall's lesser-used entrances. At one time a restaurant had occupied one of the main spaces along that corridor, but that restaurant had closed and nothing had gone in to replace it. With nothing there to draw foot traffic the corridor started to see less and less use, and the mall's owners let upkeep slip: lights burned out and weren't replaced, which made patrons avoid it even more. By the time Ken and I rushed in to make our arrest, this corridor was one of the most isolated parts of the mall. No matter what happened, it was a safe bet it would just be me, Ken, and the would-be thief.

The guy hears Ken and I running up, and he turns to face us. I move in close, stop less than three feet from the guy. I'm within striking distance, at a range at which it's almost impossible to miss. Ken's right behind me. We pull out our badges and identify ourselves as Bradlees loss prevention. We tell the thief that he needs to come with us. Before I even know what's happening, the thief reaches into his jacket pocket with his right hand and pulls out a wooden-handled revolver. He doesn't aim it at us, doesn't even pull it all the way out of his pocket, but the threat is absolutely clear. He looks from one to the other of us and in a calm, cold voice he says, "I will blow you motherfuckers away."

I freeze. For a second my mind locks up, trying to decide whether to go for the gun or run. Then, instead, I do neither.

"Sure," I say. "Do you need any help carrying your clothes to the car?"

The guy's whole demeanor changes. He puts the gun away, turns around, and pushes his score through the doors and out into the dark parking lot. Ken and I just stand there, watching him go. Then we go back to the security office to call the police. They arrive quickly. They review the tape and interview us for their report. As I'm recounting the story for the officer, it finally hits me what just happened. Up until that point I've been almost weirdly calm: the whole thing happened so fast, it was over and done with so fast, that it was like I didn't even have time to get nervous. Now the reality of the situation starts to sink in: I could have been shot tonight. I could have been killed over some clothes, for a job that's paying me a few bucks an hour. Me and my big, bad ego could have run me straight into a fight that I wasn't equipped to finish—a fight that almost certainly would have finished me.

The police took a copy of the security tape for evidence, and the next day there was a story about the incident in the local paper. The story included my name and home address. How crazy is that? My mom was seriously freaked out. This guy knew where I lived, now, knew that I'd gone to the police. What if he came after me? I told her not to worry, that the guy just wanted to get away and that he would have to be crazy to come looking to make things worse for himself. The thing was, though, the guy was at least half crazy. The next day he actually went back to Bradlees to *return the clothes hamper*. Customer service took down his information on some pretext and called the police, but by the time the officers arrived the guy—and his full refund—were already long gone. At least now they had his name... though in the end I'm not sure it made any difference. I'm not sure it did anything other than tie him to that specific theft. It didn't seem to have anything to do with them eventually tracking him down: a few weeks later we heard he was picked up for a completely separate incident of armed robbery. I know that, if nothing else, my mom breathed a little easier knowing the guy was locked up. It broke my heart to see her upset, and I was glad to be able to tell her that they'd caught him. As if I needed another reason, it was yet another flashing neon sign from the Universe: it was time to stop putting my mother through this shit. It was time to *go*.

DÉJÀ VU, ALL OVER AGAIN

If the definition of insanity is doing the same thing over and over and expecting different results, then I guess at this point you could say I'm truly certifiable. It's only a few months after Pete's trip to the ER and our near-miss with the cops, and I'm back at the Network. For a guy who's telling himself that he wants to change his life, I'm sure acting like a guy who wants to keep things exactly the way they are. I'm sure acting like a guy who's in a seriously committed relationship with his own bullshit.

And tonight, yes, of course—at this point do you even have to ask?—we're back out in the street in front of the club, this time in a full-on snow storm, fighting like wild animals. There are so many people fighting you can hardly move. Several guys are laying unconscious on the ice-covered pavement. Two snow plows are stopped and running idle, waiting for us to clear out so they can get back to work.

Let me repeat that: the snowplows can't make it down the street because there are too many people outside fighting.

In the midst of this chaos, out of nowhere, this guy I've never seen before or had a beef with squares up with me. I throw a punch at his face, but he immediately shoots underneath my outstretched arm and scoops me up in a double-leg takedown. My feet fly out from under me as this guy readies himself to slam me onto the icy pavement. Purely out of instinct, I wrap my arm around this guy's neck in a sort of modified front headlock—not quite a guillotine choke, but something in the vicinity. I don't know what I'm do-ing, I'm just reacting. As we come crashing to the ground, the top of this guy's head slams directly into the asphalt. His body goes limp. He'd knocked himself out cold. I scramble out from under him and back to my feet, still holding him by the neck. With one arm I hold his limp body aloft and with the other I start smashing down on his upper back and shoulders

93

with downward elbow strikes. One of this guy's friends—a well-known local thug nicknamed "Hit"—sees what's happening and tries to intervene. This spells trouble, as Hit's known for carrying a gun, but he doesn't get a chance to pull it: my buddy Pete sees Hit headed my way and drops him with a well-timed right hook to the jaw. It's a beautiful shot, but we don't have time to enjoy it: Hit's unconscious form hasn't even settled on the ground before some random shitbag comes rushing into the middle of the fray *swinging a metal chain*. Who the fuck carries a chain? What is this, *Street Fighter*? Everybody takes ten steps back.

One of my dear friends, who for legal reasons shall remain nameless, runs to his car. He pops the trunk, reaches inside... and pulls out *a fucking chainsaw*. Two hard pulls on the cord and the thing roars to life. There's nothing in the world that sounds like a chainsaw but a chainsaw. To this day, when I hear one start up, I think of two things: the bathroom scene in *Scarface*, and my buddy running to our rescue. The shitbag with the chain is just as surprised as we are. He stops swinging the chain and stands there, frozen, and the realization dawns: he's just been out-crazied.

I honestly have no idea what my buddy meant to do at that moment, but luckily—and I use that term loosely, here—we never have to find out. Almost immediately, several cop cars come screeching onto the scene. The crowd scatters. As we run to our cars I see Hit picking himself up from where Pete dropped him. His eyes scan the roiling crowd until they lock on us.

"The next time I see you," he yells, over the sirens and the confused noises from the crowd, "I'm going to FUCKING SHOOT YOU!"

There's no time to argue about it. We pile into the back of my buddy's car. The wheels spin and finally catch and we fly out of the icy parking lot. Out on the road I notice for the first time that my buddy has set the running chainsaw on the passenger seat beside him. This crazy bastard is fleeing the cops in some of the worst driving conditions any of us has ever seen... with a running chainsaw riding shotgun.

Somehow we make it out of there safely. I get back home, get to bed, and am roused the next morning by another call from the police asking what I know about a big fight at the Network last night. Several people were severely beaten, the detective tells me. Some of them ended up in the hospital. Some of them are in serious condition.

"Sorry," I tell him, for what now feels like the hundredth time, "I don't know anything about it."

He asks me if I own a chainsaw. I ask him if he's joking. He informs me, sternly, that he is not. He tells me he may have more questions for me as the investigation progresses. I tell him he knows where to find me.

Later that night, there's a report about the fight on the news. There was a riot outside the Network, the reporter says. There are several eyewitness reports of a man chasing people with a chainsaw. So far police have been unable to identify this man, but they are working closely with witnesses. It is expected that arrests will follow.

All I can say is: thank God this all happened before the age of cell phones. If this sort of thing happened today, my buddy would undoubtedly be in jail and viral on YouTube all at the same time. With the way things were back then, nothing ever came of it. No one—not even the guys he chased—ever ratted him out. To this day, our chainsaw-wielding rescuer remains at large.

ESCAPE FROM NEW YORK

My family had seen the news report. They knew I'd been there. They knew who'd called the house that morning, asking what I knew. They didn't say a word. They didn't have to. What was there to say? I felt disgusted with myself and finally, this time, for whatever reason, I was willing to sit with that feeling long enough for it to actually do some good.

It was a long time coming, but that night was truly and finally the last straw. After that night, I knew beyond a shadow of a doubt that I had to change... and in order to do that, I knew I had to leave. I knew what would happen if I didn't. So I called up a childhood friend—my buddy Daryl Hagen—who'd already moved out to California, and who was known for helping guys like me establish a foothold out west. I told him the situation.

"If I don't get out of here," I told him, "I'm going to end up dead or in jail."

Even though they didn't really have room for me at his house at that time, he told me they'd make room. He gave me the green light. I packed everything I owned into a small suitcase and a duffle bag, and two weeks later I left for California.

My mother and father drove me to the Syracuse airport, and they waited with me at the gate until it came time for me to board. I'll always remember the strange mix of sadness and excitement I felt, torn between my dreams and hopes about where I was headed and the knowledge of what I was leaving behind. As they made the final boarding call my mother was crying her eyes out. She gave me a big hug and a kiss. She didn't want to let me go, but I could tell that she understood that this was something I needed to do. After a long embrace, she finally released me. I turned to my father. I was expecting a handshake, maybe, a few words of goodbye. Instead, unexpectedly, my father opened his arms and pulled me into the biggest hug I can ever remember him giving me. Holding me close he said, "I love you, son."

It was the first time he'd ever called me "son." It was the first time I'd ever heard him say the words, "I love you." I was nearly twenty-one years old, and he'd never said those words to me before. It hit me to my core. My father and I had butted heads many, many times, but in that moment it no longer mattered. I'd been chasing his love and approval for so long, never feeling like I met the mark. In that one moment, finally stepping out on my own, I felt like I had it.

I made two promises to myself as I boarded that plane to California. First, there was nothing that could happen that would make me turn around and go back to New York. New York, the person I'd become, and everything I'd done there were the past, and California was the future. Second, no matter what I pursued out west—be it bodybuilding, acting, or something else that I couldn't even imagine yet—I was going to be successful.

The weight I'd been carrying on my heart and on my shoulders got lighter and lighter as New York dropped away beneath us. I was leaving behind a lot of people I cared for dearly, but I knew with absolute certainty that I was doing the right thing. I knew because, for the first time in a very long time, I felt free. I felt like the future was wide open and full of possibilities. I settled back in my seat and eagerly awaited our arrival in the land of Arnold, Gold's Gym, Muscle Beach, and Hollywood herself. I drifted off to sleep thinking of the person I'd been, and dreaming of the person I would become.

PART II

CALIFORNIA

GOD BLESS YOU, JIMMY TREEN

I arrived in California and took up residence at my buddy's place in the small town of Temecula, located just about halfway between Los Angeles and San Diego. I absolutely loved it there. Everything about it was new and exciting for me. Part of this had to do with the fact that everything was literally new: the town was still small, just a little bigger than the town where I'd grown up, but it was growing even then, with new houses and new businesses cropping up all over. There were plenty of dirt lots that soon became housing tracts and shopping centers. At that time they were talking about Temecula becoming the new Orange County. After Utica, it felt like a breath of fresh air.

I liked everything about Temecula—the weather, the gyms, the opportunities—but if I'm being honest, I think the thing I liked most of all was the fact that I was there and my New York friends weren't. I missed them plenty, but being on my own gave me space to redefine myself. I didn't have to be a tough guy anymore. I wasn't constantly drawn into situations that left me torn between my loyalty to them and my foolish pride and my understanding that nothing good could come from any of this. Out away from them, that tension—my constant companion for years—lifted from my soul.

None of this is to say that life was comfortable or easy. When I first arrived there wasn't a room available at my buddy's place, so I slept on the floor under the dining room table. Back in New York I'd been living at home, eating my mom's cooking... This was a definite lifestyle change. Still, it's funny how something so simple makes you appreciate things even more: when a bedroom finally opened up for me, I felt like a king. The previous occupant had even left me a parting gift: a single twin mattress on the floor. I moved in and called it home.

The house where I stayed was actually owned by Daryl's uncle, a guy named Jimmy Treen. Jimmy and Daryl shared the house with a rotating cast of delinquent young men from Upstate New York who, like me, were trying to get away from their bad habits and make something better for themselves out west. Without question or hesitation Jimmy welcomed me in, gave me a place to stay, and even offered me a job at his landscaping company, "TreenScape." He was an amazingly caring person, one of those guys who would do whatever he could to help someone in need. He treated everyone like family. All of us guys at the house, and even the guys from my old neighborhood, called him "Uncle Jimmy."

Jimmy's place also functioned as an unofficial halfway house for people working their way through Alcoholics Anonymous. Jimmy had struggled and been helped through his own addiction issues in the past, and this was his way of paying it forward. Needless to say, in the time I lived there, we had all kinds of characters coming through. For a while we had a guy named Curtis sleeping on our couch, and when the couch was unavailable Curtis would sleep in my old spot under the dining room table—he was there so much, in fact, that we started calling it "Curtis's Corner." Curtis was a very sweet and lovable guy who, it turned out, had been in jail for manslaughter. He had the IQ of a child and a bit of a crystal meth problem, and the story went that he'd been manipulated by a few of his junkie friends into helping them dispose of a body. He'd been up for several days on a bender, and he'd thought these people were his friends, and he'd done whatever they told him to do. From what I heard, Curtis was in charge of rolling the body up in a carpet and putting it in a dumpster. I don't believe he actually killed anyone or had anything to do with killing anyone, but I could be wrong.

Curtis spent much of his time sketching cars and women and women in cars. He carried his sketchpad around with him everywhere he went. He showed his drawings to everyone. If you met Curtis, you were going to see his drawings.

Jimmy knew Curtis from AA, and he was doing his best to give Curtis a new life. He did more than just give him a place to live. From his years of drug use, Curtis had an awful case of "meth mouth." For those of you who don't know, meth mouth is where prolonged methamphetamine abuse causes the user's teeth to rot from the inside out. Curtis's teeth were an absolute wreck, and he almost never smiled because he was so embarrassed by them. Jimmy understood; he also knew that Curtis would have a hard time getting a job and building a life for himself with his teeth looking like that, so Jimmy paid out of pocket to have a dentist fix Curtis's teeth. That's the kind of man Jimmy Treen was. That's the kind of heart he had. God bless you, Uncle Jimmy. You opened your door to me and helped me change my life when I didn't have many options. I will never forget that. Rest in peace.

LET'S GET PERSONAL

As I said, I moved out to California with the secret dream of following Arnold's path through bodybuilding into Hollywood. That was still my goal, and the driving force behind every ounce of effort spent under the bar... but it wasn't exactly paying the bills. I needed something with a more immediate return on investment: something I cared about, something that I could pursue with the same inspiration and enthusiasm and that would allow me to start establishing myself out in California. It wasn't long before personal training caught my eye.

Nowadays it seems like everybody and their brother has completed a personal trainer certification; back in the early '90s, however, personal training was a whole new career field. Back home in New York I'd never even met a trainer, and most of the people I knew didn't have the disposable income to hire one anyway. Now, though, I was in California: the land where the sun is always shining and where people wear shorts year-round. I was in the national epicenter of fitness and health. If I was going to work as a trainer, this was the place.

At that time, as the field was so new, there were very few trainer certifications available. I looked around and finally found one run by the American Council on Exercise, or ACE. The ACE certification consisted of an involved course of study touching on everything from exercise science to nutrition to biomechanics, and would conclude with a written examination. I saved up the necessary cash, sent in my registration forms, and got to work.

For the next six months, my life fell into a steady routine. In the mornings I went to work at TreenScape. I'd quickly graduated from day laborer to sales, and now I was going door-to-door soliciting jobs. This was back when people actually answered the door when a stranger knocked: knock on some random person's door these days, and you run the risk of getting shot. I'd walk up to a house, knock on the door, and when the person answered they'd find me standing there with my clipboard in hand, wearing a white polo "TreenScape" shirt and my most winning smile.

"Hi," I'd say, "I'm John Petrelli from TreenScape. We're currently working in your neighborhood, and I'm checking to see if anyone in the area would like a free estimate on any of their landscaping needs. We do everything from sodding lawns to building pools."

And I don't mind telling you... I was good at my job. I got a lot of "yeses" and fewer than average "noes." Despite what you may assume from some of my more antisocial antics in the past, whether it's personal training or selling sod, I've always been very customer-focused. Plus, I was representing Jimmy Treen, and I wasn't about to let him down. From nine in the morning until three in the afternoon I was Jimmy's envoy to the households of Temecula and the surrounding area. Then it was home to eat lunch and study for my certification, and then off to the gym to work out. I also had a job bouncing at a nightclub on Thursday, Friday, and Saturday nights from eight in the evening to three in the morning. I was plenty busy, and I loved every second of it.

After six months of working, training, and studying my ass off, I was finally ready to take the ACE certification test. The test was to be administered on the campus of San Diego State University, and on the appointed day I drove down. I was driving a brand new car: a 1993 Nissan Sentra that I'd purchased with my TreenScape money and some help from my parents. It was a simple car with a five-speed manual transmission and no power anything, but I loved that car. I felt like a million bucks driving down to the SDSU campus. I pulled into the parking lot and parked, and just about fell over from sheer disbelief. The local community college I'd attended was the only college campus I'd ever been on. For most of the academic year, going to class meant trudging through snow drifts from one uninspired building to another. It meant freezing your ass off in a building that looked like it was designed to be a DMV. By contrast, the San Diego State University campus was *beautiful*. It looked like something out of a movie: nothing but green grass, blue skies, and gorgeous coeds as far as the eye could see. The moment I turned off my engine, as if on cue, an old Volkswagen van with surfboards on the roof pulled in and parked in the spot right next to me. Two long-haired, cutoff jean-short-wearing blonde girls in bikini tops hopped out and headed to class. It was a scene straight out of *Fast Times at*

Ridgemont High. I was positively floored. It was a challenge to stay focused as I wandered around the campus, searching for the appointed classroom.

Finally, I found the right room. I collected my exam from the proctor, sat down, cleared my head, and got to work. I'd never been great at taking tests, but the hard work I'd put in studying, my recent success at community college, and my experience and my passion for training and physical fitness gave me a bit of confidence. I finished up in about two hours and handed in my test. The proctor informed me that I would be notified of the result by mail in four to six weeks. *Four to six weeks?* I couldn't believe my ears. But what could I do? Remember, this was back before the internet. There was no going online to check your score. I left the campus and headed north toward Temecula feeling like I was back in junior year of high school, waiting for the coach to post the tryout results on the bulletin board outside his door. Every day for the next two months I rushed home from work to check the mail. Finally, the day I'd been waiting for came. I eagerly tore the envelope open and read the results. All my hard work had paid off. I'd passed. I was officially an ACE-certified personal trainer.

AM I THE MEANEST? AM I THE PRETTIEST?

It's April 28, 1993—my twenty-first birthday. Little do I suspect that it's also the day I'll meet a beautiful girl who changes my life forever.

It's a Thursday night, and I've got the night off from bouncing at the club. What do you do when you've got the night off from working at a bar? You head out to a different bar, of course. My buddy Rick Chadd—another bouncer from the club, and somebody I still stay in touch with to this day— went out looking for love. When we arrive at our destination we discover that tonight the bar is playing host to auditions for a movie that's going to film in town. What more could a guy ask for on his twenty-first birthday? I get to check out the local hotties and audition for a part in a movie all at the same time.

At this point in my life I have a decent amount of experience picking up girls in bars, but I have *zero* experience acting. The focus is still on body-building—the Hollywood part of the dream is somewhere further down the line. Remember, though: it's my birthday. It feels like anything is possible.

The auditions are being held on the dance floor. That's right: in order to audition you have to go out and perform in front of not just the film's producers and director but also *everyone else in the bar*. Looking back on it now this all strikes me as staggeringly unprofessional, but at the time I didn't know any better. At the time it even seemed smart, at least for the bar: having the auditions there meant plenty of aspiring stars standing around waiting their turn, and if you're nervous about auditioning and you can order a drink to bolster your courage or calm your nerves, or just to pass the time, aren't you going to do just that?

Rick and I watch several people get up and perform. None of them do anything all that impressive. *Shit*, I think, *I could do at least as good as these guys.*

I approach the table.

"Hey," I say to the guy holding the sign-up sheet, "what do I need to do to audition for this movie?"

Dumb? Bold? Some combination of the two? Sure. I can't say. What I do know is that, no matter what this guy says, I can't back down now. Everyone in the bar saw me approach the table. I can't go back to my buddy and tell him I chickened out. In my mind I'm already committed. If the guy tells me I have to strip down to my BVDs and dance the Funky Chicken, then that's what I'm going to do.

Luckily it doesn't come to that. The guy tells me that they have two more spaces available, and that I'll need to perform either a comedic or a dramatic monologue. Monologue? I have no idea what he's talking about... but I don't tell him that.

"Sure," I say. "No problem."

"Great," he says. "Comedic or dramatic?"

"Yes."

He looks at me. "No," he says, "I'm asking, Which one?"

"Both," I tell him.

He looks at me for another moment, and then he puts my name down on the list.

"We'll call you in about fifteen minutes," he says. "You should go get ready."

Other than the third-grade school play—in which I played a groundhog and had *one line*—I've never acted in my life. Now I've got fifteen minutes before I have to step out onto a dance floor in front of a room full of strangers, in a town I just moved to, and perform something that's both comedic *and* dramatic. Well: go big or go home, right? One of my favorite movies of all time is *The Last Dragon*. No, not *Enter the Dragon* with Bruce Lee: I'm talking about *The Last Dragon* with Bruce Leroy, the "Black Bruce Lee." As a kid I'd been obsessed with this movie. I'd watched it literally hundreds of times, and—to this day, in fact—I know every line from every character from every scene... a fact I'm now counting on, as the minutes before my audition tick down. I tell Rick that he's got to help me out: he's going to recite Bruce Leroy's lines, while I tackle the masterpiece that is Bruce's arch nemesis—Sho'nuff, the Shogun of Harlem..

If you haven't seen the movie, it's basically a genre mashup of black comedy and Kung Fu flick—comedy *and* drama, as far as I'm concerned. The villain, Sho'nuff, spends the entire movie erasing the line between menace and self-parody; he steals every scene he's in, and leaves no piece of scenery unchewed. There's no way I can do either the character or Julius Carry's performance in the role justice: you're just going to have to watch that shit for yourself. You can thank me later. Right now my master plan is to get out on the dance floor, have Rick pitch me his one line, and then give the movie people and everyone else in the bar the best Sho'nuff they've seen this side of the cinema screen.

We rehearse the scene several times by the pool table, and then they call my name.

Adrenaline is pumping through my body as I walk out onto the dance floor. Rick feeds me my line, and we're all systems go for the famous confrontation between Sho'nuff and Bruce Leroy. The volume of my voice is obscene, the level of the performance is borderline psychotic... in my honest, unbiased, and completely uneducated opinion, the scene goes off without a hitch. I go for it. I'm not saying it was *good*, I'm saying it went the way I thought it *should* go. I think I did Sho'nuff proud. And the upshot of the whole thing is that, while I'm not sure to this day what the hell the other people in the bar were thinking, I do know that I caught the attention of one pretty little girl standing by the dance floor. Lucky for me, this girl just happened to have a thing for twenty-one-year-old, borderline psychotic bodybuilders with a knack for pulling off monologues that are both comedic *and* dramatic on nightclub dance floors. I'd caught her eye and, as I walked back to my seat sweating from my amazing performance, she caught mine.

To this day I'm in my friend Rick's debt, because this cute girl had a friend with her... a rather aggressive friend, who apparently was also blown away by my amazing performance—a fact she had no trouble telling me as she slid her hand into my back jeans pocket. I asked Rick if he would be willing to take one for the team and run some interference. I pried this girl's hands loose from my butt and Rick intervened just enough for me to talk to my future wife and best friend, Cheyenne Green.

We hit it off, exchanged numbers, and have been together ever since.

It's the best birthday gift I've ever received.

CHEYENNE

Cheyenne has been such a blessing in my life. She's truly a beautiful person, inside and out. She's one of the most kind and patient and caring people I've ever met... and Lord knows, with all of the craziness my dumb ass has put her through, she's had plenty of chances to prove it.

When we first started dating, I was so focused on bodybuilding that everything else in my life took a back seat—including her. For those of you who don't know, bodybuilding is an incredibly demanding sport: everything from when, how, and how much you train (a lot) to when, what, and how much you eat (a lot) to when and how much you rest needs to be planned out, and that plan executed to a T. And that's not to mention the mental side, which presents its own set of complications and considerations. Case in point: soon after we started dating, Cheyenne took on a part-time job working the front desk at the same gym where I was training. I didn't say anything about it at the time, but in my mind I knew this presented a potential issue. The thing was, I had this extensive process that took place before I ever stepped foot in the gym for a workout. First, I would write out everything that I had to accomplish in that particular workout: every set, every rep, and every weight would take place on paper before it ever took place in the room. I would visualize the entire workout, set by set and rep by rep. I would feel how hard it might be, feel the speed the weight would travel, feel how I would barely be able to complete the last repetition. Even the clothes I wore were part of it. The clothes I wore correlated to the workout I was doing. I left nothing to chance. I wore the same clothes all the time. I'd once read that Einstein wore the same outfit all the time so that his mental energy wasn't wasted on picking out clothes, and for whatever reason that made sense to me. Sets, reps, weights, clothes: I dialed it all in. And throughout this process—this anticipation of the workout to come—anger would start to build. On the drive to the gym I would crank the most aggressive music I could find and let this anger build to a white-hot intensity. Many times, when I got inside, I wouldn't even speak to my training partner. I would be boiling over with this internal anger and aggression. I'd get straight under the bar and get to work.

Looking back this all seems a bit ridiculous, but what can I say? I was willing to do whatever it took to be successful short of taking steroids, and the fact that everyone else I would be competing against *was* taking steroids meant that I had to train even harder, be even more focused. If the other people in the gym thought I was a fucking psychopath, so be it. I couldn't have cared less.

The point is, there was no way I was going to spend all of that time and energy preparing, build all of that momentum, gather all of that focus, just to lose it talking to my girlfriend as soon as I walked in the front door. Arnold himself could have been standing at the front desk waiting to shake my hand, and I wouldn't have stopped... but if that ever happened, I knew Arnold would understand. Cheyenne was another matter altogether.

But guess what? *No issue.* Cheyenne understood my intensity. She knew I was focused on my dream. Not many women will put up with that sort of thing, but I didn't have just any woman. And it went well beyond just giving me the space I needed at the gym. She brought me food when I was sick. She brought me food when I *wasn't* sick. In the off-season my goal was to consume nearly eight thousand calories a day, and I was really into buffalo meat because it was high in protein and low in fat. Cheyenne would cook full baking sheets of buffalo flank steak. She'd bring over containers of cooked vegetables and rice. She understood when I canceled dinner plans because I was exhausted from training and passed out on the couch by seven o'clock. What a ball of fun I was. She threw her full support behind me, and did everything in her power to help me make my dream a reality.

Looking back, I'm embarrassed by how selfish I was. I'm overwhelmed

Cheyenne and me on the beach, back when I had hair and before we had kids… Coincidence?

by how lucky I am. God only knows what I did to deserve someone like Cheyenne. We've been together now for more of our lives than not. For nearly thirty years, this woman has been by my side. She's my rock, my silent storm. I love you, babe.

LATE NIGHT BEEF

Getting my ACE certification was a pivotal moment in my life. It felt like a major accomplishment, and I went right to work putting together a rudimentary plan for the personal training business I was going to start. I never thought for a second that it wouldn't be successful: I had so much passion and drive, I felt like literally nothing could stop me.

I guess it's true what they say: sometimes ignorance is bliss.

I was still bouncing at the club Thursday, Friday, and Saturday nights. I'd left street fighting behind me in New York, but—if I'm being totally honest—part of the appeal of bouncing was that it kept a bit of that same excitement in my life. There were plenty of occasions when I had to toss people out of the club, or break up a fight. The worst was when two women were fighting—those fights could get nasty. Take it from me: nothing is more dangerous than a drunk twenty-five-year-old woman in stilettos attacking her ex-boyfriend's new date. Most nights I would come home exhausted, down as many quality calories as I could, and crash into bed. My go-to meal at the time was a half-pound of ground beef mixed up with four whole eggs and diced potatoes. I would eat this monstrosity and pass out.

On one particular night, not long after I'd received my ACE certification in the mail, I woke up from my post-bouncing slumber to a full-on, four-alarm emergency in my guts. I rushed to the bathroom where I threw up all of my late-night beef, egg, and potato scramble. I cleaned myself up and managed to get back to bed and back to sleep, but I was sick to my stomach all the next day and had to run to the bathroom every couple of minutes. By the end of the day I'd spiked a fever of a hundred and five and I was full-on hallucinating. When Uncle Jimmy got home from work that evening, he took one look at me and called 911.

I don't remember any of this, but apparently by the time the paramedics arrived I was saying some pretty weird shit. The paramedics kept asking me and everyone else what drugs I was on, saying that they couldn't help me if I didn't tell them what I took. And who knows: maybe if I'd told them "ground beef and eggs" I could have saved us all some trouble. My state of mind and level of comprehension and communication being what they were at the time, there was nothing to do but load me into the ambulance for a quick ride to the ER.

We arrive at the hospital and the paramedics wheel me inside and deposit me in an ER bay. A few minutes later a doctor comes in and starts examining me. He tells me to open up and say, "Ahhh." This doctor wants to put that popsicle stick thing down my fucking throat so he can get a better look. The thing is, I've got a horrible gag reflex... and I manage to tell him as much. He insists. What can I do? I open wide and say, "Ahhh." The doctor inserts the popsicle stick... and I immediately projectile vomit all over him at point-blank range. I cover his whole face, his clean white outfit. This poor bastard literally has the orange Gatorade I drank in his mouth.

Needless to say, he doesn't mention the popsicle stick again.

They collect blood and other fluids, tell me they're going to run some tests, and after a while they're able to stabilize my temperature and they discharge me. My friends drive me home, and I spend the next few days in bed. My fever approaches a hundred and five again, and my gastrointestinal problems continue. As soon as I drink any fluids, they pass right through me. I'm using the bathroom a hundred times a day. No exaggeration, a hundred times! I literally can't sleep for more than ten minutes at a stretch without waking up and running to the bathroom. Finally, my fever breaks. My other symptoms continue, though. I'm a mess, an absolute wreck.

After several days I get a call from the hospital: the test results are finally in, and they've come back positive for E. coli. The good news is that there's a treatment. I set up the appointment and I get a ride back to the hospital. A petite Asian nurse escorts me into an examination room, where the largest hypodermic needle I've ever seen is waiting for a one-on-one encounter with my buttocks. The nurse tells me to drop my drawers. I do. I feel that thick-gauge needle going into my butt cheek... and I pass out. I haven't eaten in days, haven't been able to keep any liquids in me long enough to do any good. I barely have the strength to stand, and apparently that hypo-dermic needle was the last straw. I go completely unconscious and crash, head-first, onto the tile floor.

Picture this: my feet are still on the ground, the nurse has a hold of my waist, and my naked ass is peaked up in the air like the top of a pyramid, with a big ol' needle sticking out of it. I guess the nurse managed to call in reinforcements, and together they were able to scrape my useless carcass off the floor and onto the examining table. Talk about embarrassing. I have to stay there for another forty-five minutes of observation before they'll let me go home.

At that point I have no idea how I'd gotten sick. Eventually, though, it comes out that one of the large grocery store chains in our area had been grinding up the old, unsold ground beef and mixing it in with the new ground beef. Anything to save a buck, right? Apparently I wasn't the only one who got sick. I hadn't noticed anything off about the meat I'd cooked... then again, it was three in the morning and I was asleep on my feet, so who knows? I also found out that an E. coli infection is a great way to lose a bunch of weight really fast: in those handful of days I was sick, I dropped nearly thirty pounds. It was months before I felt fully back on my feet.

WRECKED

Now that I was cured, it was time to get back to work on my new personal training business. I'd worked out a deal with a private gym to start training clients out of their facility, so now it was just a matter of finding those clients. I took an ad out in the local newspaper, hired a local printer to print flyers. I hired a couple of friends to go around to local parking lots and place those flyers on car windshields. I did all the things you did back in those days.

It was an exciting time. I was still recovering from the E. coli, but inside I felt great. Just a handful of months earlier I'd been so unhappy. I'd been out running around, getting into trouble, fucking up my life and going nowhere fast. Now I was in California starting a brand new life. I was starting my own business, one where I'd be doing something I loved, where I could actually help people and make a living doing it. And, given my ACE certification and the California fitness market, I felt like the sky was the limit. I had all the momentum in the world. It wouldn't be long, however, before I was tested again.

I remember the day like it was yesterday. I'm driving around town, running errands for the business. I have a meeting with a guy about some new business cards, and then I have to run to the printer's to pick up a new batch of flyers. I'm driving toward an intersection where I have the right of way and the cross traffic has a stop sign. A large municipal water truck coming down the cross street blows right through the stop sign, and I can't stop in time to avoid the collision. I slam right into the passenger side of the truck. Next thing I know I'm back in an ambulance on my way to the ER.

I'm more or less all right, all things considered. At least nothing is broken. The thing is, though, my neck and my back are fucked. It hurts to turn my head, hurts to twist my torso or lift anything. This would be bad enough on its own, but given what I'm trying to accomplish at the moment the timing couldn't be worse. Pretty much everything in my life depends on my physicality. How the fuck am I supposed to put anyone through a workout if I can't even rack a weight on a bar? Let alone the questions about training myself or bouncing at the club. On top of that, my beautiful new car—the first new car I've ever owned—is wrecked. Sitting there in the ER, my thoughts turn south: I just got back on my feet after E. coli, just got back to work building my business, and now this. I'm twenty-one years old, and it feels like I'm getting a crash course in what it takes to make it on your own: like life is checking to see if I really have what it takes, to see if the promises I made to myself are more than just talk. I feel like I'm being tested by God to see if I'm worthy of being on my own: to see if I'm a man or still a boy.

It breaks my heart to do it, but with no car and new hospital bills on the way, I finally break down and call home. At that moment, even this feels like a test. You kids who grew up with cell phones won't understand this, but back in the '90s we had to worry about things like higher rates for long-distance calls. Uncle Jimmy had phone service through MCI, and back then a call from California to New York cost twenty-five cents a minute. When you've only got a couple hundred bucks to your name, that adds up fast; when you've just wrecked your car and you've got medical bills coming, it's even worse. It sure doesn't sound like much now, but in that moment those fees felt like yet another obstacle standing in my path. Luckily, I'd picked up a few tricks in my time at Uncle Jimmy's that helped me negotiate the problem.

On occasion, Uncle Jimmy would get a collect call from prison. Often these calls were from friends who were due for release and needed a place to stay. Prisoners have very limited phone privileges, and those on the receiving end of their calls aren't always in a position to pick up the tab, so many prisoners learn to employ various techniques for making the most of their time. One such technique was to pack as much information as possible into the allotted audio recording. Again, you cell phone kids won't understand what I'm talking about, but the older generation might remember that when you place a collect call the operator records a short audio clip—ostensibly of you saying your name—to be played for the call's recipient. The recipient's phone rings and the operator says, "You have a collect call from—" and then plays your audio clip "—do you accept the charges?" If you were clever and you didn't have much to say, you could pack all the information you needed to convey into those couple of seconds. The recipient would then decline the charges and hang up, having received your message all the same.

I'd used this workaround plenty of times to avoid the long-distance rates and save my parents the astronomical collect call fees. When my family picked up the phone the operator would ask them if they accepted the charges for a call from "It's John, call me back." They would then say no, hang up, and call me back. Now injured, nearly broke, and with no car, I dialed the operator, recorded the message, and waited for them to call. A minute later the phone rang. It was my mom, with my sister Gina on the extension. I told them what had happened. I told them my new car was totaled and I was hurt. In that moment I was feeling the lowest I'd felt since coming out to California, but just hearing the care and concern in their voices was enough to make things seem a little better. They told me they would do what they could to help, and a few days later an envelope arrived. I opened it and looked inside. There were two checks, one from my mom and one from my sister. One was for two hundred and fifty dollars and the other was for five hundred dollars, and seeing them brought tears to my eyes. Seeing them, I felt not only their support but also their belief that I could and would get through these challenges, and it meant the world to me. In that moment my shaken faith regained its footing, and I made a decision. Those checks represented what was, to me at that time, a ton of money: life-changing money. I wanted—arguably I *needed*—to cash those checks... but I knew I couldn't do it. I told myself right then and there that if I couldn't do this on my own—if I wasn't man enough to do this on my own—then I should run back home like the child I still was. If I wasn't man enough to do this on my own, without calling my mom every time any little hurdle got in my way, then I didn't belong out here. I thought of my mother traveling all the way from Italy to America to start a new life, and that gave me strength. I thought of my father fighting in and surviving three wars, and that gave me strength. I thought of having to go back to my old neighborhood as a failure, and it gave me the resolve to never quit. I put those checks away, put my head down, and got back to work.

I still have those checks in a scrap book somewhere. Looking back now I'm not sure whether it was pure stubbornness or blind ignorance that kept me from cashing them, but—whatever it was—I'm glad I made the decision I did. I drew a line in the sand and I stuck by it, and I know for a fact that I'm a better man for it.

OPEN FOR BUSINESS

They say it's a fool who counts his problems and not his blessings; I've been foolish plenty of times in my life, but I hope to say I'm not a fool. I'd taken a couple of knocks, sure, but those were nothing compared to what I had going for me... and nothing compared to what I had working for me behind the scenes. Call it fate, call it luck, call it the hand of God or whatever you believe in: whoever or whatever was pulling the strings set me down in the perfect market at the perfect moment. Personal training was a fresh concept, and I was in a new, young, and growing community that was willing to invest in its health. As soon as my first batch of flyers went out, my phone started ringing almost instantly. I would get home from my Treen-

Scape job to find four or five messages for training waiting for me almost daily.

It's funny to think about it now. It all happened so fast, I didn't even know what to say when I returned calls or answered the phone for training. I didn't know how much to charge. Hell, I didn't even know how I should *sound*. I thought that if I used a deeper voice when I talked to people on the phone they wouldn't catch on to the fact that I was only twenty-one years old. I remember actually sitting in my room talking into the mirror, rehearsing not only what I was going to say but *how I would sound* when I said it.

The situation was a little intimidating, if I'm being honest. I'd spent a lot of time training myself, and I'd swapped plenty of tips with plenty of work-out partners, but being the guy in charge, the *hired professional*, added a level of pressure I hadn't previously experienced in the fitness world. On top of that, just in terms of day-to-day operations, there was a lot to manage, and I was learning it all in real time. There were plenty of moments early on when I felt overwhelmed, when I genuinely wasn't sure whether I was smart enough to figure it all out. Looking back, though, I can honestly say that the thing that pulled me through all of those early awkward moments (and there were plenty)—the thing that actively erased any doubts I had about myself and what I was doing and made them utterly beside the point—was how helping my clients made me feel inside. I don't know how to say it other than to say it: bit by bit, piece by piece, helping people was healing my soul. Every time someone walked through the gym's front door or left a message on my answering machine, it was an opportunity for us to go on a journey together. And sure, on the surface it was an opportunity to help them lose weight, to help them look better in a bathing suit or feel better when they squeezed into their dress for their daughter's wedding. Really, though, it was an opportunity for both of us to discover and become new, better versions of ourselves. It was an opportunity for both of us to uncover and pursue our potential, a chance for both of us to better our lives. Most people have no idea what they are capable of: a fact I knew only too well, because I had been one of those people. I'd been trapped in an identity that kept me from achieving my potential. For so long I'd been surrounded by fear, anger, and violence. I'd been unable to see any way out. Now I was living in Southern California, building my dream, working with people who were happy to see me and whose lives I impacted in a positive way. I'd traveled across the country to escape my past and now I could finally see the brighter future. I wanted to pay that forward, to give other people that same sense of freedom and power to redefine themselves in the pursuit of something better. I wanted to give people that same sense that the possibilities were endless. Maybe it was seeing the positive impact Uncle Jimmy had on the lives of the people he helped, or recognizing the positive impact he'd had on me in my own life; maybe it was the years of collected guilt still weighing on me over the person I'd been, the people I'd hurt, the violence I'd been a party to; maybe it was the memory of the promise I'd made to the Judge and the DA—a promise I'd largely broken and ignored; maybe it was nothing more than the desire to finally be someone who made his family proud, after years of disappointing them. Maybe it was all of that or none of it. All I know is that I felt driven, inspired and compelled. Helping my clients, being the absolute best I could be *for them*, quickly became an obsession.

I worked up my courage and charged my first client twelve dollars an hour. I felt like the luckiest guy in the world when they agreed to the price without batting an eye. I'd spent countless hours baling hay for five dollars an hour in the blazing sun and gut-checking humidity of Upstate New York. In my time working in loss prevention at Bradlees I'd faced down death for a whopping seven bucks an hour. Now I was making nearly twice as much for personal training, and I didn't have to worry about getting shot. Truly, I was in the land of opportunity. And it only got better: word spread, I got busier, and as I got busier my rates increased. Eventually I had a completely full schedule and I was making *forty dollars an hour*. For a kid in his early twenties in 1993, this was pretty amazing. I was able to move out of Uncle Jimmy's house and into my own place, and this afforded me other opportunities to pay it forward: a couple of my friends from back east, Joe Palumbo and Nick Fazio, also wanted to start new lives, and I invited them to come out to California and stay with me. I have so many great memories from that time, and I owe them both a huge debt for all the laughs they gave me and the lessons they taught me.

It was a wonderful time in my life. I was succeeding in a new venture that fed my soul. I was having a positive impact on the people around me. I was falling in love with Cheyenne. That moment of doubt I'd felt sitting in the ER with a jacked-up neck and back and a totaled car, feeling scared and sorry for myself, felt well behind me. Still, for all that, I wasn't satisfied. If you know me then you know I never am. I felt like I'd only begun to scratch the surface of my own potential, and I wasn't going to let up until I found out just how far I could go.

MUSCLE MANIA

With my business up and running and my car accident injuries fully healed, I decided I was ready to refocus some of my energy on my big dream: it was time to take a run at becoming a professional bodybuilder. I had my old training partner from New York, Les Shibley, come out and live with me, and we trained like savages.

Looking back on it now, I can say that I'm truly proud of two things I achieved in bodybuilding. Number one: I can honestly say that I never saw anyone train harder than we did. And number two: I can honestly say that I never cheated and took drugs.

That second one is a bigger deal than you may think. I was in for a rude awakening when I started training around some of the top pros. I was shocked to discover that, despite their massive size and chiseled physiques, they weren't actually training all that hard... instead, they were hitting the needle hard. And it didn't stop there: with some of them, steroids were just the tip of the illicit substance iceberg. Here I am training like an animal, washing down eight cans of tuna a day with a glass of spring water—meanwhile Miloš the Serbian shitbag is pin-cushioning his ass with needles and snorting cocaine as a "pre-workout." Understand: I was no wet-behind-the-ears greenhorn. I knew that the sport of bodybuilding had a steroid problem, but I simply had no idea the scope and scale of the issue. It became very clear very quickly that steroids were what *all* of these guys were using to take them to that next level, and that was a line I simply wasn't willing to cross.

I trained hard for a solid year, bringing my weight to over two hundred and twenty pounds. For reference, just a few years earlier I'd tipped the scales at only one hundred and seventy pounds. And I was *strong*. Fair warning: this is the part of the book where I go full Al Bundy from *Married with Children* and brag about all the stuff that I can't do anymore, so if you're not interested you can just skip ahead. Here are some of the most notable lifts I completed:

Incline bench press at four hundred pounds. It was on a Smith Machine, so an argument could be made that it was slightly lighter than four hundred. I would regularly rep three fifteen on a traditional incline bench for a set of eight to ten. Max squat of four ninety-five. I did sets of ten to twelve with four hundred and five pounds at the end of a workout that went from leg extensions to squats to leg presses to leg curls and then went back to squats again. I did a set of full squats with three hundred and fifteen pounds on my back. Full range of motion, with my butt going all the way to the floor. I did that for twenty-three full reps. I shoulder-pressed the one-hundred-and-twenty-pound dumbbells for sets of ten, and on a couple of occasions did sets of four to six with the one forties. I chest-pressed the one hundred and fifty pound dumbbells for five reps, and I regularly did seated dumbbell curls with the eighty-five pound dumbbells. All of this through sheer hard work and determination. I was the biggest and strongest I'd ever been, and I had my sights set on one of the biggest amateur shows in the nation: Muscle Mania.

At that time, Muscle Mania was touted as the nation's largest and most prestigious "drug free" competition... though it wasn't long before it became crystal clear that the "drug free" part was a load of utter bullshit. For instance: in the registration paperwork I signed months in advance of the event, the organizers had stated that each athlete would have to take a polygraph test before competing in the morning's prejudging. That never happened. I never even saw a polygraph machine at the venue. Then, in our mandatory pre-competition athletes meeting, the promoters made a special announcement: "Because there are so many athletes competing today, it wouldn't be realistic to drug test everyone. Instead, we're going to randomly pick and test ten percent of all athletes." It turns out that testing and clearing ten percent of the competitors is all it takes to qualify as an "all-natural" competition. There were one hundred and twenty athletes competing that day. Ten percent meant six men and six women. And the guy who ended up winning my division? He didn't even attend that "mandatory" meeting, meaning that he had zero chance of being tested. What do you want to bet this six-foot tall guy had a little "help" achieving his competition weight of two hundred and thirty-eight pounds? This competition was "all natural" all right: just like horseshit.

I was in third place after prejudging... but I was also livid. I was so pissed off with the state of affairs, in fact, that I didn't even show up to the evening performance. I didn't bother to pick up my trophy. I truly let my anger and insecurities get the best of me that day. I should have stood there proudly, knowing that I was probably the only one on stage who hadn't used steroids to get there. I was just so mad and insecure. I couldn't let anyone see me receive anything less than first place—not after all the days where I couldn't walk back to my car after nearly dying under the squat rack. Instead, the friends who'd come to see me compete didn't see me at all.

If I could have a dozen days back in my life, that would be one of them. I loved bodybuilding, but that experience killed any desire I had to compete. Just on a basic level, I've always believed that working out should be about building better health, and the truth is that there is absolutely nothing healthy about what goes on in competitive bodybuilding. That experience made it clear to me that if I wanted to be the "best in the world" in that sport I would have to cheat, too. Instead, I made the decision to let that dream go—and my life has been all the better for it.

LOOK OUT, HOLLYWOOD...

I'd given bodybuilding twelve months of the hardest training of my life. For a solid year, I gave it absolutely everything I had. Now, though, that phase of my life was over. I'd made my run and come up short—but I'd also seen behind the curtain and realized that this thing was not what I wanted to be. Now it was time for me to regroup and refocus my energy on the next part of my dream. Look out, Hollywood, here I come.

I started making trips from Temecula down to San Diego to study acting. I would train clients all day, and then I would hop in my car and drive down to my classes. I got work as an extra on a couple of TV shows filming around San Diego, and I was also able to convince an agent in San Diego to give me an audition for representation. Somehow I managed to trick them into believing that I knew what I was doing, and we signed a contract. Soon after that, they started sending me out on auditions.

The auditioning process was pretty brutal, if I'm being honest. It mostly consisted of me sitting in my car for long hours in traffic just to go to some small office and suck at reading for "Security Guard #1." I was a good actor in the car on the ride out to the audition, and I was absolutely great again on the long ride home, but the two minutes I actually spent in the office were another story. In those two minutes, I always managed to blow it horribly.

I swear, there was Academy-Award-level shit going down on those painful three-hour rides home. Over and over I'd say my lines: "Ma'am, where do you think you're going? The restrooms are on the *east* end of the building." I'd say them to the steering wheel. I'd say them to the cars passing by. I'd say them to the empty passenger seat. The people in the cars next to me must have thought I was fucking nuts. The two minutes I'd spent in the casting office would be playing over and over in my head on an endless loop. They haunted me for days. I relived them every time I looked at my silent pager. I would try to tell myself that it didn't matter, that they'd seen my potential, and that today would be the day I'd get the call from my agent: "John, even though you sucked ass in the casting office, they'd like to hire you. You start filming tomorrow." Of course those calls were few and far between. Still, what I lacked in acting ability at that time I more than made up for with persistence. When it comes right down to it, I will put my head down and work past the point that most normal people throw in the towel. So I kept at it, and eventually—between the classes and the experience I gained working and auditioning—I got better. I booked a few roles on different shows, and I was able to put a bit of a résumé together. It was a start, and it was enough for me to attract the attention of a small agency in Beverly Hills, just a stone's throw from the movie capital of the world. They'd seen my work, they said, and they wanted me to come in so we could talk about my future.

I can still vividly remember driving to that appointment. I was so nervous that I literally sweated through the shirt I was wearing on the drive down. Luckily this was pretty standard, and I'd come prepared. I had another shirt with me. I changed in the parking lot and went inside.

Part of the reason that this agency was small was that they were new, basically just starting out. They were in the process of building out their roster, which meant both that they were willing to take a chance on a newbie like me and that, when I got up to their offices, I found a whole room full of aspiring actors who were also scheduled to interview and audition that day. All the men were going to work from one scene, and all the women were going to work from another. If I remember right, they were both from some soap opera. I got the sides and had about fifteen minutes to figure out what was going on before they called me into the room.

I was so nervous that I could barely see straight, but somehow I made it through the whole scene without fucking up. When I finished there was silence. Finally, after what felt like an eternity, they asked me to step outside while they talked. I don't know what was said inside, but when they called me back in it was to let me know that they wanted to see more. They gave me another scene—a comedy scene, this time—and sent me off to prepare. Ten minutes later I was back in the office. Once again, I managed to make it through the scene without any major blunders. The agents looked at each other, looked at me, asked me to take a seat... and offered to sign me as a client. All of the work I'd put in—the acting classes, the brutal auditions, the bit parts, the extra work, the endless hours sitting in traffic—had all been preparing me for that one moment. I was good enough or young enough or handsome enough or a small slice of all three enough to convince this little agency in Beverly Hills to take a shot on me. I was over the moon. That day, my three-hour drive through rush-hour traffic flew by. I was celebrating all the way home.

...HERE I COME

Sitting there in that Beverly Hills office and signing the representation contract, I made my decision: I would find an apartment, pack up my stuff, and move up to LA. I intended to be one-hundred-percent available for any audition the agency could book for me, and living way out in Temecula presented a major hurdle to that plan. If I was going to do this, I had to be close to the action. And, as luck would have it, the very next week I landed a small part as a mobster in a very low budget movie that was made for the film festival circuit, and I ended up meeting a guy on the set who was living in LA and in need of a roommate. I was in need of a room, so we made a deal.

Leaving Temecula was harder than I'd thought it would be. I was excited to start this next chapter of my life, but I was also sad to leave a group of clients who, in our time working together, had become more like family. I'd met some truly wonderful people in Temecula—people who'd helped me as much as, if not more than, I'd helped them. When they took a chance and hired me to be their trainer—when they decided to place their trust in some twenty-one-year-old kid from New York—they'd changed my life, and I will be forever grateful to them.

In LA, I hit the ground running. I'd spent a decent amount of time and effort already trying to educate myself on the ins and outs of how things worked in Hollywood, but I knew I had much more to learn. I kept my eyes open and my ear to the ground, and quickly discovered a way to give myself a leg up. At the time, when a casting director was casting a TV show or film, a fax would go out from the casting director to the various agencies saying that they were casting this or that film or show and that they needed this or that type of actor or actress. All of the agents would then either put in a call to the casting director, if they had a relationship with that casting director, or they would pull a bunch of headshots and résumés and stuff them into a manila envelope for a courier to deliver to the casting director that same day. All this couriering amounted to a significant expense for all talent agencies, but for a major agency it was just another item in the budget. For the tiny agency I'd just signed with, however, this expense comprised a serious consideration. I saw an opportunity. I offered to help mitigate this problem by delivering any packages that contained my photo to the intended casting director's office personally and for free. I knew that if my picture was in a packet it meant that the casting director was actively looking for someone that looked like me, or that I at least fit the description of the "Police Officer #2" or "Italian Hitman #4" role they were casting, so why not show up to their office so they could see me looking like Police Officer #2 in person?

Then as now, the movie business is crazy competitive. There is way more talent than there are jobs, and there's more talent arriving all the time. Back then, depending on the job, it was totally normal for a casting agent to see twenty or thirty people for the first round for a given role. I've been in more crowded rooms than I can count with people who could be my brothers or cousins, all of us gunning for the same twenty-second, two-line job. And that doesn't even take into consideration the fact that some of the jobs that went out on the casting sheet never even made it to that point: those slots were filled by agents who had enough juice to place their talent in the room, sight unseen. Others were filled by talent that the casting agent or assistant already knew from previous jobs. The rest were thrown to the thousands of us aspiring unknowns to fight over. Imagine hundreds of packages with literally thousands of headshots and résumés shuttled back and forth around LA for any single role and you start to get the picture. As far as I was concerned, if there was anything I could do to make myself stand out, then I *had* to do it. Showing up in person was a simple way to audition before the audition. And sure, I was out of pocket on the gas, but fuck it. I'd saved up a good chunk of money from all my personal training work, I didn't have another job to go to, and this was what I wanted to do. I had to go for it. I logged countless miles on my (new) ruby red Nissan Sentra and delivered a mountain of manila envelopes all over town, and it wasn't too long before it started to pay off.

And I should also mention: my agent absolutely loved the idea. Who wouldn't? I was saving them money and, when I started getting gigs, it was also *making* them money. It was a total win-win... for them.

I'm kidding, of course. It was a huge win for me as well. I was getting work, building the life I wanted, and I was learning a valuable lesson: if you want to be valued, then *make yourself valuable.* For years I'd been a violent hoodlum with a chip on his shoulder, causing problems and contributing nothing. I'd focused on the opportunities I'd been denied, the people who'd told me I wasn't good enough, as though their approval was something I was owed. Once I started focusing on what I could give—as a trainer, as a guy with a spare bedroom in his house where his New York buddies could stay and take a shot at a new life, as a partner in the effort to get this agency off the ground—the Universe started giving me everything I could have ever wanted, and more.

Don't get me wrong, though: just because I showed up in person to deliver the packages didn't mean I was a shoo-in. On a couple of occasions I actually had casting directors tell me to "Grab the sides for"—whatever the part was—"take a few minutes, and come back into my office and audition when you're ready." At that point I could have taken a month to prepare and I still wouldn't have been ready, and I blew several opportunities. But I kept at it and, once again, whether out of some higher virtue or just plain hardheadedness, I absolutely refused to quit.

And it turned out I didn't mind the couriering. I didn't mind it so much, in fact, that I got a job delivering packages as a legit courier. It was another opportunity to get my face seen around studio lots and casting directors'

Ready to rumble! "Boxing" headshot from my portfolio.

offices, whether my headshot was in the packages or not. It certainly couldn't hurt, and I was putting names to faces and making connections. I was learning how the sausage was made at lightning speed.

Day after day, I got up and got after it. I'd wake up early, go work out, then I'd come home and read the fax of the day's breakdowns. I wasn't supposed to have them, but I paid a guy to get me a copy. Then I'd put on my courier shirt, head to my agent's office to get the morning's packages, and head off to the casting directors' offices and the studio backlots.

This was all before 9/11, and security wasn't as tight as I'm sure it is now. Back then I could make my delivery at some small bungalow way in the back of the lot at Paramount or Warner Bros., and then spend hours just walking around the place. I'd learned early in life that if you just act like you belong most people won't question you. This was true in New York, and it was ten times truer in Hollywood. A studio lot is a place where literally anybody could be someone important. There are so many different people walking around: the sound guy, the head of the makeup department, a bigshot producer, a director... Nobody knowing who I was meant that nobody knew who I *wasn't*. Once I realized this flaw in the system, I exploited it to my full advantage. And it was absolutely amazing. Here I was, a kid from a town of less than two thousand people, a kid who used to bale hay for five bucks an hour, and now I was walking around the backlot of Warner Bros. Studios. I saw big-time movies being filmed. Movie stars that I'd been watching my whole life passed by me, smiled and said hi to me. It was mind-blowing.

And, naturally, I raided the craft services table. I can't tell you the number of times I just walked up and helped myself to a free lunch. Was it stealing? Sure, maybe technically. Can we call it a gray area? I was doing what I had to do to get by... and I make sure to pay it forward now. Seriously. Coming from an Italian family, where a huge part of our love and culture revolves around food and sharing food, it hits my heart on several levels when I hear about or see people going hungry. If you've got a cause that deals with food and feeding hungry people, you can count me in. Hell, I've bought extra meals at takeout places and dropped them off to the homeless guy sitting out front with the cardboard sign asking for spare change for food. Recently our church started a massive "Feeding the Hungry" campaign: my family and I joined several hundred other congregation members to pack boxes of non-perishable food. It may sound crazy, but over a single weekend we packed nearly two hundred and fifty thousand meals. Those meals went to feed needy people in over seventy countries. The point being, these days I tend to think I've at least evened the score... Plus, I don't think Warner Bros. ever missed those sandwiches.

I was quickly learning that, in this town, it helped to be bold... which was fine by me. Remember, you're talking to the guy who did Sho'nuff to a bar full of strangers. I can do bold. I was willing to try anything—including cold-calling casting directors. And, believe it or not, this was how I managed to book a job on *General Hospital.* I found the number for the casting director, called her up, and said, "Hi, my name is John Petrelli, I'm an actor who just arrived from New York, and I'd like to come in and meet you so I can show you what I can do." I expected her to blow me off, to demand to know how I got her number and tell me never to call her again... but she didn't. She scheduled a meeting. Two days later I was in her office auditioning, and a week later I was filming. How's that for "Fortune favors the bold?" I only had five lines, but they were the most important lines in the world to me. I remember sitting in my dressing room—*I had my own dressing room!* —looking in the mirror, and being overcome with pure, unadulterated gratitude. I literally could have been in jail. I could have been working a job I didn't give a rat's ass about, dredging my way through life and wondering what could have been if I'd only had the balls to try. Instead I was *here.* The lesson I'd learned taking my one-hundred-and-seventy-pound frame up to two hundred and twenty pounds was showing itself to be true all over again: if you're willing to put in the effort, you can literally will anything into reality.

That stint on *General Hospital* felt like a crowning achievement for sure, but I was still far from satisfied. I kept pushing, and over the next few years I went after and booked speaking roles on nearly every daytime soap opera. I also booked a couple of commercials, and I even had a role on a TV show opposite the one and only Pamela Anderson.

At that time Pam was starring in an action / comedy series called *V.I.P.* as Vallery Irons, the head of an eponymous personal security agency. I was hired to play the nameless "Hunky Pool Guy" in an episode involving terrorists from the former Soviet Union impersonating a band and ransoming some hostages for US treasury codes in an attempt to destabilize the capitalist system (you get all that?). It was a pretty cool gig. I had my own Hunky Pool Guy pickup truck, and Pam and I even had a scene where she commented on my "big pool hose"... pretty racy stuff for network TV. I was so nervous going into it that I almost crashed the Hunky Pool Guy truck. Understand: back then, as far as I and a lot of other people were concerned, Pam Anderson was the crème de la crème of hot chicks. I'd actually made a comment once in front of Cheyenne about how hot Pam Anderson was, and I know it made her a little uncomfortable that day when I reported to the set. For the record, on that score, I'd like to say the following. First, Pam is a sweet lady. She was very nice to me, and a joy to work with. Second, to Cheyenne: by the time that moment came to film my scenes with Pam, my heart already belonged to you.

CHEYENNE MOVES TO HOLLYWOOD

When I walked away from bodybuilding and moved to Hollywood to pursue acting, Cheyenne stuck with me. We had a long-distance relationship for almost two years. But, as some of you reading this already know, a long-distance relationship can be challenging. Even though we were only a few hours apart, many times our work schedules kept us from seeing each other for weeks at a time. I was making friends and connections in Hollywood, going to events and parties, and I know it was stressful for her to sit and wonder what I was getting into while I was out on the town and she was at home. Even though Cheyenne had nothing to worry about, let's face it: there are plenty of opportunities for a guy in his twenties in Hollywood to get into trouble, and it was only natural for her to worry. It couldn't go on forever, and after nearly two years it had reached a breaking point. To me, the solution was obvious: I suggested that Cheyenne quit her job and move to Hollywood to join me.

At that time Cheyenne had a great job working for a semiconductor company. I was working steadily as an actor, but I didn't have anything approaching what you'd call "job security." Still, Cheyenne took a leap of faith. She left her family and her job so we could be together.

If I'm being totally honest, the truth is that I wasn't LA's only selling point. Cheyenne had always secretly wanted to try her hand at acting, and I think seeing my success gave her the boost of confidence she needed to give it a whirl herself. I imagined that I, having worked in Hollywood for years at this point, would be helping her career... but it turned out I had it backwards. Cheyenne was simply much, much better than I was. Her success came much quicker than mine did, and it wasn't long before she left me completely in the dust.

This girl is an advertiser's dream. She's drop-dead gorgeous, and with a very unique and striking look. Her mom is part Hispanic, part Filipino, and part Native American, and her dad is half black and half white. That's right: our kids can go to school anywhere for free. They cover just about every minority racial demographic in one take. Add to that how poised and articulate and talented she is, and it's not hard to see why she was in such demand. As soon as she was settled in LA I set her up with my commercial agent, and before long her phone was ringing off the hook with commercial bookings. She'd be in New York one week as the spokesperson for Gold Bond, and the next week she'd be in San Diego filming a car commercial. Our agent started kidding me that I should hire her for acting lessons. Personally I couldn't have been happier: Cheyenne is a natural talent and a very hard worker, and she deserves all her success and more. Plus, all of that success meant something else: it meant that she was in Hollywood to stay.

MODEL? WHO, ME?

The world of talent work comprises a fairly broad spectrum of gigs, platforms, outlets, and opportunities. TV work, movie work, commercial work, print work, and modeling all orbit in the same general solar system, and I wasn't inclined or in a position to turn down any opportunity that came my way. All of which is to say that I did plenty of print work back in the day, mostly for magazines like *Men's Fitness* and *Men's Health*. Leaf through some back issues from that era and you may find a picture of yours truly jumping rope, holding a Gatorade bottle, or jogging on the beach with some hot chick in a bikini. The point being: I was no stranger to this kind of work, so when a call came in from my print agent telling me that they were sending me out to a casting, I didn't think too much about it. I figured it was probably another fitness magazine shoot. I hopped in my car and headed over.

It turned out, though, that this particular casting wasn't just another fitness magazine shoot: the casting on this particular day was for the world of high fashion. Now understand: at this point I had zero experience in the world of high fashion. In fact, I had no fashion sense whatsoever. Unless you consider camouflage pants and a leather fanny pack high fashion, I'm not your guy. These people were looking for an Italian guy to be in a worldwide Dolce & Gabbana campaign with Gisele Bündchen—yes, that Gisele Bündchen. I figured I had about as much chance of booking this gig as I did of winning the lottery.

The audition was with some guy named Steven Meisel. I had no fucking clue who Steven Meisel was, but it was pretty clear that everybody else at the audition did. It was pretty clear that, to everybody else at the audition, Steven Meisel was a big fucking deal. Okay, fine. I got in line and I waited. I waited for a long time to meet Mr. Big Fucking Deal Steven Meisel. I hate waiting in lines. Grocery store, movie theater, you name it. I simply have no patience for that shit. So imagine my state of mind. It's nearly two hours before it's finally my turn to meet the high-fashion God Steven Meisel. I walk in, sit down, and hand Steven Meisel's assistant my modeling book. I'm all business. As far as I'm concerned we all know how this is going to go, so I figure we should get it over with as quickly as possible and get on with our day. These people have already taken two hours of my life, plus drive time. I figure the sooner we're done here the sooner I'm home, writing this day off as a total loss.

Steven Meisel's assistant hands Steven my modeling book. For those of you who don't know, a modeling book is a model's portfolio. A proper modeling book is filled with images from all the different campaigns and ads that the model has appeared in. My modeling book has none of that. There are plenty of pictures of me doing chin-ups and dunking basketballs, but that's about it. To top it off, to take my book to the next level, I've strategically placed a picture of my mom as the very first page. My mom had been out to visit earlier that year, and she happened to come when I had a photoshoot for some fitness product. I brought her to the set, and at the end of the day I asked the photographer if he could take a few pictures of us. The one I've picked to lead my modeling book is a great one of me giving my mom a big hug. Also, just to push the whole thing over the top, in the upper righthand corner of the page I've included a wallet-sized picture of my nephew, William, on his first day of kindergarten. Clearly, I'm taking this modeling thing very seriously.

Steven Meisel opens my modeling book, takes one look at the picture of me and my mom, looks at me, and says, "What kind of photo is *that?*"

I look him dead in the eye and reply without hesitation: "That's my mother. You got a fucking problem with that?"

Now, I'm obviously joking... but it's immediately *obvious* that this fact is only *obvious* to *me*. The silence in the room is *deafening*. No one says a word. No one cracks the faintest smile. Not any of the assistants, and not Steven himself. For a moment we just sit there, our eyes still locked, stone-faced. It's a good ol'-fashioned Wild West stare down. Then, Steven closes my book and hands it back.

"Thank you," he says, "I've seen enough"

I go back out to my car and I call my print agent, a woman named Shelly. Shelly is an absolute sweetheart of a person, and I hate giving her bad news. There's no point in putting it off, though. The agency's policy is that I call them after every big audition, even when I know it's a "no." Shelly answers the phone and asks me how it went. I tell her what I already knew going in: that I have a better chance of winning the lottery than of booking this job. I tell her that I joked around with Steven a bit, and it turns out he's got zero sense of humor.

I can tell that Shelly is disappointed, but she's always positive and super nice. She tells me not to worry about it, that we'll get the next one. I hang up with her and I head to my next appointment, a workout with a personal training client. Not fifteen minutes later I'm cruising down the 10 freeway when my phone rings. It's Shelly.

"Guess what?" she says. "Steven Meisel loves you. You're his first choice."

It turns out that this cat is so used to people kissing his ass all day long that he actually found me refreshing. He appreciated the joke. He wants to work with me. Two days later I'm on the backlot of Universal Studios shooting a Dolce & Gabbana campaign with Gisele. They made Universal Studios look like old-world Italy, complete with cobblestone streets and outdoor cafés. The photos we shoot that day appear in ads in fashion magazines all around the world. My ugly mug is everywhere: in the center and on the back cover of magazines, on billboards, you name it.

And Steven Meisel? It turns out he's a really cool guy. He actually has a great sense of humor. This cat wears the same thing every day: black pants, black boots, black hat—his whole ensemble is black on black on black. I called him "Zorro" on my first day on the set, and he laughed his ass off.

Gisele was also very cool to work with. It was amazing to see a supermodel at the top of her profession work. She owned the camera, she owned the scene, she owned whatever clothes they had her in. She brought it all to life. I, on the other hand, felt like a fucking clown. They stuffed me into wool turtlenecks and shiny, pointy-toed dress shoes. Honestly, who buys this stuff? I felt so uncomfortable. The shoes made my size-twelve feet look ridiculous. I felt like the Joker from Batman. Then again: what the fuck do I know? Dolce & Gabbana seems to be doing just fine.

The whole thing was just crazy. You have to realize, not too long before that my mother had been cutting my hair and dressing me for school. I'd been a four-foot-eleven freshman sporting a cheesy thin mustache, a bowl cut, and a fresh crop of forehead acne. A regular teen heartthrob, right? Hard to imagine why *Tiger Beat* didn't track me down and throw me into the next boy band. Back then I was so intimidated by girls that if they were even standing near my locker I would turn around and walk the other way. I went to class with the wrong books to avoid the possibility of having to actually *speak* to one of them. The thought that just a handful of years later

Me and my mom: the picture that got me hired by Steven Meisel.

that kid would be modeling for a worldwide high fashion campaign with Gisele Bündchen is *absolutely fucking insane.* Yet another reason why I truly believe: anything and everything is possible.

But the story gets even better. At the end of our week of shooting, Steven Meisel took me aside.

"Let me ask you something," he said. "Would you be interested in doing a shoot for *Vogue?*"

Would I be interested? You bet your fucking ass. Next thing you know, I'm in *Vogue.* After that shoot Steven hires me for a shoot for *W* magazine. In all he hires me a half-dozen more times. I end up working with Carmen Kass, Amber Valletta, and a handful of other supermodels. My extended family back in Italy sees my picture in Italian magazines. A friend of mine hops off a plane in France and my face is staring back at him from a billboard. It was bananas. And after my work with Steve had run its course, I was able to book a bunch of other jobs because of all the exposure. I made thousands of dollars a day for doing basically nothing... all because I wasn't afraid to bust Zorro's balls at the audition when he talked shit about my mother.

In the end, though, I found that I didn't have any real passion for modeling. The money was good and the exposure was cool, but somehow I could never get completely comfortable with the idea that my whole job was to look attractive in front of a camera. Not that I ever complained. Remember: I'm a guy who knows what it is to bale hay and muck horse stalls for five bucks an hour. I felt blessed to be making a living looking into a lens. Even still, the whole experience felt like a big ol' chocolate Easter bunny: all shiny and sugary on the outside, and hollow as hell on the inside. Who was I helping with all of this posing? What was I adding to people's lives? Compared to helping my personal training clients and seeing them grow toward their potential, modeling ranked a far distant second. I stuck with it for a while, but by the time my dumb ass turned down a chance to meet Annie Leibovitz the writing was on the wall. It's true that I had no idea who she was, but even if I had, given the headspace I was in at that time, I'm not sure it would have made any difference. By then I was truly only modeling for the money, and apart from my lack of interest the amount they were offering me for the shoot was less than I was making as a trainer, and so I told them to go pound sand. Next time, Annie. These are the things that happen and the choices you make when you're doing something for the wrong reasons. I'm grateful that I had the chance to do it. I feel blessed to have had these experiences. For just a little while, it was very cool to be Derek Zoolander. In the end, though, the whole thing made me realize even more that my true passion lies in helping people. For that alone, if nothing else, I'm very grateful for the experience.

PART III

THE GOOD, THE BAD,
AND THE UGLY

CONFESSIONS OF A HOLLYWOOD TRAINER

A funny thing had happened. Four or five months after my big LA move, a casting director called my agent. He'd seen my headshot and résumé, he said, and not only was he interested in casting me for a recurring role on a daytime soap opera, he was also wondering if he could hire me as his personal trainer. At that time my work life was split between acting and my regular courier gig: I hadn't trained anyone since leaving Temecula. I hadn't made any effort to reestablish my personal training business in LA; I was one-hundred-percent focused on acting, and things that related to and directly supported that dream. Still, when he asked me I didn't hesitate. The hours I'd spent working with my clients in Temecula were some of the most rewarding of my entire life, and the prospect of doing that work again called to me on a deep level. And it stuck: from that single client, through word-of-mouth, referrals, and connections I'd already made, I built back to a fully-booked training schedule in under four months. I was still an aspiring actor, making the rounds at auditions and booking parts, but I was quickly becoming something else: a proven fitness trainer in a town where people expect the best, where look is everything, where a star's health and fitness can mean the difference between a successful shoot and an over-budget catastrophe, where a sold-out, global arena tour can all hang on a pop star's physical stamina. The lesson was as clear as it was simple: if you want to be valued, add value.

I didn't fully see it then, but looking back on it now I truly feel that that casting director's request was the Universe's way of guiding me back to the thing I was meant to do—the thing I've been doing now for almost thirty years, for everyone from some of the biggest names in the entertainment business to ordinary folks like you and me. And let me tell you: it's been a crazy ride. I've been to some wild places, seen some unbelievable things, and had some unforgettable experiences that have profoundly enriched my life. I've learned some invaluable lessons: about the life-changing potential of belief, about the vital importance of connection, and about the soul-mending power of forgiveness, acceptance, and love. I've also seen some things that, when I think of them now many years later, still make me laugh my fucking ass off. I'd like to share some of these experiences with you now. My name is John Petrelli, and this is my confession.

ANGUILLA

I've been very lucky in my career to meet and work with some amazing, interesting, and highly successful people. These people have given me a lot: friendship, wisdom, and some incredible opportunities. Two such people are Brad Korzen and Kelly Wearstler, the design and real-estate development power couple responsible—in the words of The Hollywood Reporter—for "LA's high-end boutique-hotel culture." I met Kelly and Brad through Barry Jay of Barry's Bootcamp, the now international chain of high-intensity interval training facilities (which, last I heard, is close to becoming a billion-dollar company). Barry was one of my clients—I had the privilege of teaching him martial arts and boxing, and we worked together for quite a while. Kelly and Brad both attended Barry's fitness classes regularly, and when they asked Barry for a recommendation for a personal trainer, he sent them to me. It was, as they say in the movies, the beginning of a beautiful friendship.

Kelly is an amazing combination of athleticism, intelligence, and beauty, all wrapped up in one of the sweetest personalities you could ever meet. She is way tougher than she looks, and can make it through the hardest workouts I can dream up with a smile on her face. And Brad is no slouch either: when I first started training Kelly, we would head into their home gym around six in the morning for an early workout, and Brad would already be there finishing up his hour-long workout and cooling down on the treadmill with a four-mile run. In a word, they're both savages. I've also been blessed to work with Brad's father, Erwin, a person who truly left a lasting impression on my soul.

At the time the story I'm about to tell you happened, we'd known Brad and Kelly for years.

Cheyenne and I were stuck in some God-awful LA traffic, on our way to Cheyenne's parents' house for Christmas, when we got a call from our friends. They'd recently built a luxurious hotel on the small Caribbean island of Anguilla, and were now days out from their scheduled grand opening. As with most projects of this magnitude, there'd been some major challenges, and now—with a sold-out hotel and hundreds of millions of dollars on the line—they were asking us if we could hop on the next plane down to Anguilla to help.

A high-end hotel is an entity unto itself, where anything a guest wants or wants to do can be provided or arranged. Hundreds of employees and dozens of affiliated service providers represent you, your hotel, and your brand—a harrowing prospect when you consider how one bad interaction or service experience can color—or even define—a guest's stay. In this case, Brad and Kelly had hired some local talent to run their hotel's health and fitness offerings, and things had not turned out as planned. Now, with just days before guests were due to arrive, Brad and Kelly were asking me to create and institute an entire fitness program for the hotel's guests to have at their disposal. They needed a variety of fitness classes, enough to fill about eight hours a day, and they needed me to teach *every one of those classes every day*. Also, in the mid-afternoons, they needed my help teaching the security staff some basic protocols in communication and self-defense. Additionally they wanted Cheyenne to come down and serve as the lead massage therapist at their in-house spa. Cheyenne had been Kelly's massage therapist for years at this point, working on her almost every week, so Kelly knew firsthand what Cheyenne brought to the (proverbial and literal) table. In her downtime, Cheyenne would also be teaching some of the newer massage therapists the hotel had on staff.

They needed all of this, they said, and they needed to know that it would all be done with the level of skill and professionalism that their guests would expect from a top-tier facility. They didn't want to entrust the job to anyone else.

Our plan had been to take the next week off and spend some much-needed downtime relaxing with Cheyenne's family. Truth be told, the last thing either of us wanted to do was hop on a plane, miss Christmas with the family, and go back to work... but we could also hear it in Brad and Kelly's voices that they truly needed us. So without even discussing the terms of our deal, I hit a U-turn on the freeway. Next thing you know we're at LAX, checking in for our flight.

Yes, Virginia, there is a Santa Claus... and this year, if you're Brad Korzen and Kelly Wearstler, his name is John and Cheyenne.

We had a layover in Puerto Rico, and from there we hopped on a private jet that was going to take us all the way to Anguilla. The weather didn't get the memo about our travel plans, though, and after a ton of rain and turbulence we were diverted to the island of St. Martin. But Brad and Kelly didn't have time to wait out the weather: they made some calls, and the next thing

Cheyenne and I knew we were boarding a Zodiac—the same kind used by the military—and braving the choppy waters over to Anguilla.

Wow, I remember thinking, as we cruised along. *This personal training thing has been really good to me. Here I am, halfway around the world, taking a Zodiac across the ocean at first light.* It took me back to my childhood, when I used to lay in bed and dream up crazy scenarios exactly like this one: of secret missions and covert operations, the kind where high-ranking officials call in the one operative who's guaranteed to get the job done... I pictured Cheyenne and I as the Special Forces of our profession, coming in to save the day. Probably because of my father's service to our country, I'd always had a deep affinity and admiration for the small percentage of men and women who put their lives on the line so that the rest of us can enjoy the freedoms we enjoy. Cruising along across the ocean, I thought of the path I hadn't taken... and the debt we all owe to those who did.

On the flight down I'd designed a system of classes that both fit what Brad and Kelly needed and gave me the intervals of intensity and recovery that I knew I needed to physically complete the hundred or more hours I'd agreed to teach over the coming two weeks. Once we arrived, though, it was immediately clear that there was a whole lot of work that needed to be done... and fitness classes and massages weren't even on the list.

It turned out that the weather system we'd encountered on our way down—the one that had made it impossible for us to land on the island—was actually a tropical storm that had torn through the entire region. By the time we arrived, the look on the receptionist's face said it all: they'd been in a pitched battle with Mother Nature for several days, and their side was losing the war.

We got the full story from Brad and Kelly in a high-paced debrief as we toured the scene. First, the power had gone out. This was no big deal, as the hotel had sufficient backup generators to keep things running smoothly. Which they were... until the torrential rains caused the generators to arc and go offline. At the same time, the rain was washing a massive amount of debris into the storm water system, clogging and backing up the sewer lines. This backed up the plumbing. You heard me right: by the time we arrived, this luxury hotel had no power and no plumbing. For the guests who'd arrived for the grand opening, this was far from the dream vacation they'd imagined. This was closer to an all-out nightmare. The staff was working around the clock doing whatever they could, but many of them had little or no experience in the service industry. Combine that with no plumbing, limited electricity, and even more limited sleep, and you've got a recipe for hot tempers and all-out disaster on your hands.

In all, Cheyenne and I were on the island for ten days. We did anything and everything we could. We taught staff, ran classes, gave massages, helped guests, ran errands. We ran on limited sleep and a steady drip feed of pure adrenaline. We weren't the only ones: everyone did. It was the order of the day. I learned a lot in that time. I watched Brad stay cool as a cucumber as complaint after complaint came his way. This guy had every reason to crack, to snap at people, to fall into self-pity. He had a huge financial stake on the line, and Mother Nature had just dumped a load of whoop-ass in his lap. I never saw him flinch. It was an amazing lesson in leadership. As the top guy you set the tone for your organization, and I've never witnessed a better illustration of that principle. Because of Brad's example, I saw people in every position and from all walks of life rise to the occasion. I take my hat off to him, and to all of them.

We all worked very hard, and by the end of the first week things were finally under control. By the end of ten days, things were in much better shape... and Cheyenne and I were fully exhausted. I can only imagine how Brad and Kelly felt. We hopped on a plane and headed back to Los Angeles, where our regular jobs and clients were waiting for us.

At Brad and Kelly's request, I ended up coming back to Anguilla three more times. Each occasion was its own unique adventure. Each trip involved instituting a fitness program for the hotel guests as well as teaching self-defense to the security staff. Thank God for the martial arts: Jiu-Jitsu, Krav Maga, and all the other disciplines I've studied over the years have served me in so many ways. Among other things, those skills and that knowledge—along with my high-percentile knowledge of physical fitness training—have given me something unique and valuable to offer people like Brad and Kelly. It's been a powerful lesson in the principle that commitment to excellence and a relentless drive for personal growth can make you a very valuable commodity... and that value can lead to some unforgettable experiences.

My last trip out to the island was once again over the Christmas holiday. Brad and Kelly had a very extravagant party planned for New Year's, and they'd spared no expense. DJs had been flown in from Europe. A world-class fireworks show was going to light the sky over the hotel at exactly midnight. Elite socialites had flown in from all over the world to celebrate. Honestly, I couldn't have cared less about any of it: after working for two weeks straight without a day off, the only thing I cared about was some time off and some much-needed sleep.

It's seven o'clock on New Year's Eve, and I've just officially finished work for the day. I make my way back to the villa where I'm staying to pack for the early morning flight back home. Just as I hop in the shower, the doorbell rings... and it doesn't ring once. It rings twice, three times, four times... there's a pause and then it rings four more times. Someone is insisting that I answer the door. Someone needs me to respond.

Honestly, my first thought is that there's something wrong back home. Images and scenarios are flashing through my head as I quickly cross the room and open the door. I find the hotel manager standing on my doorstep with an apologetic look on his face.

"John," he says, "I'm so sorry to bother you. I know you just finished work. I need to ask you a big favor. A huge favor. May I come in?"

151

I let him in. I'm wearing nothing but a towel. He doesn't seem to notice. He's got other things on his mind.

"I'm very sorry to ask this," he says, "but is there any chance you could work tonight? It'll only be for a couple of hours, and I'll pay you an additional full day's pay. We were just notified that some very important guests will be flying in for the party, and we need you to be their personal bodyguard."

All I want to do is FaceTime with Cheyenne. Our first son, Hunter, is about six months old, and I just want to see their faces for a few minutes before I pass out. I'm dead-dog tired. All the air is out of my balloon. But... Brad and Kelly need my help. I start counting in my head how many hours of sleep I can possibly get tonight if I take the job. I have to be up at four in the morning for my ride to the airport, and this gig will go until at least midnight...

Before I can tabulate everything in my head, the hotel manager blurts out, "Please, John! I will give you two day's pay! And I promise it will only be a couple of hours!"

What the hell. I was going to say "yes" anyway. You ask for my help, I'm going to help. I'd just needed a second to reorient, to think through what I needed to get done before I could report back. Lesson learned: sometimes the best way to negotiate is by saying nothing at all.

"No problem," I tell the manager. "I'm happy to help."

His whole demeanor changes. He visibly relaxes. "Great," he says. "Thank you!" And then he hits me with the details of the gig: "You'll be working with Michael Jordan, Derek Jeter, and NASCAR driver Jimmy Johnson. They're flying in for the night on Michael's jet, and I will feel much better knowing that you are heading their security detail."

At this point I've worked with and met plenty of famous people. I've found most of them to be very personable and above all, normal. If they keep their distance from the general public, it's only because they expect to be allowed their personal space in exactly the same way you do—and fans don't always understand that. When you're working security for high-profile individuals, it's important that you *do* understand: that you know how to maintain a buffer between them and anyone they might not want to deal with, but also that you know how to stay close without invading their personal space yourself. When I work with this type of client, I am always conscious of their privacy and their right to their personal "bubble." That being said, I grew up watching Jordan and Jeter, and I'd be lying if I said I wasn't excited to meet them. I wasn't familiar with Jimmy Johnson at that time, but I can tell you that he's one of the nicest people I've ever met.

I finish getting cleaned up and I head back out to work, and soon Jordan, Jeter, and Johnson arrive. People are understandably excited. Jordan, Jeter, and Johnson are very gracious and friendly to everyone. They sign autographs, shake hands, and pose for photos. After about an hour of this they ask me if I can create some space for them so that they can eat dinner without any interruptions. Absolutely. I start letting people know that it's time to give these guys some privacy.

This is when things start to go sideways.

My good friend Matt Amerosa has a term for the specific kind of attitude you get from wealthy people who are used to getting whatever they want whenever they want it. He calls it "Veruca Salt Syndrome," after the character from *Willy Wonka & the Chocolate Factory*. "Daddy I simply must have an Oompa Loompa!" I suddenly understand why I've been offered two day's pay for a couple hours of work: it's my job to somehow thread the needle between giving Jordan and company their privacy and communicating that disappointing fact to a hotel full of liquored-up Veruca Salts, each of whom expects *and has been promised* a VIP experience. To make matters worse, several of the worst offenders have been taking my boxing classes for the past week… This is going to be interesting.

Allow me to set the scene. The hotel's restaurant is built right on the beach. It's high tide, and the ocean is literally at your feet. The setting sun has painted the evening sky a breathtaking blend of pinks and blues. The DJ is rocking the tunes, people are enjoying exquisite meals. Jordan, Jeter, and Johnson are relaxing at a secluded table...

Suddenly, in what appears to be a planned and coordinated effort, several women in their mid-thirties and forties descend on the area. They dance their way toward the table, gyrating their hips to the pulsating Euro techno beats pumping out of the hotel's high-end sound system. Inch by inch, they close the distance. They're staring hard, looking for eye contact with the men. One woman in particular is making a hard push toward Derek Jeter. She clearly wants to get up close and personal with him... and it clearly doesn't matter that his girlfriend is seated right next to him.

Let me say for the record: when it comes to physical confrontation, I feel very comfortable dealing with men. I feel very comfortable with the prospect of going hands-on. Yes, I could certainly end up on the wrong side of the exchange, but it wouldn't be the first time. I'm okay with that. I'm less okay with the prospect of having to get physical with a thirty-five year old female socialite in stiletto heels. I can tell you, though, that this is a very dangerous creature indeed, one that can go from a seductress with a smile and a hip thrust to a ferocious tiger in a split second. I've never seen anything like it. Ah, the wonders of entitlement and alcohol. I position myself for intercept and I kindly ask the woman to please back up a bit and give the gentlemen a little space to enjoy their meal. I shit you not, this woman turns to me and says, "Just so you know, sweetheart? I'll knock you and that ugly bitch"—here, referring to Derek Jeter's girlfriend—"out, just to have his babies."

Honestly, I think she's joking. Who says that?

"In that case," I say, trying to roll with the joke, "you might have to wait until after dessert."

The woman doesn't laugh. She doesn't crack a smile. She's dead serious.

She's still moving with the music, still doing her seductive dance. She looks me straight in the eye and she says, "Why don't you *go fuck yourself?*"

This, from a woman who dines at Michelin-starred restaurants. Who would look down on you for putting your elbows on the dinner table. Honestly, I'm not mentally prepared for this. But the night is young, and it only gets worse. Next up? Several men who've been taking my boxing classes all week, and with whom I thought I had a friendly rapport. These guys go absolutely apeshit when I inform them that no, unfortunately I won't be able to introduce them to Jordan and Jeter, as the gentlemen would like some privacy. I instantly become public enemy number one. When Veruca Salt doesn't get what she wants, things go south quickly. Names, threats, curses, insults... I hear it all that night. Still, through all of it, all I can think of is my family back home. I miss them dearly. I've missed my son's first Christmas, working here on the island. Now, in less than twenty-four hours, I'll be back with them... I just have to get through this first.

After several hours of absolute nonsense, Michael and company are ready to head back to their private villa. I bring in two other members of the security team to help with the transport. We escort Derek, Michael, Jimmy, and their significant others through the crowd to where three golf carts are waiting. Everything goes smoothly in transit and we arrive at the villa without incident. We exit the golf carts and approach. A member of my team leads the way, the guests are in the middle, and another security guard is shadowing. I take up the rear. Just as the first guard opens the door to the room, a drunk guest comes flying down the dark pathway, blows past our point man, and runs directly into Michael Jordan's villa.

Private dinner? Check. Drunk guests intercepted? Check. Successful transport? Check. Safe and secure in one of the hotel's finest and most private villas? *Fuck.*

Seriously, though, what the fuck? Why? What's your actual plan? You think this is how you meet your sports hero, and show him that you love him? I'm upset and embarrassed for this imbecile all at the same time. We secure the guests back in the golf carts and then I have to go into the villa and pull this drunk idiot out. He isn't going to go quietly, though. I end up chasing him around the kitchen island, then into the living room, then back into the kitchen. His shirt is unbuttoned all the way down to his fat, hairy navel, he's dripping with sweat, his face is red, he's running around with a half-empty Corona bottle in his hand, and the whole time he keeps yelling some drunken, incoherent nonsense about the Chicago Bulls ruling the world. Finally I corner him in the kitchen and I start speaking to him like he's a five-year-old.

"Come on," I say. "You know you can't do this. You can't just break into someone's room and start screaming at the top of your lungs. You know that what you're doing is wrong." I'm closing the distance as I talk, getting ready to make my move. I think I've got him. The guy's backed against the kitchen counter, and he's got nowhere to go. Nowhere to go, that is, but *up*. This moron downs the rest of his beer, climbs up on the kitchen counter, takes his shirt off, and starts chanting, "Jeter! Jeter! Jeter!"

Even John Belushi would have been embarrassed.

At that moment another member of our security team enters the room. He's escorting a woman who I've never seen before. This woman takes one look at the guy on the kitchen counter and yells, "Steven! What the hell do you think you're doing?"

The imbecile on the counter freezes in mid-chant. His eyes lock on the woman and he just stands there staring at her, frozen in fear. It's like watching a child getting busted by the school principal. Honestly, it's pretty satisfying.

The woman walks over, picks Steven's stained and sweat-soaked dress shirt off the kitchen floor, points her finger at him, and lets him have it.

"Steven! You put your shirt back on and you walk out of this house! Now, Steven!"

Steven climbs down off the kitchen counter. The woman literally grabs him by the back of the neck and marches him out of the house. She stops outside so Steven can put his shirt back on. Then she walks back into the kitchen, comes over to me, places several one hundred dollar bills in my hand, and says, "I'm so sorry you all had to see this."

Then, before I can say anything, she's gone.

Later the hotel manager tells me that Steven runs a major international company, and that he has been a huge pain in the ass for the entire duration of his stay at the hotel. Nothing the staff did or could do was ever good enough for him. Go figure.

We clean up Steven's mess, sweep the place to make sure no other crazies have snuck in during the confusion, and then we escort Jordan and his crew back inside. We apologize, wish them a good night, say our goodbyes and leave, and early the next morning I catch my flight and finally head home to my family.

The whole way home I think about how bizarre the last twenty-four hours have been. We tend to envy the super famous, but flying home on the heels of that experience I start to consider just how challenging it must also be to be someone like Michael Jordan or Derek Jeter. I'd been offered a brief glimpse into that world—a brief glimpse into what, presumably, happens to them all the time—and it is more than enough to last me for a good long while. To think that, to a greater or lesser extent, this is how it is for them *each and every day*: that each and every day they have people coming up to them wanting their attention, their acknowledgement, their time and energy; that each and every day there are people in their faces with requests, demands, propositions... It has to be exhausting. And it has to be incredibly challenging for them to effectively navigate that boundary between genuinely appreciating their fans on the one hand and, on the other, respecting their own very basic human need for personal time and personal space... especially in a culture where members of the general public often feel that they are owed something for their support, their game ticket and merchandise purchases... I'd had my own dreams of being super-famous: flying home from my New Year's adventure in Anguilla, for the first time I'm actually glad that I'm not.

Oh, and for all you memorabilia hounds? I do have one souvenir from that night: a video of Michael Jordan and Derek Jeter dancing on the table-top while Euro techno beats bump in the background and fireworks explode overhead.

It's not for sale.

RICK YUNE

Everyone has their favorite James Bond, and everyone has their favorite Bond villain. Mine is Zao, the North Korean henchman with the "sparkling personality" in *Die Another Day*... then again, I'm biased.

I first met Rick Yune, the actor (*and* screenwriter *and* producer *and* martial artist *and* former model) who plays Zao, back when he was in training for his role in *The Fast and Furious*. At that time I was meeting clients at a private gym facility set up exclusively for one-on-one sessions between trainers and clients. Rick was working out there as well with another trainer, and—to put it kindly—she was in over her head.

To be totally fair to her: I love Rick to death, but he is very demanding... and, though he has many virtues, at that point in his life patience was not one of them. Rick's trainer was constantly consulting me in regards to Rick's training, and finally—after about a month of this—she asked if I'd be willing to step in and take him on as a client. She thought it might be a better fit, she said. Turns out she was right: Rick and I hit it off, I got him in the best shape of his life, and we've been friends ever since.

Rick lives in Europe now, but back when we were both living in Los Angeles he and I would train at least four days a week. If he was getting ready for a movie, we would train up to six days a week. Let me tell you: this guy puts in as much effort as many of the top-level athletes I've trained. He's worked his ass off to be where he's at, and I couldn't be happier for him for all he's achieved.

Through our many years of training and friendship, Rick has shared a lot about himself that has helped me understand his outlook and what motivates him. Growing up, Rick's family life was filled with chaos and instability. His childhood was filled with violence, both at home and on the street. He was the only Asian kid in his neighborhood, and it made him a target. It made him stand out when all he wanted to do was blend in—a struggle I, in my neighborhood full of Italians, never even had to consider. Within this constant bombardment, TV and movies became an escape: a chance to enter a world far removed from the horror that surrounded him. Even here, though, he found more of the same prejudice he faced in his daily life. So many early American movies portrayed Asian men as emasculated coolies, indentured labor "hopping to" at the command of their white bosses. Even though the great Bruce Lee—who was a hero to so many of us—started to break down these stereotypes, there was still much work to be done. It made him angry, and that anger drove him to seek the next level in his own life: to set new standards for himself and in so doing show the world what a powerful Asian leading man can do. It motivated him to face down and overcome the monumental challenges that stood between him and his goal... and the end results have been seen by hundreds of millions the world over. In my humble opinion—even though I know there is much more greatness to come from my friend Rick—I feel he has done exactly what he set out to do. How many of us can say that?

When I told Rick I was writing this book, he gave me a great deal of support and encouragement... but he was also quick to point out the opportunity and the responsibility that a project like this represented. What I wrote had the potential to impact the life of anyone who happened to read it, he said, and that could mean someone who was struggling. It could mean someone who was going through the same hardships he and I had experienced growing up: someone feeling as lost and directionless as we'd once felt. I needed to write something that would inspire people from our old neighborhoods, he said: something that would speak to anyone out there who was desperate, whose life was filled with anger and violence. I needed to write something that would let them know the truth: that if you surround yourself with people who lift you up and want you to succeed, if you change your mindset, and if you're willing to put in the work day in and day out, *you can do anything.* That if a delinquent Italian kid from a town with the population of two thousand and a Korean kid who grew up in a world of chaos and uncertainty can set and achieve incredible goals, then so can you.

In our years of friendship, I've been lucky enough to accompany Rick on some pretty incredible adventures, and have had the opportunity to see exactly the kind of person he is firsthand. Case in point: once, while we were on a trip to Thailand together, Rick had an offer to take a (paid) trip to either Phuket or Ko Pha Ngan—both very well known for their wild beach parties and night life. Instead, Rick had the inspiration that we take a trip to Cambodia—at his expense.

The idea didn't exactly come out of nowhere. During our stay in Thailand, Rick had been invited by the King and Queen of Thailand to a party held at the Grand Palace: an opulent complex of buildings located in the heart of Bangkok. I got to tag along, and so I was there for King Bhumibol Adulyadej's tour of the ornate and lush interior and exterior grounds. To say I was in disbelief of the wealth I was surrounded by is an understatement. I was in absolute awe. Room after room and garden after garden stood as a testament to the monarchy's affluence. Don't get me wrong: I would trade everything in that palace—and more—for my life with my family in a heart-beat. But the sheer scope and volume of the treasury on display was stag-gering. I kept thinking, *How the heck does a kid from a small town in Up-state New York end up here, in the Thai presidential palace?*

The setting made an even more powerful impression on Rick. Later that night, standing on a balcony out away from the other partygoers, he pre-sented me with the idea of going to Cambodia. In addition to a (somewhat disputed) border, the two countries share a long and complicated history, with the smaller and poorer Cambodia usually finding itself on the worse end of the countries' exchanges both politically and economically. Rick wanted to see firsthand the contrast between our current regal surround-ings and daily life for the Cambodian people.

I'll be honest: at first, I needed a bit of convincing. Not because I wanted to stay here, lulled into an affluent daydream (I didn't), and not because I wanted to head to one of the aforementioned party destinations in Thailand (I most certainly did not). The simple fact of the matter was that I didn't know what to expect in Cambodia. My father spoke very little of his time in the military until the last years of his life, but of the little he did share, sneaking his platoon along the Ho Chi Minh trail in and out of Cambodia with the aid of South Vietnamese natives was one story I remembered vivid-ly. The thought of traveling through that same unknown jungle made me feel a bit uncomfortable... and my good buddy Rick could tell. He could sense it, could smell it... and that made him push me even harder. He re-minded me of something I already knew, something I was constantly saying to him in our training sessions back in the States: whether mentally or phys-ically, growth happens when you get outside your comfort zone. He had me there—and I'm grateful that he did. Before I knew it we were on a plane and Thailand, the presidential palace, and the never-ending beach parties were falling away behind us.

Rick had arranged for a liaison to meet us at the Siem Reap airport.

Thom would be there to help us navigate the country, and over the next couple of days Rick and I would be very glad that he was there. Within seconds of landing one thing became immediately clear: we weren't in Kansas anymore. There was a tension in the air that was palpable. Everywhere we looked, young soldiers toting AK-47s stared back at us. Standard operating procedure in Cambodia, maybe, but it certainly didn't make me feel any more at ease. I was way out of my element, operating on high alert... and Rick knew it. He took great pleasure breaking my balls each time I overreacted to any unexpected sound or shout. At one particular moment I actually started covering my mouth with my hand when I was talking, so that no one would hear me but Rick. Like we were in *The Sopranos*, and the FBI lipreader was in a far-off building trying to decipher what the hell I was saying. Rick looked at me with wide eyes and started laughing his ass off.

I couldn't really blame him, but his laughter didn't exactly calm my nerves. Of course it also didn't help matters that blending in was nearly impossible—and not because of my Italian ass. At this point Rick's face was plenty recognizable, and everywhere we went it felt like all eyes were on us. I had the unshakable sense that something bad could happen at any time... and in the days that followed I would come to understand why.

Cambodia is a country of ancient culture and startling beauty. With Thom guiding us, Rick and I explored the magnificent temples of Angkor Wat, the largest religious monument in the world. We stood in awe of what this civilization had been able to construct, and all without the use of modern technology. But Cambodia also bears the unmistakable and un-ignorable scars of modern warfare. Everywhere we went we saw dozens upon dozens of amputees: victims of landmines left behind by soldiers and stumbled upon by children out playing in the fields. Just try to imagine. Imagine having a childhood where you have to worry about stepping on a landmine—where you have friends or siblings or classmates who've lost limbs that way. Imagine being a parent who has to worry about your son or daughter stepping on a landmine buried somewhere in the fields around your village. It broke our hearts. Every time we stopped to get something to eat, we bought extra food and passed it out to amputees.

True to his word, Rick asked Thom to take us out of the tourist areas to a place where we could see how the working people lived. Initially, Thom advised us against this. He told us that it wouldn't be a great experience. We insisted, though, and Thom finally agreed. We headed out of town, out to a fishing village set amongst rice fields. All I can say is this: in my life, I have seen many different types of poverty, from the inner cities of Newark, New Jersey and the Bronx to Mexico. What we saw that day in Cambodia was different from anything I had witnessed before. We saw whole families living in houses made of cardboard. We stopped by workers standing chest-deep in the foul-smelling water flooding the rice fields. When I tell you that the smell almost knocked me over, you can take that for what it's worth: remember that I'm a guy who spent a good portion of his childhood working in horse barns. I'm no wilting flower. On top of that, as soon as we stepped out of the car, biting mosquitoes and flies attacked like they had been waiting their whole lives for this very moment. All of this had us retreating back to the car in minutes... and yet here were children. Young men and women working all day long, chest-deep in putrid flooded rice fields, just to make enough money to live in a fucking cardboard box. Their ox wading through the fields right beside them, defecating in the same water they were standing in. My own complaints and problems, whatever they were, seemed impossibly small and petty in comparison. To this day, anytime I start to feel sorry for myself over anything that's going on in my life, I think back to those people and that village. Those images are forever burned in my memory, and—maybe selfishly—I'm glad they're there. They've offered me a perspective that few I've encountered have.

Our brief trip was soon coming to an end, and we were ready to go. We were blessed to have the ability to leave, to climb aboard an airplane that would take us back to America's unimaginable prosperity, and that fact was not lost on us. As Thom drove us back to the Siem Reap airport, Rick and I made the decision to give him all the money we had left in our pockets. It wasn't much by American standards, but we knew it would mean a lot here, where the average annual income was about twelve hundred dollars. At the airport, when it came time to say our goodbyes, we made our move: we handed over all the money we had. We would have given him more if we had it. Thom hugged and thanked us, and couldn't have been more grateful. He wished us safe travels and drove off. With a sigh of relief we walked inside. But as we checked in we were greeted by a surprise: there was a departure tax to leave the country. That's right: we had to pay a tax to leave. I'd never heard of anything like this before in my life, and apparently neither had Rick. Neither of us had a dime on us. We'd given Thom every cent we had. And—naturally—they didn't accept credit cards.

Our plane is set to leave in thirty minutes, and without cash to pay the tax we're stuck here. Immediately Rick and I start rifling through our carry-on bags, checking our pants pockets for any missed bill or errant coin. What we find isn't nearly enough to get one of us back home, let alone both of us. For the first time in either of our lives, we're literally asking strangers for money. How quickly the tables can turn. Of course, we've got one major thing going for us: Rick's famous mug. Before long one of the ladies working behind the ticket counter recognizes him, and asks if we need help. We explain the situation, and promise her that if she loans us the forty dollars we need we'll send her the money as soon as we land back home. Out of the kindness of her heart, she agrees. We rush through check-in and barely make the last call for boarding.

A day later, back in the States, I turned on the TV to see rioters crowding the streets of Phnom Penh. All of the tension I'd been feeling in the air had finally boiled over, and in the end would result in massive damage to Thai-owned businesses and to the Thai Embassy itself. The newscasters named resentment over Thailand's role in Cambodia's economic hardships as a driving force behind the upheaval. I thought back to the conditions I had witnessed, and I didn't wonder at the anger I saw being vented on those Cambodian streets. I realized again that I'd been given a rare gift: a window into a world I never would have imagined. My friend Rick had pushed me to get out of my comfort zone in ways that, even in a few short days, had radically opened my eyes and shifted my perspective. For that, and for his many years of friendship, I am profoundly grateful.

DISCOMFORT ZONE

There are plenty of clichés that get thrown around the fitness world, and even if you've never worked out a day in your life you're probably familiar with some of them. For example, I think it's a safe bet that no one reading this has completely avoided hearing the phrase "No pain, no gain" in their lifetime. Or how about, "Pain is weakness leaving the body"? Or, "That which doesn't kill you makes you stronger?"

Tired or not, these clichés endure for one very simple reason: they're true. In fitness as in anything else, growth happens where comfort ends. New challenges mean new adaptations which collectively mean a new you—and that's true whether we're talking about you achieving a new max rep or learning a new language. It's a principle I've tried to embrace in every facet of my life... and my chosen profession has offered me some unique opportunities to test that commitment. For example:

I have a client—who, for reasons that will become obvious, has asked to remain nameless—who's a major international star, the kind of guy whose face you see on billboards overlooking Hollywood Boulevard. In our time training together we've become good friends, and I've been lucky enough to tag along on some of the incredible adventures his line of work affords him. If I say that I'm incredibly grateful to him, that should not also imply that these adventures have been without their challenges... or that traveling with him is a walk in the park. In fact, the contrast between our two personalities is never more fully on display than under these circumstances. For starters, my buddy is *much* more spontaneous than I am. He moves at the speed of light, and many of our adventures have involved last-minute plans and split-second decisions—not my usual *modus operandi*. Thomas Edison said that what you are will show in what you do, and if you've read this far then you already know me as the guy who preplanned and visualized every step, set, and rep of his bodybuilding training. That's who *I* am. My buddy? He's a whole other kind of animal. Case in point:

My buddy hits me up early on a Friday morning and tells me that he's just been invited to a big party at The Palms Casino in Vegas, that a high-end magazine is throwing a big bash for a bunch of famous and infamous Hollywood celebrities, that he's got a plus-one and he needs to know if I'm in.

"When?" I ask him.

"We have to be at Van Nuys Airport in a couple of hours," he says. "There's a private jet."

I'm still half asleep. I'm processing at quarter speed. High-end magazine party, Vegas, Van Nuys Airport...

"*John*," he says, "are you in?"

"What the hell," I tell him. "Let's do it."

I hang up and I call a couple of friends in San Diego. I figure if I'm going to Vegas then we might as well make a weekend of it. I don't have to ask twice: these nut jobs immediately hop in their SUV and start driving the seven hours to Vegas. Meanwhile I pack an overnight bag, make arrangements at work, and zoom out to the airport. My buddy meets me there, and we head to the plane.

If you've never flown private, let me tell you: it's pretty damn cool.

There's none of the regular bullshit. There's no security check. They take you out to the private jet in a golf cart. A drink of your choice is always waiting for you. The flight attendants are gorgeous. I'm not kidding. They must hold casting calls for these jobs. Everyone looks like a model.

There are a few other people already on board, and I immediately recognize a bunch of them. Lindsay Lohan, Paris Hilton, Lance Bass, Tara Reid, David Alan Grier... This crew is trouble in the making. The flight attendants tell us to take our seats, and we're wheels-up and on our way to Vegas.

When you actually get up close and see how the sausage is made—when you see how life works for people at the height of fame—it becomes very easy to see how so many young actors end up so messed up. Celebrity is a crazy thing. It seems like the more money you make, the less money you have to spend. Celebrities are flown around on private jets, handed free clothes, fed meals at top-end restaurants, given drugs and sex... you name it. Even as a plus-one I got hooked up with a good amount of swag: dinner in some of the finest restaurants, clothes, luxury suites, money for the strip club... all that and more came my way. Luckily by then I was mature enough to handle it. I was mature enough to understand that when people shower you with tons of unearned free shit it goes against the laws of physics... and that sooner or later the Universe will come knocking on your door to collect its pound of flesh. If I'd had access to women, alcohol, drugs, money, and private jets back when I was in my teens, God only knows where I'd be. I was a douchebag all on my own, paying a homeless guy twenty bucks to buy me a five-dollar bottle of Olde English 800. If I'd had any help—if I'd had casinos flying me out and sending magnums of Dom over to my private table, like I saw happen with certain underage starlets on this trip—I'm pretty sure I'd be dead.

On this trip—in addition to the free rooms, free food, and swag bags—the casino gives us two thousand dollars of "funny money" *each* to spend at their strip club. Funny money is like company scrip: it's "money" that's only good in this particular strip club. Outside the club it's worthless, but inside the club it's as good as cash.

You can believe this or not, but the fact of the matter is that I've never been a big fan of strip clubs. I can't separate my mind from my body enough to enjoy the experience. I get hung up on the fact that this is what these poor girls have to do to make ends meet. This place is full of hot chicks in the absolute prime of their stripping careers, but my mind won't let me just relax and enjoy the experience. *Why would this beautiful girl want to do this?* my mind wants to know. *She's barely twenty years old. She has her whole life ahead of her. She has the world in the palm of her hand. She could do or be anything, so why does she want to do this?* I feel like I want to save all of them. But that's usually when another voice chimes in. *These girls know exactly how you feel,* this other voice says, *and they're going to play that impulse for every last dime you've got!* The first voice protests. *These girls aren't like that!* it says, and back and forth and around and around we go. Instead of watching the show, my pathetic ass is tuned in to the battle going on between my ears. None of which is helped by the fact that, on this particular trip, as soon as we walk through the door, all stripper eyes lock on us. Famous faces attract attention. The dancers leave Mr. Shady in his trench coat. Never mind the singles he's been feeding them all night. His small change is not going to stop the call of the great migration. Tonight, we are the Promised Land.

The manager leads us across the floor to a VIP section they have cordoned off in the back. And let me just say that, necessary as this step probably is, for me it's strike two. I just don't get the whole VIP thing. You go out because you want to be around people. If you don't want to be around people then you don't go to a club full of people, right? You stay home. But then you set yourself up in a special little area, behind a little velvet rope that separates you from all the people you came here to be around. It seems nuts to me. We settle in behind the velvet rope and we look out at all the people on the other side, who are all looking right back at us. I feel like a gorilla in a fucking zoo. That's what I'm thinking when, despite the "boundary" between us and the general population, I overhear the chatter from one of the nearby tables, where one of the girls is working her regular mark.

"Baby," the mark is saying, "I can't pull eight hundred dollars out of the ATM without my wife knowing about it."

The stripper counters: "But honey, you *always* pull out eight hundred. Am I not worth it anymore?"

The counter is effective. The mark has no defense. A few seconds later he's punching his PIN into the ATM. Out flutter the bills, and he forks them over. The stripper takes him by the hand and walks him off to a private room for, presumably, eight hundred dollars' worth of blue balls. I watch them go, wondering how long it's been since this guy's wife has had a new pair of shoes.

I don't have long to ponder this injustice, though. The strippers are circling heavily, swarming us like bees on honey. A beautiful brunette fixes me in her sights. She comes over, leans in close, and whispers in my ear, "Are you having a good time?"

Before I can spit out a single word in reply she pushes my legs apart, drops to her knees between them, and starts dancing. She rubs herself against my inner thighs. Her eyes are locked onto mine. I'm mesmerized. I'm toast. I instantly fork over the whole fucking wad of funny money. Two thousand (fake) dollars for fifteen seconds of dancing. I point across the VIP area to where another member of our group is sitting by himself.

"All I want is for you to dance for my friend over there," I say.

That does the trick. The stripper moves on. I take my seltzer with lemon and I remove myself from the VIP area. I find a seat off by myself, back against the wall, where (I hope) I'll be left alone. I feel better already. I've never liked being at the center of attention. I've always been more comfortable being the fly on the wall... but this reads differently in a strip club. Suddenly, without meaning to, I've become the creepy guy in the back who just wants to *watch*. My friends notice, and they let me have it. After some well-deserved ridicule I bid them goodnight. I catch a smelly cab back to the hotel and I'm in bed before the clock strikes twelve. Viva Las Vegas.

Nobody gives a shit, not really. It's forgotten as soon as it happens. Still, that trip is on my mind when my buddy invites me along on another adventure. This time he has a film in the Bangkok International Film Festival, and the organizers are flying him out and putting him up. He wants to know if I want to tag along. I don't make him ask twice.

From its inception in 2003 up to the 2006 coup d'état, after which its budget was severely reduced, the Bangkok International Film Festival was one of the biggest in the world. Accordingly, this year, my buddy isn't the only big name on the bill: we travel as part of a group that includes members of a popular boy band, Vivica A. Fox, sports anchor Bryant Gumbel, and martial arts movie star Steven Seagal. The organizers mean to make sure that these celebrity guests have everything they might need or want, and to that end—in addition to the other significant amenities they make available—they have placed a couple of local liaisons at the group's disposal. Basically these guys are there to get us anything we ask for, take us anywhere we want to go, and generally help us get out and explore the local culture. They're also tasked with making sure we have a good time: a tricky proposition, as one man's good time is another man's nightmare... especially when it comes to me, and especially when it comes to Thailand.

Before I get into this story, let me just say the following: I'm not a big "group activity" guy. In general, in social situations, I tend to turn into a bit of an introvert. Just about the worst place you can take me is a dance club. I'd much rather go out to a nice meal and enjoy some conversation with a few friends. I'd much rather be someplace where you can actually hear what the other people are saying. Of course, at this point I'm also very aware of the fact that holding on too tightly to this mentality can mean you miss out on some pretty incredible experiences... and here I am in Bangkok, at one of the biggest film festivals in the world, as part of a group with local liaisons at our beck and call. It's unlikely that I'll ever be in this situation again, and I want to make the most of the experience. Accordingly, I make a conscious decision: tonight, I'm going to stretch myself. I'm going to get out of my comfort zone. I'm going to go with the flow. When my buddy tells me that the group is heading out and asks me if I want to come along, I tell him yes. I tell him I'm happy to go wherever the group wants to go, do whatever the group wants to do. Tonight, I'm along for the ride.

Where does the group want to go? You guessed it: a dance club. *Perfect.* The only thing worse than bad techno is bad techno in a foreign language. Still: in for a penny, in for a pound. No early bedtime for me this time. Let's do it. I can't fucking wait.

We pull up to the club and our group files inside. They're pumping thick smoke out of the ceiling vents, and the whole place is as foggy as the San Francisco docks. Immediately my Spidey Sense starts tingling: all I can think of is how to protect everyone if some crazed Thai crime boss bursts through the fog and tries to take all of these celebrities hostage. In reality, of course, our hosts and all the people in the club couldn't have been any nicer. They show us through the club to the back, where they've cordoned off a special VIP area for us.

Ah, my old friend the VIP area. Am I annoyed? Not tonight. Tonight I'm stepping out of my comfort zone. Tonight I'm here to have a new experience, to grow as a person. To be part of the fun. I take my seat behind the velvet rope, and I work to quiet the voice in my head nagging me with the thought that I would have been happier—or at least a hell of a lot more comfortable—if I'd just stayed back at the hotel.

Fortunately, we don't stay at the club long. Unfortunately, we only leave that club to head to a different club. Fortunately, we don't stay at that club long, either. Unfortunately, the next stop is a karaoke bar. Fortunately... but you get the picture. It's hours and hours of this shit. In all I think we hit every club and bar in the vicinity, and everything in between. And I'm there for it all. I'm part of the fun.

As we go along, I notice something. No matter where we go, this group of transexual men in their twenties follows us. The really crazy thing is, they're all dressed like American women from the 1950s. It's like a bunch of girls from Arnold's on *Happy Days* are trailing us—except they're all men. No matter where we go they're right behind us, smiling at us. We'll go into a club, hang out for an hour, and then head out the back door to avoid the crowd... and there they'll be. And it continues, no matter what we do or where we go, no matter how fast or slow we walk. There's no escaping them. Maybe the thinking is that if we don't find what we're looking for in the club, we'll go for option number two: a 1950s-era Thai transsexual with the big red bow in his/her hair.

Actually, now that I think about it, I'm sure that's not so crazy. I'm sure plenty of drunken sailors have gone for option number two. Simple economics of supply and demand. Things probably look different when your shore leave is running out and you're still all alone. As they say: any port in a storm. I can't imagine these gents were following us around because that strategy had proved *in*effective.

Finally, our group has had enough of the nightclubs. They're ready for a change of scene. They ask our Thai liaisons to take us to—what else?—*a strip club*.

By now it's probably three in the morning. Our Thai liaisons guide us through the maze of streets and deposit us in a kind of town square, where a bunch of local hustlers for the strip club scene swarm us. They overwhelm us with their patter. They're each working as hard as they can to convince us that their club is the one to see, the one we don't want to miss. They bombard us from every angle with every kind of strip club sales pitch you can imagine:

"Best pussy show!"

"Best pussy in all Thailand!"

"Number one pussies!"

They're all trying to out-pitch each other. All of a sudden a kid who looks to be all of thirteen years old and who barely speaks English pushes his way through the crowd.

"Hi," he says to us. "I Herman. Promise to take you to best pussy show in all Thailand. Girls shooting darts out of their super number one pussies."

Um... What the fuck did he just say?

"Herman show you dart flying out of pussy show," Herman says. "For real. Much fun to have."

What can you even say to something like that? The group is—perhaps understandably—intrigued. We fork over the necessary cash. Herman tells us to follow him. He leads us down several blocks to an old industrial build-ing. He ushers us inside and leads us up a rickety wooden staircase, down a dimly-lit hallway, up another cramped staircase, past several dangerous-looking characters—one of whom gives Herman a high five—and up to a large steel door. The music from the other side of the door is deafeningly loud, even out in the hallway. Herman hands over our cash to the lug stand-ing guard. The lug hands Herman a few bucks from the wad and Herman runs off. The lug then opens the door and shows us into the room. We've finally arrived. It's time to see the show.

In the center of the room, up on the stage, several women are working the pole. Fanning out from this focal point is the seating: a varied mix of bleacher seating and plastic lawn chairs. Up front, this club has a "VIP" sec-tion all its own: a couple of tables pushed right up against the stage. And guess what? Every seat is full. The place is packed. We spread out and find standing room against the back wall, and we settle in to watch the show.

And what a show it is. The ladies up on stage look like they've just returned from their seventh tour of Afghanistan. They're notably older than standard US protocol, too: nobody up there is younger than thirty-five, and I'd bet money that at least one of them is a few klicks past forty. Understand: this isn't old in the real world, but in the world of strippers this is *ancient*. Las Vegas this is not.

This motley crew is finishing up as we arrive. The changeover is signaled by David Lee Roth's "Yankee Rose" blasting out of the speakers at eardrum-shattering volume. Within this cacophony, the next two ladies take the stage. They are decked out in red, white, and blue. They head to opposite sides of the stage, take off what little clothing they have on, drop to their backs, and proceed to insert what appears to be a dozen or so sparklers each into their vaginas.

Are you with me so far?

An assistant comes on stage. The assistant has a lighter. The assistant lights the sparklers. The sparklers ignite in every color of the rainbow. That's right: a symphony of flaming colors for your viewing pleasure. The assistant then grabs a handful of these flaming vagina sparklers and starts handing them out as gifts to people in the crowd. The people in the crowd go nuts. Some yahoo in a Stone Cold Steve Austin tank top takes a handful of these sparklers and places the handle end—the end that was oh-so-recently tucked deep in the recesses of a Thai stripper's vagina—in his mouth. His buddies go apeshit.

The sparklers burn out. Now it's time for phase two of the fireworks portion of the evening's entertainment. This event's incendiary of choice? The classic Roman candle. The strippers face off, insert and ignite. Suddenly colorful fireballs are being lobbed back and forth across the stage. They land on the stage, fall onto the bare wooden floor, roll under chairs. They just keep coming. I am one-hundred-percent certain that any minute now the whole place is going to go up in flames with all of us inside. I'm looking for an exit and I'm trying to figure out how I'm going to get our group out of here once the panic stampede starts. OSHA regulations? Fire codes? This is Thailand. To this day I have no idea how the fuck the place didn't burn down.

The Roman candles fire their last salvo and go dark. Somehow we've made it through the preliminaries—now it's time for the main event. The ladies swivel back around. Nether regions are once again staring the audience dead in the face. The ladies insert long bamboo poles into their vaginas. While that's happening, several of the other strippers head out into the audience to pass out balloons. A couple of guys from the boy band jump at the chance, and take several balloons each. My Spidey Sense—which has been tingling nonstop since the second we stepped foot in this deathtrap— goes into overdrive. I start to drift away from our group. I don't know exactly what's coming, but I can guess well enough to know that it's not safe to be anywhere near those balloons. But moving away is no easy task, either: the room is smokey, dimly lit, crowded and extremely loud, and with all these distractions I take my eyes off the stage.

ZIP! POW!

I look up in time to see shards of the burst balloon drop from our boy-band friend's hand. The crowd goes bananas. I look past him and I see a primitive-looking dart embedded a quarter-inch into the drywall behind him. This is the kind of projectile you'd expect to see sticking out of a monkey's neck in a National Geographic documentary and *it's penetrated the fucking drywall.*

ZIP! POW! ZIP! POW!

Two more balloons explode just to the left of my face. I'm thinking about my buddy's manager and agent, about what I'm going to say to them if their client gets taken out in some den of iniquity on the other side of the world. I'm thinking about how this boy band is going to explain to their fans that they have to cancel the European leg of their world tour because several of their members have suffered grievous bodily harm at the hands of a dart blown from a Thai stripper's vagina. I look over and I manage to catch my buddy's eye, and an understanding passes between us. We duck and cover.

POW! POW! POW! POW!

Darts are flying everywhere. The crowd is going nuts. The balloons don't stand a chance. Chris Kyle wasn't this accurate.

The hail of projectiles ceases. There isn't an intact balloon in the house. The ladies stand and take a bow. The crowd is in an absolute frenzy. The strippers who handed out the balloons now pass through the crowd collecting tips. I'm not sure how much they collect, but I can tell you that it is at least enough for the ladies to take the next month off and give those vaginas some well-deserved rest. I later got word that the guys from the boy band loved the show so much that they actually flew a couple of the strippers out to Miami to perform at one of their birthday parties. Too bad this was before *America's Got Talent.* These ladies would have cleaned up.

Even though we get back to the hotel insanely late, I have trouble getting to sleep. I lay awake in my hotel bed processing the night's events. *How does this sort of thing even happen?* I wonder. What series of events leads a person to *that*? Do you start off at nineteen or twenty with just regular pole dancing and stripping? Then you age, and the younger talent starts getting all of the attention, and you decide to come up with a creative way to stay relevant? Maybe you put some sparklers in your vagina. Maybe you and another performer battle it out with some strategically placed Roman candles. But how long does that last? How long before everyone is cribbing your act? How long before you need something new, something fresh, something even more exciting and extreme? And thus the blow dart pussy show is born.

Because—and let me be clear, if I wasn't already—none of the ladies in tonight's show had been what you'd call "spring chickens." If they were a

Vegas casino, it would be a loooooong Uber ride down the strip to their location. And the years had not been what you'd call "kind": we're talking stretch marks, scars, even what I'm pretty sure were healed-up bullet wounds. All of that set on top of bunioned feet stuffed into stripper heels several sizes too small. And yet the more I think about it, the more I come to feel something approaching admiration for these women. Lying there in that lucid haze somewhere beyond all-out exhaustion but just shy of sleep, I even start to feel that I understand them. What we'd witnessed up on that stage was nothing short of a pure manifestation of the burning will to survive, and that is a primal instinct I understand very well. There have been times in my life when I was down to my last can of sardines, flat broke and with no idea what I was going to do. Luckily I didn't have to resort to launching fireworks out of my ass to make ends meet then... but I also didn't have an audience that was willing to pay good money to watch me do it. These ladies saw a problem and they found a solution. The sun had set on their stripping careers, and they'd figured out a way to become headliners again. Our dumb asses had paid money up front, walked eight city blocks, and risked being burned alive to see them. These ladies could teach Tony Robbins a thing or two about turning lemons into lemonade.

And that, my friends, is the kind of shit my sick mind comes up with. I can't shut it off. I can't make it stop. I'd probably be better off getting shit-faced on cheap, sugary vodka drinks, kicking back, and just enjoying the show. Taking the burning sparklers from the assistant and putting them in my mouth to give my buddies a laugh. I know it will be a long time before I can tell Cheyenne what I've seen, or what I thought as the whole strange spectacle played out before me. It will be a long time before I can tell her that I'd thought of the birthing class we took in the weeks before our first son, Hunter, was born, and about what the instructor told us then: that a mother goes through different stages in the delivery room, the final stage being that she doesn't give a shit anymore. No more concern for being

177

naked, no more worries about having your legs up in the air and your hoo-ha hanging out—a strange kind of zen. These ladies *live* in that place. We should all be so lucky.

MR. ACTION HERO

As I said, most of the celebrities I've met have been very gracious and very cool—a few have not. In fact, believe it or not, I have several stories that involve one particular major action movie star. And when I say major, I mean *major*. This guy was a huge box office draw back in the day. You have no idea how badly I want to tell you who this douchebag is, but my attorneys have advised me against it. Apparently you can get sued for telling the truth about someone's bad behavior. Accordingly, for legal purposes, the subject of this chapter will be known simply as Mr. Action Hero.

Honestly, part of me thinks that some people won't believe me anyway. It can be hard to digest and accept the fact that your movie hero is a real-life asshole. Trust me, I understand. Growing up, I was the guy's number one fan. I vividly remember coming out of the movie theater after seeing one of his seminal movies. I was so amped, so totally floored from the experience, there was so much adrenaline rushing through my body, that I immediately forked over another six bucks of my hard-earned paper-route money to see the movie a second time. It was the best money this fourteen-year-old had ever spent.

To a young, impressionable kid, this guy had it all. He had muscles, he knew how to fight, he saved everyone from the evil villains, and he always got the girl. I wanted to be like him... Hell, I wanted to *be* him. Little did I know that my reverence and admiration were setting me up for a fall.

My first encounter with Mr. Action Hero happened on one of my trips to

Thailand. I was lucky enough to be seated in first class and even luckier—I realized as I scanned the cabin—to be seated just a few feet from my childhood hero. A smile came over my face as I remembered the countless hours I'd spent rewatching and mimicking the different fight scenes from his movies. I damn near wore out the VHS tapes rewinding them over and over. And now here he was, in the flesh, seated less than an arm's length in front of me, *for eighteen hours*. This was literally a childhood dream come true.

But... fourteen-year-old John and professional John had some things they needed to get straight first. As I explained in the Anguilla story, part of my job is knowing how to treat celebrities: how to give them their space and respect their privacy. Every fiber of my being wanted to go up and ask Mr. Action Hero for an autograph, but my professional side took note of the signals. He was wearing dark glasses *inside* the cabin. He seemed to be sleeping or trying to sleep. He was very clearly putting out the vibe that he wanted to be *left alone*. So I complied with this unspoken request. I refrained. I didn't say one word to him. Instead I waited for a signal, an opening, some sort of cue that would let me know that it was okay... and I was still waiting when, eighteen hours later, our wheels touched tarmac. We'd landed in Bangkok. The flight was over. Mr. Action Hero gathered his belongings, walked off the plane and down the jetway, and I was sure that my once-in-a-lifetime opportunity had walked off with him.

I wish now that it had.

It turned out that Mr. Action Hero and I were staying at the same hotel. All week long, everywhere I looked, there was Mr. Action Hero. It would have been easy to ask him for a photo, but I left him alone. Even when he was greeting other fans and being cordial, I left him alone. I didn't want to be just another fan. I wanted to share with him what his movies had meant to me. I wanted to let him know what a positive influence he'd been in my life. Martial arts meant so much to me, and he and his movies had played no small part in that journey. I wanted us to connect as fellow martial artists. A photo or an autograph would have been fine, but I wanted something more.

Toward the end of the trip, I was sitting in our poolside cabana when who should sit down in the next cabana over but Mr. Action Hero, his crew, and a couple of the local ladies. I figured this might be my last opportunity to introduce myself, so I mustered up my courage and walked over. I was maybe ten feet away when everything turned south. From ten feet and closing I watched as Mr. Action Hero leaned down, placed a rolled-up dollar bill in his nose, and took a bump of cocaine off the magazine lying on the table.

Did you hear that sound? No, not the sound of Mr. Action Hero snorting coke, the other sound. The one that sounded like something busting into a million pieces? That one. That was the sound of little prepubescent John Petrelli's dreams shattering.

Without breaking stride I hit an immediate U-turn and sat back down. I couldn't believe what I'd just witnessed. I was stunned. But it only got worse from there. From under our sunshade I watched as Mr. Action Hero's attitude and behavior quickly deteriorated. Within minutes he and his crew were hassling the staff, bullying the waiters, harassing the towel boy, and acting generally obnoxious toward anyone who happened by. I was speechless. I was angry. I was heartbroken. How could my childhood hero act this way? He was supposed to be a martial artist, supposed to be living a life of discipline and honor. Finally, I couldn't take it any more. I got up and left the pool. I didn't know what else to do. I was disoriented and upset. In the course of less than five minutes I'd gone from being excited about finally meeting one of my idols to seeing him act like a total scumbag. All I could think to do was remove myself from the scene. To this day I feel ashamed that I didn't say anything to him or his group, that I didn't stand up for the staff.

These things happen, right? Our childhood heroes disappoint us. We realize that the characters they play in movies are just that—characters—and that the real person lurking behind the mask might not be who we'd like them to be. Maybe part of growing up is accepting this fact—accepting that there is no Santa Claus and there are no superheroes, only fallible people like us—and moving forward. Maybe I'd judged the guy too harshly, I thought later. After all, I'd certainly seen him act graciously toward a number of fans at the hotel. I'd seen him pose for pictures and sign autographs. Maybe I could chalk the whole thing up to a bad day, a bad crowd, a rough patch in his life. One event doesn't make a pattern. I'd certainly made my share of mistakes in the past, and at key moments I'd been lucky enough to receive the benefit of the doubt. Couldn't I afford my childhood hero the same?

Fast forward a couple of years. I'm living in West Hollywood. A good friend of mine needs a place to stay while he gets back on his feet, so I let him crash on my couch. This friend is working a bunch of odd jobs to make ends meet, and one of them is as a bar-back at a popular nightclub. One night while he's staying with me, the nightclub hosts the LA Lakers. The Lakers have just won another championship, and the event is going to be huge. They're expecting a ton of celebrities to attend.

At around one o'clock in the morning my cell phone rings, waking me out of a dead sleep. It's my buddy. I can barely hear him over the sound of the Lakers party still going full-tilt in the background. His voice is frantic.

"John," he says, "I need your help! You have to get down here immediately!"

I tell him to calm down. It takes him a second. I ask him what's going on.

"I need your help," he says again. "I need your help *kicking Mr. Action Hero's ass!*"

For a second I wonder if I'm really on the phone with him, or if I'm still asleep and dreaming. I don't care who you are: your help putting a beat-down on your childhood action hero is not the sort of request you expect to receive on a middle-of-the-night phone call. Welcome to Hollywood.

"Wait," I say, "what the hell are you talking about?"

"This punk motherfucker just crossed the line," my friend says. Then he says one of the greatest sentences I've ever heard in my life: "If it wasn't for Shaq, I would have punched his fucking lights out!"

Add that to the list of things I never thought I'd hear.

"What the hell do you mean, Shaq?" I say. "You mean Shaquille O'Neal?"

I'm almost laughing at this point, but my buddy is dead serious.

"Yes," he says, "what other Shaq have you heard about? Just get your ass down here!"

This guy has been a friend of mine for years, since we were kids back in New York. Back when we were teenagers, whenever he got into trouble, he would call me up and ask for my help. The house phone would ring at two in the morning and it would be my buddy telling me that he was in a jam, and could I come help him sort it out? I remember how pissed my mom always was: me and my hooligan friends, waking everybody up in the middle of the night. Still, what are you going to do? When your friend needs your help, no matter the hour, you go and you help, and in the end you're glad he called. You're glad to be the kind of guy whose friends know that he has their back.

I throw on some clothes and I hurry down to the club. The whole ride over my mind is racing. Now I'm fully invested in the reality of what's happening, and I'm running through the practical concerns and considerations. I talk it through out loud. In his movies, Mr. Action Hero appears to be a really good standup fighter, always kicking people in the face, so it's probably best to take him to the ground and negate his striking ability. The first punch he throws I'm going to duck under and hit him with a double-leg takedown. From there I'll work into a dominant position and see what happens. Maybe I'll hit him, maybe he'll give me an opportunity for a submission. I won't know until I get there. I'll have to wait and see.

That's right: the whole drive over to the club I'm trying to work out how to *kick Mr. Action Hero's ass*, because right now that is my actual, practical, number-one concern.

But why? What happened? My buddy was in too much of a hurry, and the club was too noisy for him to explain the situation over the phone. I don't get the full story until much later, over steak and eggs at NORMS on La Cienega Boulevard in the wee small hours of the morning. As my buddy tells it, the party is going in full swing. The place is packed and everyone seems to be in great spirits, celebrating the Lakers' big win. This is a private event, so it's an open bar and the alcohol is flowing. My buddy is working his ass off. A couple of the other bar-backs called in sick at the last minute, so he's doing triple the work. Two of the club's bars are on the second floor, but the only ice machine is down in the kitchen on the first floor. My buddy is basically spending the entire night running back and forth between the ice machine and the bars. Each trip means maneuvering through the packed crowd and up the stairs while carrying two five-gallon buckets of ice. He's just finished topping off the ice for one of the second floor bars when all of a sudden Mr. Action Hero throws his empty scotch glass into the ice bin. Glass shatters everywhere. The bin is now a mixture of broken glass and ice, and there's no way to tell which is which. The whole thing has to go.

"What are you doing?" my buddy asks Mr. Action Hero. "That's not the garbage." He tells Mr. Action Hero that now he has to clean out all of the ice and broken glass and haul new ice back up from the kitchen. Mr. Action Hero responds to this by placing his hands in front of his face in the prayer position and saying in the worst Asian accent, "Oh so sorry, oh so sorry, many apologies, many apologies."

My buddy doesn't even know how to respond to this—so he doesn't. He bites his tongue and gets back to work. He empties the ice bin as fast as he can, hauls the mix of ice and broken glass back down the stairs to where he can dump it, fills the two buckets with clean ice, and hauls the hundred pounds of ice back through the sea of people and back up the stairs. He makes his way over to the bar and refills the ice bin. Just as he's dumping in the last of the ice, Mr. Action Hero—the heartless motherfucker—throws the beer bottle he's now half-emptied into the bin. Beer and broken glass spray all over my buddy. The ice is ruined *again*.

My buddy goes ballistic. He goes right after Mr. Action Hero. He doesn't get very far though, because they're separated by none other than Shaquille O'Neal. That's right: fucking Shaq has to step in and play sheriff. The bouncers arrive soon after, and they end up tossing Mr. Action Hero out of the club. Meanwhile, my buddy runs to grab his cell phone and calls me.

By the time I arrive at the club Mr. Action Hero is long gone. I never find out if my strategy would have worked against that famous spinning split kick. Probably it's for the best. Either way, the whole episode certainly clarifies my impression of my former childhood hero. This guy wasn't having a bad day that afternoon in Thailand. This guy is an asshole.

If you're not convinced yet, though, I've got one more story for you. I happened to mention my crazy encounters with Mr. Action Hero to another longtime friend and client of mine—who has asked to remain nameless— and he came back with one of his own.

"You're not going to believe this," he told me, "but that son-of-a-bitch tried to stiff me on a tab when I was working at the Four Seasons in Beverly Hills."

My buddy is a big star now, but back before he hit the big time he was working as a bartender. He told me that one day he was working when Mr. Action Hero and two other guys came in. They all ordered herbal tea and bottled water, and after hanging out for a while they got up and left without paying. My buddy figured they just forgot, so he followed them outside. When he caught up with them they were already waiting at the valet stand for their car.

My buddy calls over to them, "Hey, guys, I don't know if you're aware, but you forgot to pay for your drinks."

Mr. Action Hero turns to him, looks him up and down, and says, "Yeah, we're aware."

"Well, look," My buddy says, "I'm not paying for it. If you guys don't pay for it, it comes out of my paycheck."

And what does Mr. Action Hero, the movie badass, do then? He takes a threatening step toward my buddy, like he's going to kick my buddy's ass just for asking. One of Mr. Action Hero's associates steps in and holds Mr. Action Hero back.

"Then he basically told me to go fuck myself," my buddy said. "I told him, 'Look, you might kick my ass, but those drinks aren't coming out of my pay.' So the other guy goes into his pocket, pulls out some cash, and throws it on the ground. He tells me, 'There's your fucking money.' I had to literally pick the money for this tab up off the ground."

So much for childhood heroes. If I've got basically nothing to do with the guy and even I have three stories about him acting like a huge asshole, just imagine how many more incidents like this there must be.

Yep, there it is: the sound of young John Petrelli's heart shattering into a million pieces.

And I guess while we're on the subject of celebrities treating people like crap, let me tell you about an incident I had with...

MS. FANCY PANTS

This incident happened during one of my work trips to Anguilla. As you now know, the hotel saw a decent amount of traffic from celebrity clientele, and during this particular trip a major daytime talk show host happened to be staying at the resort. Once again, my attorneys have advised me against using the name of the party in question, and God knows I don't want to spend all of my time in court defending true statements... Accordingly I'm just going to call this piece of work Ms. Fancy Pants.

I'd been seeing Ms. Fancy Pants around the hotel all week long. I'd seen her sitting by the pool, in the lobby, at the restaurant eating lunch. Each time I saw her I made it a point not to approach her. As I've said, I have some idea of what it's like for celebrities to get hassled all the time, and I understood that one of the best ways to show your appreciation for them is by just giving them their space. I also understood that, if you've come to this hotel, whether you're a celebrity or not, you're on vacation. You're not here to meet your public. You're off the clock. You want to be left alone.

The thing is, though, that Ms. Fancy Pants and I have a friend in common. One of Cheyenne's massage clients was Ms. Fancy Pants's talent manager, and a few years earlier he'd mentioned that Ms. Fancy Pants was looking to hire a personal chef. He'd asked Cheyenne if we knew of anyone who would be a good fit and who he could recommend. Our friend Umberto is an excellent chef, and we didn't hesitate to give Ms. Fancy Pants's manager his contact info. As luck would have it, Umberto and Ms. Fancy Pants hit it off, and they ended up working together for several years. I believe they even wrote a cookbook together, that Ms. Fancy Pants featured on her show.

For whatever reason, I felt the need to let Ms. Fancy Pants know about our connection. I should have known better.

On my last day at the resort I'm walking down a private bike path to my hotel room when who should come along but Ms. Fancy Pants. She's headed in the opposite direction, coming straight toward me. As we get closer I start imagining the conversation in my head—imagining how happy and appreciative Ms. Fancy Pants will be once she finds out that it was me and Cheyenne who referred Umberto to her.

She seems so nice, I think. *She's always so upbeat on TV. I'm sure she'll be happy to know that Cheyenne and I are the ones who helped her out.*

And anyway, when are you ever going to get a chance to speak to Ms. Fancy Pants again? This is one of those "small world" stories that people tell their friends. I've got to say something. What can go wrong?

What can go wrong indeed.

We approach and begin to pass each other. The bike path is so narrow that we each have to turn sideways to give the other room to walk by. She's literally two feet in front of me. Our eyes meet, and in that instant I decide it's now or never.

"Hello," I say.

Ms. Fancy Pants doesn't reply. Instead, she freezes. I stop, too. We're standing there in the path, both of us turned sideways to let the other pass, neither of us moving. She's staring me dead in the eye. My gut tells me to let it go, to just keep moving, but my dumbass ego wants so badly to let her know my stupid story.

"Hi," I say again. "You don't know me, but I actually referred your chef, Umberto, to you—"

I don't get the rest of the story out. Ms. Fancy Pants cuts me off. Looking me straight in the eye, she says, "You know what, buddy? I don't have time for this kind of shit!"

Then she turns and walks off down the bike path.

I'm so shocked that, for a moment, all I can do is stand there. Like that moment with Mr. Action Hero in Thailand, my brain is stuck somewhere back in the version of this meeting that I imagined and has locked its gears trying to catch up to the far-less-pleasant reality. I feel so stupid. I feel like I should have known better—like I *did* know better—and I went ahead anyway. I walk back to my room feeling like an absolute fool.

Later, though, I start to feel differently about it. I understand that we all have our off days, but as a professional—hell, as a human being—I'd never treat anyone like that. And sure, maybe she felt bad about the exchange after it happened. Maybe it's the one moment in her life she'd like to have back… but I doubt it. I doubt that she even remembers it. I doubt that it stands out from the avalanche of other similar incidents. Because my gut tells me that she probably does this sort of thing all the time: that she probably treats her staff like shit and walks around with a huge sense of entitlement. A few years later, when reports came out about her talk show set being a toxic work environment, let's just say I wasn't surprised. Turns out Ms. Happy-Go-Lucky Fancy Pants ain't so happy-go-lucky when the cameras aren't rolling.

And yeah, I know I'm not running a huge risk of being invited on her show to promote this book, but I'm going to say it here anyway: Sorry, Ms. Fancy Pants, I just can't make it. Turns out I don't have time for your kind of shit either.

MR. ACADEMY AWARD

One of my dear friends and clients had worked with Wolfgang Puck and the Academy Awards for many years, and she extended an invitation to Cheyenne and myself to attend the Academy Awards and the exclusive party afterwards. She didn't have to ask twice.

The Academy Awards is everything you've seen on TV and more. It was one of the few times in my life that I've been truly starstruck. At one point Anthony Hopkins was sitting right next to me, and I couldn't even remember his real name. All I could think was, *This is Hannibal Lecter*.

The first stop after the awards ceremony itself is the Oscars Governors Ball. Literally all of the top actors in the world gather together in one place to have dinner and celebrate the Oscars and the end of the awards season. There we had the pleasure of meeting Tom Hanks, Ben Affleck, Ang Lee, Benicio del Toro, Jeff Bridges, Willem Dafoe, and many others. Everyone was extremely cordial. They simply couldn't have been nicer.

By the time dinner was served, the place was absolutely bursting with positive energy. Ben Affleck was telling jokes, Tom Hanks was chatting with Cheyenne. It seemed like everyone was having a great time... everyone, that is, except Mr. Academy Award.

You guessed it: lawyers again. My hands are tied. For what it's worth, though, let me just say that I'm a big fan of Mr. Academy Award's work, and a few hours earlier I'd been glad to see him win the Academy Award for Best Actor in one of that year's biggest films. In his acceptance speech he'd been charming, affable, gracious... Now, though, he seems like he's about had it with everyone.

The Academy press has been making the rounds all evening, taking photos of the winners with their trophies. As far as I've seen, everyone has been very happy to oblige them... everyone, that is, except Mr. Academy Award.

Mr. Academy Award is sitting one table over from ours, eating dinner. At one point he looks up and he sees a photographer taking his picture, and he goes ballistic. He pushes his chair away from the table and he charges at the photographer. At this same moment Cheyenne is making her way off the dance floor, back over to our table. She doesn't see what's happening, doesn't realize she is walking directly into the path of the oncoming award winner. I feel the hair on the back of my neck stand up as I get up out of my chair. All I can think is that if this guy knocks my girl over, I'm going to deck his halls for him. Luckily it doesn't come to that. Mr. Academy Award misses Cheyenne by inches and he goes chest to chest with the photographer. He doesn't even notice her. He's oblivious to any and everyone else— Cheyenne, the other guests, his peers and colleagues. He seems oblivious, even, to the fact that this photographer is part of a corps hired by the Academy to take photos at the Ball. The same Academy that had just awarded him the Oscar for Best Actor, and in so doing sent his per-project asking price to the next level. Behind him I can see Tom Hanks spinning his son around the dance floor. He's smiling ear to ear. Meanwhile, Mr. Academy

Award is yelling at the photographer at the top of his lungs, scolding him like a child. What a contrast in personalities.

Cheyenne and I enjoyed the rest of our night. It was an amazing experience, and one for which we will always be grateful. For me, it was also an important lesson in perspective and gratitude. Imagine a night where your friends, peers, and colleagues gather and award you their highest honor. They throw a party to celebrate you and the handful of others at the top of your chosen profession. They deck the venue out in the best of everything for your enjoyment, and all they want in return is to take your picture. What do you choose to focus on? Which part of that experience defines the night for you? It made me sad that someone could have so much and act so small. To this simple farm kid, it was a powerful reminder that even though someone appears to have the world at their fingertips, they may be battling demons you know nothing about. It was a powerful reminder to focus on the good and be grateful. I thank Mr. Academy Award for teaching me this lesson.

To be fair to Mr. Academy Award, though, I have to say that I only ever had this one interaction with him. As I've said, one event does not make a pattern, and I know that, if the shoe were on the other foot, you could very easily isolate any one of a hundred different events from my youth and from that conclude that I'm a horrible person. Most people are not all good or all bad, and I hope that I caught Mr. Academy Award at a bad moment. I want to believe that his batting average is better than his performance on that particular outing.

And I'm glad I didn't have to fight him. Because who knows? He was still in pretty good shape from his Academy-Award-winning role back then. Maybe he would have whupped my ass.

EXTREME HANGOVER

This next story concerns a trainer who, for legal reasons, I will simply call "Todd." For several years Todd and I trained clients out of the same gym space: a small, private facility on the corner of La Cienega and Holloway, right in the heart of West Hollywood. During that time, I always got along with Todd. I found him to be funny, free-spirited, charismatic, and knowledgeable as a trainer. One day, in between clients, Todd approached me with a somewhat personal request. He was lacking motivation in his own training, he said. He'd taken some time off to nurse a few old injuries, and now he felt like he needed a trainer to help him get started again. Todd told me that he'd been watching me train my clients for a long time, and he was impressed with the amount of thought and detail I put into my training. He asked if I could fit him into my schedule for three sessions a week. I was honored. Here was another high-level trainer asking me if I could train *him*. Moreover, he'd picked me out of a gym full of skilled trainers. I immediately accepted, and we got to work.

Todd and I sat down and devised a plan for how I could best be of service to him. We covered everything from training and nutrition to the psychology behind some of the bad choices he'd made in the past, and how he could avoid making them again in the future. When you're making a plan for overcoming your vices, honesty is imperative, and I was impressed with Todd's openness throughout the process. We talked about everything. It was a challenging time in Todd's life: he'd just ended an unhealthy relationship, he was frustrated with his injuries, and he was generally unhappy with his physical state. However, he was willing to put in the time and effort needed to make the changes he wanted to make. Week after week he worked his ass off, both inside the gym and out. He trained hard, cleaned up his diet and his habits, and together we made tremendous progress.

About a year into our training, we each caught the attention of a different TV production company. Both companies were looking to create a reality show centered around weight loss and fitness, and both were looking to hire a lead trainer. The producers who wanted me were working on a US version of a successful European show called *You Are What You Eat*; the producers who were interested in Todd were developing a show that became... well, for those same legal reasons, let's just say it became a show you've probably heard of.

It was a long but exciting process, and throughout it all Todd and I kept each other in the loop on how things were going on our respective ends. I think we both appreciated having someone to confide in and who understood exactly what we were going through, without any of the weirdness that would have come if we'd been up for the same gig. Finally, after weeks of preliminaries, the *You Are What You Eat* producers told me that I was their guy, that they wanted me as the trainer on their show. I was off to shoot the pilot.

Todd, however, was not so lucky. After an extensive auditioning process the producers had it narrowed down to just two candidates, Todd and another trainer, but the stress of the experience was wearing on Todd. What was worse, the producers simply refused to make up their minds, and the uncertainty dragged on and on. In those weeks our training sessions became as much about Todd's mind as about his body: about reminding him that all he could do was show up and do his best every day, and reminding him to let go of worry about everything that was out of his control. We continually worked to keep him focused, keep him positive, and keep him out of his head.

Finally, after several weeks, during one of our Friday morning sessions, Todd informed me that the producers would likely be making their decision later that day. Todd's anxiety levels were understandably super high, so that day he asked if, instead of our intense workout, we could just sit and talk.

We talked all through that hour, and I reminded Todd that he'd done everything he could do, that he'd given this whole undertaking his best effort, and that no matter what happened he should feel proud of himself. I left the meeting feeling like no matter what the producers decided, Todd was going to be okay.

Just goes to show you what I know.

Later that evening, Todd called me. It was clear the second I picked up the phone that things had not gone the way we'd hoped. Todd was an emotional wreck. He'd clearly been drinking. The producers had picked the other trainer, and he was crushed. Nobody could have felt more for the guy than I did: nobody knew better than I did how much he wanted this, or how hard he'd worked to get it. However, that didn't mean that I was going to join his toxic pity party.

"Are you done crying?" I asked, after Todd stopped venting.

There was silence on the other end of the phone.

"Good," I continued, "then let's cut the shit." I proceeded to spell out for him in simple chapter and verse what needed to happen next. I told him that this was no time to throw away everything he had worked so hard for, both in the gym and in his personal life. I told him that he was a fucking mess, and that this shit had to stop. I told him that, no matter what anyone told him, *he did not know what the future held.* "What if they come back tomorrow and they tell you that they've changed their minds?" I asked him. "What if things didn't work out, and now they want you instead? Or what if they have a different show that they want you for? Are you going to be ready to take that call? It's time to dry up and start acting like a big boy."

I was pretty hard on him, and I imagine it came as a shock. Clearly he'd called me looking for sympathy, support, and consolation... what he got was something else entirely. But remember what I told you at the very beginning of this book: I'm not a good trainer, I'm an *excellent* trainer, and an excellent trainer doesn't tell you what you want to hear—he tells you what

193

you *need* to hear. By the end of our conversation, I was confident that Todd and I were back on the same page. I knew there was a chance he'd hang up the phone and go right back to his destructive behavior, but I also knew that there was no longer any confusion between us about my feelings about the situation. Given the respect I believed Todd held for me, I hoped that would be enough to steer him in the right direction.

Monday morning I got another call from Todd. This time he was fucking ecstatic. The producers weren't able to come to terms with the other trainer, and negotiations had fallen apart. They were forced to move on, and Todd got the call. Fortunately he'd taken my advice about pulling it together, so he was ready when that call came. When I saw him at the gym later that morning he greeted me with a big hug. He told me that he was very thankful for everything I'd said to him. I told him that I was glad I could help—that that's what friends are for. And to this day, despite what happened next, that's genuinely how I feel about it. I'm glad that I had the chance to help him in his time of need. I'm proud to have had a hand in that.

Unfortunately, *You Are What You Eat* never got picked up. I've actually never even seen a copy of the show. No biggie. Getting one of these things to run is a long shot, and I knew that going in. Todd's show, on the other hand, was picked up, and became something of a cultural phenomenon. I was happy for Todd. Todd is a great trainer: now he had an outlet for sharing that with the world and potentially helping millions of people. What was there to not love?

Todd and I continued training together three days a week until his filming schedule got too hectic. We kept in close contact, though. We talked multiple times a day about what was happening on our respective projects. We'd help each other out with creative suggestions, strategies, and general encouragement.

At one point, shortly after the first season of his show started shooting,

Todd called and asked for a favor. Todd knew that Cheyenne was a massage therapist, and he wanted to know if Cheyenne would be willing to come in and massage his whole team. Todd's team was competing against another trainer's team, and he was looking to get an edge on them in any way he could. The production didn't have a large budget, he said, so they couldn't offer her any compensation. She would have to donate the time.

Cheyenne is a fantastic massage therapist and an even more amazing person. Even though she didn't know Todd that well, she agreed to the gig simply because he was a friend of mine and he'd asked for her help. She drove all the way out to Malibu and was almost to the location when Todd called and canceled. Something had come up on-set, he said, and it wasn't going to work out. He didn't need her anymore. She could turn around and go home.

He didn't even offer to pay for her gas.

These things happen, and you know what they say: Friends don't count favors. It was certainly annoying, but—with a major TV production going in full swing—we were willing to chalk it up to factors outside Todd's control. Todd and I had been friends for years at this point, and this one lapse, however inconsiderate, didn't seem to amount to much when viewed against the scope of our relationship. Little did I realize it was just a preview of things to come...

A couple of years go by, and Todd and I don't see each other as often. We stay in touch, but as Todd finds his groove on the show he needs my advice less and less. I'm glad. It's not that I minded giving him advice, but I was glad that he'd found his footing and was thriving. The show turned Todd into a major fitness celebrity, and I was glad for that, too. I always wanted him to be successful.

A few years into the show's run I'm visiting my family in New York, and I get a call from my sports agency. The other trainer on Todd's show is leaving, they tell me, and the producers are looking to hire a new trainer to take her spot. They've been trying to get me in front of the production team, they say, but they're having a hard time getting me an appointment. They know I'm good friends with Todd, and they're wondering if I'd feel comfortable asking him to get me in the door for an audition.

My old buddy Todd? The guy who used to call me ten times a day looking for advice and help? I'd absolutely feel comfortable asking for a favor. I hang up with them and I give Todd a call. I get his voicemail.

"Hey, Todd, it's Petrelli," I say. "I'm sure you've heard that they're looking for a new trainer on your show. I'd love the opportunity to work alongside you, buddy. I know together we can help a lot of people. If you can put in a good word for me with the producers, that would be great. I'll handle everything else once I get in the room."

Todd calls me back… just kidding. *He never calls me back.* I leave him a half-dozen messages over the course of the next week and I don't get so much as a text message in reply. He's gone full zero dark thirty on me. I'm shocked.

Weeks go by, and there's still nothing from Todd. Finally my agent pulls a bunch of strings and gets me in the office for the interview. As you can probably surmise, it didn't work out. Again, no biggie. TV is a tricky thing, and sooner or later you realize that casting decisions are influenced by a thousand variables almost all of which have nothing to do with you. If it's right it's right, if it's not it's not.

…or at least that's how I feel about it until I hear from a mutual friend that Todd *intentionally ignored my calls* because there was "No way in hell" he was going to let me on "his" show.

"He was worried you were going to steal his thunder," my friend says. "If it had been up to him, you never would have stepped in the room at all."

Son of a bitch.

Fast forward six months, and by chance I run into Todd at a random social event. This motherfucker's face drops when he sees me.

"Hey, John," he stammers. "I heard you've been trying to get ahold of me?"

Long... awkward... pause. He's looking at me, trying to gauge my reaction. I give him nothing. He swallows and continues.

"The thing is," he says, "I changed my number. Let me give you my new number."

This piece of shit didn't even think through his lie before he answered. You changed your number? How did you know I was trying to get ahold of you, then? Also, *I left messages on your voicemail.* I *heard your voice* on your outgoing message. Did you leave your voice on the outgoing message for *someone else's* phone number? This slimy weasel sure knew how to get ahold of me when he needed my help. He knew how to get ahold of me when he needed support, advice, feedback, a shoulder to cry on. Ignoring my calls was the second "fuck you." The first one was making me ask in the first place. If I'd been in his shoes, his name would have been the first thing out of my mouth when the producers announced the vacancy.

They say that success changes you. I don't think that's necessarily true. In my experience, with the people I've worked with, I've found that success only makes you more of what you already are. If you're a self-absorbed coward who goes through life afraid that everyone is trying to take things from you, success won't solve that. Money won't fix it. Neither will chiseled abs, big tattoos, and shiny fake teeth. I was angry at Todd for a long time. I was angry when I first wrote this. I feel differently about it now. These days I tend to feel sorry for Todd. They say it's lonely at the top, and it certainly seems like it is for him. Lonely, isolated, afraid that someone is going to come and push him off of his rarified perch... Seeing all of this taught me a valuable lesson about the kind of person I want to be. If it's lonely at the top, then the only solution I can see is to bring people along with you: to continuously try to raise up the people around you so that you can all be at the top together. It also taught me that it's not just tough times that show you who your true friends are: it turns out that—in Hollywood, at least—good times can do the same thing.

LATITUDE

I've had a lot of crazy experiences with the famous and the aspiring famous in my years in Hollywood. I chose to include the preceding story and the ones about Mr. Academy Award and Mr. Action Hero and Ms. Fancy Pants because I feel they illustrate the point that—just as you'd expect—movie and TV magic is just that, and things aren't always as they appear. However, looking back on these stories now and considering them together, there's another point that stands out even more in my mind and that I feel I need to emphasize. It's easy for us to see celebrities on TV or on a movie screen or a magazine cover and assume that they have it all: that they're secure and established in a way we feel we're not and will never be. It's easy to feel jealous of them and even resent them, and celebrate their mistakes and bad behavior as proof that they aren't really better than us after all: that underneath the big fame and the fans and the money they're still so very small. Even a quick look at TMZ.com or at the local supermarket's tabloid rack will show you this in no uncertain terms: we like nothing better than to see the rich and famous fall from what we perceive to be their high place on the human pecking order. It is very easy for us to forget that, at the end of the day, these larger-than-life figures are fallible humans just like us, and that they deserve the same compassion we'd hope to receive if we were in their shoes. And this is not simply a matter of principle: if I've learned one thing in all my years, it's that in order for any of us to grow—to do better—we need the space and the latitude to admit our mistakes and learn from them. We need others around us who are not only willing to call us out for our mistakes but also willing to hold that space: to let our past mistakes and misdeeds be the past when the work is done, and accept the new, better version of ourselves that we've worked so hard to become. If you've read this far then you already know that I've been blessed to receive this grace and compassion at many moments in my life, and I'd be sorely remiss if I was unwilling to offer it to others—even those who seem to have it all.

Nowadays we live in a world where it feels like anyone's life and career can be destroyed for something they said or did twenty years ago: for mistakes they've made that, it seems, we feel should follow them forever. But are we all so perfect that we can demand this from our fellow travelers on this human journey? As I said in my story about Mr. Academy Award, I do hope that I happened to catch these people at bad moments: that their average is better than their performances on these particular outings. If not, however, I hope that I'd have the wisdom to approach them with a clean slate should our paths ever cross again: to give them the same freedom to try again, past mistakes and all, that I'd hope they'd give me.

ZIGGY

Tired of stories about celebrities behaving badly? Then I've got just the thing for you.

I get a call out of the blue from the William Morris Talent Agency. If you don't know the name, the William Morris Talent Agency was an agency that represented some of the biggest names in film, television, and music. It merged with another agency and was renamed in 2017, but during its one-hundred-and-nine-year run it was regarded as one of the premiere agencies in show business. The person who called wouldn't tell me how they got my number, but they did have a bunch of questions for me about my training philosophy. I answered their questions and after ten or fifteen minutes the caller asked me if I'd be interested in meeting one of their clients, a guy by the name of David Marley.

David Marley? Sure. Why not? I had no idea who David Marley was, but I'm always happy to meet a new client. We set our meeting for eleven the next morning, and I didn't think too much more about it.

Eleven o'clock comes around, and David shows up at the gym for an initial consultation. We shake hands and he introduces himself as "Ziggy." I ask him if David is still in the car. He laughs, and thus begins our great friendship. Nothing like a little anonymity, a chance to meet person-to-person instead of celebrity-to-fan. It's not just an act, either: at this point in my life I've heard of Bob Marley and I know some of his songs, but I'm mostly into old-school rap like Public Enemy and rock like Metallica and Guns N' Roses. I don't know Ziggy or his music at all; to me, this morning, he's just another client... which makes him the most important person in the world.

I genuinely think it was this attitude that laid the foundation on which our friendship would later grow. Initially, even though he was friendly, I could tell that Ziggy was somewhat guarded. It was only later, when I came to understand the full scope of his and his father's celebrity, that I understood the reasons for that distance. Bob Marley is an absolute icon, a globally-recognized figure, and there's no denying how much Ziggy looks like his dad. On top of that, it's not as though that look is inconspicuous: with his long Rasta dreads, the only place Ziggy might blend in is Jamaica... but he's a huge star there, and Bob Marley is Jamaica's favorite son, so I imagine that there it's even harder.

When we first teamed up, Ziggy was a bit of a physical train wreck. I know he's going to want to kill me for saying that, but it's true. He understood the importance of fitness and proper nutrition—hence the call to yours truly—but his lifestyle at the time just wasn't conducive to maintaining those habits. For a long while we seesawed up and down. Don't get me wrong: I have great respect for how challenging it can be to travel across the country on a tour bus, performing every night in a different venue, let alone trying to stay fit and healthy while you're doing it. Poor and broken sleep, long periods of inactivity, rushed meals with sometimes limited options, stress and fatigue: the odds are truly stacked against you. It's imperative that you have a solid plan to meet these challenges. And it took some time before we dialed it in. Back in the day we'd have to start all over again from scratch after every stint on tour. Life on the road and all of its compromises and demands would take their physical and mental toll. Now, though, I'm proud to say that Ziggy has dialed it in. He went from being a client who would work pretty hard in small stints to one who kicks ass on a continual basis. Nowadays when he returns from a tour he's in as good a shape as when he left—if not better. I can wholeheartedly tell you that this man is in the absolute best shape of his life physically, mentally, and spiritually. I know it shows in his music—just ask his eight Grammys.

Ziggy's an athlete at heart, and these days our workouts vary widely. Lately we've been incorporating a lot of Combat Sports into our training: Thai boxing, Krav Maga, and Gracie Jiu-Jitsu. I pity the fool that mistakes Ziggy's kindness for weakness—this man hits hard and has a mean right cross. He's quick with his hands and he pieces together combinations exceptionally well. We've been able to utilize the maturity of his mindset and his physicality to develop the athleticism of a man in his twenties. How many people do you know who are in better shape in their fifties than they were in their twenties? I only know a few, and Ziggy is one of them.

I've been lucky enough to be Ziggy's friend for a long time now. I've had the privilege of traveling with him, of attending his wedding, of seeing his beautiful kids grow from infants to young adults. I've been privileged to witness his quiet greatness. You'll never hear about it in the media, but Ziggy silently helps many, many people. He loves kids, and it is evident in his actions. It's one of the many things we share—I believe that one day we'll collaborate on a project to help the youth stay healthy.

One particularly memorable trip I took with Ziggy was to Hawaii. We spent two weeks on the beautiful island of Maui training, relaxing, and soaking up the *aloha*. Every morning started with two hours of yoga. Let me be clear: this was *not* my idea. I'd previously struggled under the misconception that yoga is easy. This trip cured me of that misconception. By the end of that first week I'd had such an assfull of yoga that I didn't want to even eat yog*urt*. I was downward dogged out. Yoga is no joke. I know the teacher took special pleasure in grinding up Ziggy's fitness trainer. Fair enough. After this marathon of suffering we would head back to our respective cabins to relax until lunchtime. The property where we were staying was amazing—little bungalows perched on a stretch of lush green lawn on top of a cliff overlooking the ocean. Most days I'd cook lunch for us, and then we'd head out for a couple hours of cardio. We'd play soccer or football, do some martial arts, or just go for a run on the beach.

In addition to being absolutely breathtakingly beautiful, Hawaii has some of the best fishing in the world, and I was taking full advantage. Every morning I'd wake up early, gather my fishing gear, and head down to the reef to catch us some fish for lunch. It took some pleading, but after about a week I finally convinced Zig to come along. Ziggy is a little more conservative than I am when it comes to potentially dangerous activities, and knowing this I strategically omitted some details about the approach from my sales pitch. Specifically, I strategically failed to mention that access to my preferred fishing spot was a bit... rugged. From the clifftop you descended the forty or so feet to the beach via a broken-down old rope bridge, at a certain point passing over a tidal pool filled with beds of jagged coral. Once you were across you waded the thirty or so feet through the calm waters of another knee-deep tidal pool, avoiding the sharp coral, to a rocky outcrop that climbed out of the lapping ocean and made a perfect perch for beach casting. Like the badass he is, Ziggy rose to the occasion—but I think it's fair to say that he felt slightly duped, and that he wanted me to know it. I owed him one.

In my defense, the fishing was worth it. By the time Ziggy joined me I had my system dialed. A freshwater stream flowed into the ocean not far from where the bridge touched down, and I'd start off by fishing the stream for freshwater prawns with strips of squid I bought in town. I'd keep a few of the prawns for lunch and then I'd use one for bait to fish the ocean from the outcrop. Once I caught a fish with the prawn, I'd use that fish's innards for bait, and from there I'd keep the cycle going. Ziggy and I had a blast fishing all morning—we had so much fun, in fact, that we didn't notice how quickly the tide was coming in. We didn't notice until after the rising water had fully enveloped the bridge's beach end and turned the formerly knee-high tidal pool between us and it into a roiling, rip-current nightmare. We were stranded.

I thought maybe we could swim back across to the bridge, and hopped in the water to test my theory. Almost immediately the rip currents pulled me sideways and slammed me into the coral, gashing my leg in the process. I turned around and fought my way back to the outcrop. Swimming back to the bridge was not an option.

The bridge descended at a fairly steep angle from the clifftop, but even still the bottom end sat a good distance from the base of the cliff itself. From our present position on the outcrop, Ziggy and I were actually closer to the cliff's base than we were to the point where the bridge met the beach. All that stood between us and it was a short stretch of calm and coral-free tidewater. Which would have been a moot point—climbing a forty-foot cliff of dirt clods and crumbly volcanic rock was no better than swimming through the tidal pool's rip currents—if not for one thing: from our perch on the outcrop, we now noticed two old ropes hanging from the clifftop and reaching all the way down to the beach. Looks like we're not the first pair of morons to get stranded at high tide: someone has rigged an emergency exit. But bear in mind: when I say old, I mean these ropes looked like they could have been hung there by Captain Cook himself. They were discolored and badly frayed. We had no way of knowing if they would bear our weight, and no way of knowing what they were attached to above. On the other hand, we were out of options... so straight up the cliff we went. Forty feet is a long way to fall, so once I started I didn't look back. The only way I knew Ziggy was behind me was his voice: he was cursing at me in a language I'd never heard before the whole way up.

Luckily, we made it all the way to the top without breaking the ropes— or our necks. Ziggy didn't join me the next morning when I went out, and even though I keep asking he hasn't gone fishing with me since. Even after all that, as far as I'm concerned, it's his loss.

As I said, it's been a privilege to work with Ziggy and get to know him. Among other things, he's helped me develop a greater respect and appreciation for many other kinds of music, and find inspiration in places I never knew existed. I feel very blessed to call him my friend, and to have been able to accompany him on his journey.

SEBASTIAN

This chapter is about my good buddy, Sebastian Maniscalco. Sebastian and I met many years ago when we were both hired for bit parts on *Days of our Lives*. We'd both been hired for what is called "five-and-under" roles: roles where you speak an absolute maximum of five lines. Speaking a sixth line bumps you up to the next pay scale—what they call a "day player"—so the studio makes sure that doesn't happen. In this case, it was a good move on their part: casting us both in "five-and-under" roles might be the only way to get the two of us to shut up.

In this particular episode, we were both playing passengers on the Orient Express. I remember sitting down near him on that train car set and striking up a conversation. Immediately I felt at ease with him, like this guy would fit right in with all my buddies back home. When we broke for lunch, he and I headed over to the NBC studios cafeteria to grab a bite to eat. By the end of lunch I somehow knew that we'd be in touch for a long time… My Spidey Sense was right.

We have a lot in common. We have a similar twisted way of looking at things. We both grew up with Italian immigrant parents, who raised us with a kind of "Old World" mentality. If you've seen any of his comedy, you know that Sebastian masterfully mines all of this in his act. He can take one of his Italian immigrant father's quirks and turn it into an hour of pure comedic gold. It goes without saying that he's one of the funniest people I know. He's one of the funniest people anybody knows. It's been amazing to see his career progress.

Sebastian is a grinder. He's got a work ethic you wouldn't believe. Here's a guy who would work loading boxes for UPS all day and as a bartender at night, and would sneak away to do a fifteen minute set at The Comedy Store and then head right back to pouring drinks. This shit doesn't come easy to people. It takes years and years of hard work. At this point Sebastian's been hugely successful—he's done several Netflix and HBO comedy specials, and he just finished shooting a movie with Robert De Niro as his co-star—and it's no accident. This guy *works*.

When he started making a living as a comedian, Sebastian had the foresight and awareness to invest in his product—himself. His health and physical fitness became a top priority. In Hollywood, your appearance is judged every day. On top of that, despite what you may think, the job itself is physically demanding. Watch the guy's act and tell me he's not working. I'm honored that he hired me as his trainer. We've been working together for a long time now. I've even made it into some of his comedy routines. If you've

Sebastian and me, at Madison Square Garden.

seen his special *Aren't You Embarrassed?*, I'm the guy in the routine who has a compound bow in his house for "home invasion." If you've read his book *Stay Hungry*, you also know that I introduced him to his wife. I still consider it one of my greatest accomplishments that I somehow managed to convince Lana Gomez to go on a date with this greaseball. It's a true "Beauty and the Beast" story. Thank God women are attracted to a sense of humor.

In early 2018, Sebastian called me. He was going on tour, he said, and he wanted me to come along. This would be a major commitment: months on the road, dozens of cities. We chatted about it for a while, and then I hung up with him and called Cheyenne.

"Sebastian wants me to go on tour with him," I told her. "What do you think?"

There was silence on the other end of the line while she thought it over. Going on tour with Sebastian would mean a big commitment for me, but it would also mean a big commitment for her: by then we had two young boys, and my absence would cast Cheyenne in the role of solo parent. But Cheyenne also understood that this was a big opportunity, and that it would very likely be the experience of a lifetime.

"Okay," she said, finally.

"Great," I told her, breathing a big sigh of relief. "I'm glad you're on board, because I already told him that I'm in."

I'd always had a romantic vision of how it would be to travel around the world on a comedy tour. Now I know the reality. An entertainment tour is a nonstop output of energy. It's constant movement. I'm not sure exactly how many flights we took on that tour, but it feels like it must have been close to a hundred. If I didn't fully understand it before, the tour made me realize and appreciate just how hard Sebastian works. None of which is to say that it wasn't absolutely amazing. Being backstage at some of the greatest venues in the world—Radio City Music Hall, Air Canada Center, Cesar's Palace, The

Greek in Hollywood, Madison Square Garden (for four sold-out shows!)—while thousands of people crack up at your buddy's jokes is truly something special. I feel very blessed to have had that experience.

What Sebastian does is truly a remarkable thing. Think about the power of communication, the power of laughter. Think about what it is to tell a story that literally millions of people can relate to. To hone that talent into a razor-sharp skill through tens of thousands of hours of training. To be willing to fail over and over for years until you create a hundred-million-dollar routine. And that's truly what Sebastian's work is: a hundred-million-dollar product. I don't mean just Sebastian's pay or the pay for the dozens of people he employs, I mean all of it. The ticket sellers, the stadium ushers, the parking attendants, house security, restaurants, the waiters, the chefs... not to mention how much money gets dropped at the casino tables on the nights he has a show. Money dropped by people who came to the casino to see *him*. Think about the fact that on any given weekend he plays a place like Caesar's, it's normal for *thirty thousand people* to enter the casino just to watch him. How many of those people stick around to hit the blackjack tables or the slot machines after the show? Add in hotel rooms, bar tabs, taxi fares, and everything else that goes with a weekend in Atlantic City or Vegas and you start to realize: this guy is a moving economy. Think about the fact that he *built* that himself out of sheer talent and relentless hustle. Think about all of that, and you start to realize what a special person Sebastian Maniscalco is.

I wish you all the continued success in the world, my friend. I can't think of anyone who deserves it more.

At Sebastian and Lana's wedding. Thank God women are attracted to a sense of humor.

MARTY

Over my years as a trainer I've developed working relationships with several of the luxury hotels in the Beverly Hills area. At these high-end hotels, what the guest wants is what the guest gets, and when a guest wants a personal training session I'm one of the people these hotels call to make it happen. Of these hotels, my favorite is Hotel Bel-Air. It's truly a beautiful property: set in the heart of Bel-Air, tucked away in a small residential pocket, surrounded by lush gardens and amazing trees, and dripping with old-Hollywood charm. It's a holdover from a bygone era, one of those places that could never be built with today's zoning restrictions. I absolutely love it.

Aside from the beautiful venue, working at places like the Hotel Bel-Air offers other significant perks. As you might imagine, many of the people who stay at Hotel Bel-Air are very successful, and some of them have been at the top of their game in their chosen profession for many, many years. I love hearing success stories, and if you're willing to share your story and any wisdom you've gained along the way I'm always more than eager to listen. Also, in case you're wondering, a familiar set of themes seems to crop up in all of these stories: hard work, perseverance, a willingness to go the extra mile to help people, and a genuine desire to offer a solution to a problem—to add value.

One such person I had the privilege to know and work with was Marty Handelsman. Marty had been in the textile industry, but was so successful that he was able to retire early. Now he and his wife, Jill, devoted much of their time and energy to the performing arts, contributing to various causes and investing in productions on Broadway. They lived in Long Island, New York, but during that time they were spending three months out of every year in residence at Hotel Bel-Air. I first met Marty one day while I was in the hotel's gym training another client. Marty was working out on a punching bag, and he was going at it pretty hard. I cracked a joke about his punches, and he laughed. We immediately hit it off. I found him to be warm and intelligent, with an incredible amount of life experience and wisdom to share. I looked forward to seeing him every year, when he and Jill came to stay at the hotel.

When the incident I'm going to relate happened, Marty and I had already been working together for several years.

Marty and Jill have just arrived for their annual stay at the Bel-Air and, as I haven't seen him in almost ten months, Marty and I spend the first part of our workout catching up. He tells me all about what he's been working on and how things are going back in New York while he walks on the treadmill. He casually mentions that he'd had some chest pain a couple of months earlier, and that it was bad enough that he eventually went to see his doctor. The doctor ran a bunch of tests and couldn't find anything wrong with him. Apart from advising him to continue working out and eating healthy, there wasn't much the doctor could do for him. He told Marty to return if the pain came back or got worse, and sent him on his way.

Back then, the protocol I used with all of my clients was a short warm up followed by stretching. I had a mat I would roll out on the floor, and I would have my clients get down and run through a basic stretching routine. Marty and I have come to this part of the workout: he's warmed up, and I have him hop off the treadmill. No sooner does Marty lie down on the mat than his eyes roll back in his head. His body goes limp, and in an instant he's completely unresponsive. Marty is having a full-blown heart attack.

At that time, the Bel-Air's gym was isolated from the rest of the hotel. To make matters worse, we're the only two people in the gym, and there is zero cell phone reception.

A million thoughts start running through my head all at once. I need to get help, need to call 911, but I would have to leave Marty and run somewhere else on the hotel grounds to find someone or get a cell signal. And there's no way I can leave Marty: it's clear that he needs help *now*. It's time to start CPR. As a licensed personal trainer I'm required to be CPR certified, and I'm also required to take a CPR course every two years to keep my certifications current. That being said, CPR is not something I practice every day. I jump into action, but I'm only a few seconds in before I start to second guess myself. How many breaths? How many chest compressions? My mind is racing. *You got this*, I tell myself. *Just do compressions and breaths, compressions and breaths.* I dive back in. I'm doing my best. I guarantee you, though, that it is not textbook. On top of that, I don't know if what I'm doing is making any difference or if it's already too late. I'm doubting myself.

Maybe I should have gone for help, I think. *Maybe they'd be here by now, and they'd know exactly what to do. Maybe then an ambulance would already be on its way.*

I stop doing CPR long enough to check Marty's pulse. I feel nothing, zero, nada, zip, zilch. I pinch his nose, lock my lips to his, and deliver more rescue breaths. Then it's back to compressions. Back and forth, back and forth, breaths and compressions. Minutes tick by. Apart from the sound of my efforts, the gym is eerily silent. And then I witness something that I've never been able to fully describe. Marty and I are nose to nose. I can see his chest rising and falling with each breath I breathe into him. I can smell his cologne. His eyes are literally an inch from mine, and I'm looking directly into them when his limp body goes through a violent contraction. Like he'd been hit by a stun-gun, like he'd been struck by lightning, I feel a tremor of vitality in his body again. His jaws clinch down hard and I pull back just in time to avoid getting bit. The eyes that have been staring off into nothing for minutes now have become suddenly electrified. We look at each other, and I can feel him staring through my eyes and into my soul. I can only compare it to the moment when I looked into my sons' eyes for the first time: he wasn't there, and then all of a sudden he was. I take a deep breath in. I feel my heart rate drop. Time seems to slow and expand. I want to talk to him, to make sure he knows that even though I'm scared as I can be, I'm going to do everything in my power to make sure he's all right, but I can't seem to form the words. In that moment I'm sure it doesn't matter, though: staring into each other's eyes on the floor of the gym at Hotel Bel-Air, I am absolutely certain that he hears me all the same—that he knows and understands.

At that moment, a man and a woman walk into the gym. They stop just inside the doorway. As though by instinct, without anyone saying a word, they seem to sense it: something has happened here. There's been a serious incident. I'm glad they get it, but I also need them to stay calm. I need them to go and get help *right fucking now*, but I need to convey this information without scaring the living shit out of Marty. Still kneeling on the exercise mat beside Marty I calmly tell them to go and get security, and to tell them to call the paramedics. Luckily the security office is the closest building to the gym. The man quickly turns and runs to go do it. Help will be on its way soon. But any relief I feel is cut short: Marty heard what I said and understood what it meant. It freaks him out... and he has a second heart attack.

The silence has returned. Marty is unresponsive. I dive back in. Breaths and compressions, breaths and compressions. At some point I realize that I can feel the woman standing behind me, watching in silence. She never says a word. I don't know if she was in shock. She never talked or told me her name. I guess maybe she thought she could help best by staying out of the way.

More minutes go by. Finally I hear the faint sound of an ambulance's siren in the distance. The sound grows steadily louder as the ambulance gets closer. Marty is still unresponsive. The ambulance is now directly outside the gym. I hear the tires screech as they stop just outside. I hear voices, someone directing the paramedics. I hear the back doors of the ambulance open. I never stop CPR. Breaths and compressions, breaths and compressions. I hear the clatter outside as the gurney's wheels hit the ground. Marty regains consciousness for a second time just as the gym's door bursts open and the paramedics arrive on the scene.

I get out of their way. I explain to them what happened. They immediately take over. They take Marty's vitals. His heart rate is thirteen beats per minute. His blood pressure is dangerously low. He tries to sit up, but the paramedics make him lie back on the floor. They ask him a series of questions and for the first time since he went unconscious, Marty speaks. It's so damn good to hear his voice. I drift back out of the bubble of professional care the paramedics create. I don't know what to do. For a moment I'm overcome with guilt that this happened on my watch. The paramedics don't let me linger here. They need information. How long was he unconscious? Did he hit his head? Is he on any medications? I tell them what I know. I tell them it felt like he was out for at least ten minutes. I know now that it was much longer.

It's time to move. They load Marty onto the gurney and quickly wheel him out. The ambulance speeds off, bound for UCLA medical center. Before I know it everyone is gone. Marty, the paramedics, the man and the woman. I'm all alone, sitting on the gym floor. I feel a tear running down my cheek. I'm overwhelmed with a thousand thoughts and feelings all crowding my mind at once. Fear, guilt, elation, hope… and that moment when Marty and I seemed to be communicating without words and without any possibility of misunderstanding. More tears come and I let them fall. If my friends back in New York could see me now: tough guy John Petrelli, crying like a baby.

There's paperwork to fill out in the security office. There are questions to answer about the incident. Even though I'm surrounded by security personnel I feel all alone, lost in my own world. What happened plays over and over in a loop in my mind. *What went wrong? Did I do enough? Did I do the right things?* A tremendous sense of guilt and responsibility hangs over me like a cloud. I fill out the forms and answer the questions as best I can. I leave and I get in my car and I call Cheyenne. I tell her what happened. I try to explain. I know I didn't do a good job. There seem to be no words.

I leave the hotel and I drive over to UCLA to see if I can find out any more information about how Marty's doing. The staff are able to tell me that he's alive, but that the paramedics had to paddle-shock him back to life several times on the short ride to the ICU. They tell me that the doctors are working on him now, that someone will let me know if and when I can see him. I thank them and I wait. After several hours a nurse comes and tells me that visiting hours are over, and that I should go home and get some rest. I thank her and I leave. I don't remember much about the ride home. My mind and my body are in two different places. My body is in the car, but my mind is still back in the gym at Hotel Bel-Air. Back at home I try again to explain to Cheyenne what happened. I do a better job than I did the first time over the phone, but only slightly. Then I literally collapse from exhaustion.

I should have enjoyed it: it's the last good night of sleep I get for weeks. The cloud hanging over my head doesn't leave. I'm an absolute fucking wreck.

We learn later that the doctor back in New York misdiagnosed Marty's condition. Marty had a bad valve in his heart, and he missed it. Marty was primed to have a heart attack at literally any moment. Luckily, the nurses tell me, he wasn't alone when it happened. Luckily he was with someone who knew CPR.

"Marty was very lucky," they tell me, "that you were there."

"Thanks," I tell them, "that means a lot."

But it doesn't, really. It doesn't move the needle at all. The guilt I feel has settled around my mind like a helmet that all of their placating words can't so much as dent.

The doctors take great care of Marty, and after several weeks in the ICU and a surgery to install a pacemaker he's finally ready to leave the hospital.

To celebrate, he invites me to come have lunch with him and Jill at the Bel-Air. I gladly accept. That morning, on my way to the hotel, I head down to one of the local bakeries to pick up Marty's favorite cake. I know, right? Just what every heart attack survivor needs: a cake from his fitness trainer. I'm driving down Ventura Boulevard with the cake in my passenger seat when suddenly an SUV cuts across three lanes of traffic and slams into the front driver's side of my car. All of the airbags deploy. For the second time in my life, my car is totaled. Miraculously, though, I make it out with only minor burns from the airbags and cake frosting on my face.

I call Marty and Jill. I tell them what happened, and that I can't make our lunch date. I let them know that I'm physically fine, but that my car is totally out of commission. We reschedule for later that week, and then I spend the rest of the day calling my insurance company and getting a rental car and dealing with all of the other nonsense that comes with a car accident.

A few days later I head over to Hotel Bel-Air for my rescheduled lunch with Marty and Jill. This time, thankfully, the commute goes off without a hitch. It's so good to see my friend back on his feet again. It's clear from the amount of weight he lost in the hospital that he's been through a serious ordeal, but now he's up and in great spirits. Over lunch he tells me that he'd been lying in his hospital bed for weeks trying to think of how he could ever possibly repay me.

"The doctors told me that I would have been dead if you weren't there," he says.

All I can think in that moment is that if I hadn't been there—if I hadn't put him on that treadmill or moved so quickly past what he told me about the chest pains he'd had—then maybe none of it would have happened in the first place. I tell him that I just did what I was supposed to do, and that we should both consider ourselves very lucky. Marty just shakes his head at that, though.

"John," he says, "as far as I'm concerned, that car accident you had the other day was a clear answer to my question. I don't believe in coincidences. This was an answer from the Creator of the Universe. Jill and I would like to buy you a new car."

For a moment I'm too stunned to speak. All I can think is that it's too much, that there's no way I can possibly accept such a generous gift—and especially for something over which I still feel such guilt.

"Thank you," I say, "but I can't accept."

"Please," Marty says. And then he bestows on me another of the bits of wisdom I so cherished receiving from him from his long and successful life. He explains that there is a circle of energy in life: a natural flow of giving and receiving within which things are made to flourish and grow. I'd given him something tremendous, a new lease on life, and now he needed to give in order to complete the cycle. Anything else would go against the current, the Universal way. Only when he'd given me this gift, he tells me, would he be able to truly heal.

"So, really," he says with a smile, "I'm asking you for something again. I'm asking you to accept. Choose any car you like. The sky's the limit. Anything."

For the first time in weeks, the dark clouds that have gathered above my head begin to part and the light to shine through. I look into Marty's eyes. Not far from where we're sitting, just a handful of weeks before, both of our lives had changed. On that day, for one brief moment, I'd felt like I was communicating directly with him, my soul to his, and I'd felt like he understood. Now it is my turn to understand what Marty is telling me: that there is no need for my guilt or fear; that we are living now as before in a great gift that we'd all been given, and that the only thing to do is to pay it forward to others and accept it, gracefully and gratefully, when it is paid forward unto us.

"Thank you," I say. "I accept."

And—jackass that I am—you know what I say next?

217

"You know," I say, "you had *two* heart attacks. I had to perform CPR *twice*. Maybe it would be better for all parties involved if I had a boat to tow behind my new car."

And then, sitting there in the bright Southern California sunshine, we laugh until our laughter mixes with tears of gratitude and joy.

I drove the new SUV that Marty and Jill bought me for many years. It was a constant reminder of how important it is to help when help is needed, to train enough so that you can be truly helpful when that moment comes, and that no day is guaranteed: a constant reminder of how blessed we are to wake up every single day of our lives, and to never take one second of it for granted. Thank you, Marty, for everything.

Left to right: Marty Handelsman, Cheyenne, Jill Handelsman, and myself, at the Hotel Bel-Air.

THE WILD RULES

I was in the gym one day when I noticed a poster on the wall advertising tryouts for a wilderness-based reality show. The poster said something like, "Do you have what it takes to live in the wild without any equipment? Can you find your own food and make your own shelter?" It said they were looking for ex-military, land navigators, rock climbers, strongmen, and weekend warriors who were willing to be airdropped into a remote part of the world. The winner of the show would take home a bounty of solid gold bars worth one hundred thousand dollars. I jotted down the information and when I got home that evening I pulled up the application online. Along with all of my information the application required me to make a five minute video explaining why I thought I'd win the show. I slapped together a video and sent it in, and two days later I got a call from the producers asking me to meet them later that day.

I drove over to their offices in Santa Monica. I was expecting a brief meeting, something like a regular TV audition, but I was in for a surprise. This wasn't an audition, this was a full-on *test*. Over the next couple of hours I was interviewed, assessed, screen tested, and run through a full physical and psychological evaluation. Not really sure how I passed all of that—if you've read this far you know I'm fucking nuts, you'd think that would've raised some red flags—but the very next day I received a call inviting me to participate in the show. Who knows? Maybe they figured I was just crazy enough to make the show interesting.

Things moved very quickly. By week's end I and the other contestants were going to be deposited in some remote area of the world. I had just enough time to set things up with work and gather up all the gear on the list the producers had provided. The producers had been very secretive about where the show would be filmed, but I could tell by the items on the list that we were not bound for a tropical paradise. This was all extreme cold-weather gear. As soon as I got home from the store I put it all on and I started training. I never let myself get out of shape, but for the next five days I cranked my cardio up to the next level. I also knew that if my gear was going to fail, I wanted to know about it before I got on the plane. I figured there would be no chance to secure a replacement or make adjustments once I left town. I ran the streets in three layers of clothes, hiking boots, and a backpack. This is in southern California in the middle of summer, where the temperature regularly hits the hundred-degree mark. The people driving by must have thought I was a fucking lunatic. I guess they weren't wrong.

The bigger challenge was maintaining my body weight throughout all of this training. I can lose weight at the drop of a hat, and I knew there was a good chance I'd have minimal food while on the show. I had to keep some fat reserves on my body. Accordingly, for those few days, all my meticulous diet awareness went right out the window. I ate everything I could get my hands on, and I mean *everything*.

I didn't know exactly what I was in for, but I knew I was doing everything in my power to be ready.

And oh yeah, did I forget to mention? There was one more preparatory measure I had to take. The producers had some papers they needed me to sign. Among them: a liability waiver stating that I understood the very real possibility that I'd be dying on the show. Yeehaw. Let's make some fucking TV.

After a week of six-hour workouts and bags of groceries consumed, Cheyenne dropped me off at LAX. I gave her a final hug, hoisted my gear, and headed off to check in at Alaska Airlines.

As luck would have it, standing in line waiting to check in was a buddy of mine, Paul Vinson. Paul's a former world-class wrestler—not a WWE entertainer, but a legit top-level freestyle wrestler who'd once ranked fourth in the world. When I first met Paul he was working as a plumber and harboring dreams of breaking into show business. I had Paul send me a couple of headshots, which I passed along to my commercial agent; my agent took a meeting with Paul and the next thing I knew I was seeing Paul on TV every two minutes. He was in commercials, on game shows, he even had a gig as the spokesperson for a vacuum cleaner. He booked way more stuff than I ever did. When I saw him standing in line with a pile of gear identical to mine, it didn't take long for me to put two and two together, and I was psyched: I still wasn't sure what we were going to face on the show, but I knew I had a potential ally in Paul.

The flight from LAX takes us as far as Seattle, Washington. From there a connector flight takes us over to Vancouver, Canada, where we meet up with the show's producers. They inform us that we will now be hopping on a small prop plane and heading out into the wilds of British Columbia. This is the last time we'll be allowed to use our cell phones, and I make two calls: one to my family back in New York and one to Cheyenne. I tell them all that I love them, and the general area where I believe I'm headed. Beyond that, there isn't much to say. I don't know any more. I don't even know how long I'll be gone. Production is set to run for up to two weeks, but if I blow it I could be home a lot sooner than that.

We board this six-seater airplane and we're off, flying over dense forests, rivers, and huge glaciers at low altitude. I don't remember now exactly how long the flight was: the incredible scenery and the excitement have turned it into a blur in my memory. It could have been twenty minutes or it could have been two hours. The extreme turbulence we encounter barely even registers, I'm so jazzed.

Finally we make our descent. The "runway" is just a tiny dirt track in a clearing. As we approach the landing zone the pilot suddenly pulls up hard on the controls, aborting the landing. Just before touch-down he noticed a mamma grizzly bear and her two cubs feeding in the brush right next to where we were set to land. There are few things more dangerous in the wild than a protective mama grizzly bear, and I guess the producers figured it wouldn't be good to start the show off with all of the contestants getting mauled. We circle back around until the noise of the plane sends the three bears running off into the dark timber. We touch down and rumble along the dirt track to a stop. The pilot kills the engine and we deplane. The landscape is awesome in the truest sense of the word. The silence is deep and overwhelming. If anyone thought we were headed to the Four Seasons, that dream is now officially over.

The format of the show is simple: two teams, each composed of six people from different backgrounds, compete at a variety of tasks while enduring the challenges of wilderness existence. The backgrounds the producers have decided on for this season are military, navigator, hunter, fisherman, strongman, and weekend warrior. I'd been chosen as the weekend warrior from New York. When the producers heard that I was originally from New York they'd automatically assumed the City, and I wasn't about to correct them: not if it meant giving up a shot at a hundred thousand dollars in gold. Standing by the dirt runway deep in the Canadian wilderness, I offer up a quiet prayer of thanks for the Balios and all of the countless hours I'd spent hunting and fishing on their farm; I know I'll need every ounce of that experience and more to win this competition.

I've come into the competition with an unknown skillset, which works to my advantage. However, I've also come in with a major weakness: I don't understand how reality shows work. I haven't considered or studied the game strategy part of it. I don't understand things like creating allies, lying, cheating, and plotting against your own teammates. I also don't understand how the sausage gets made: how, once everything is filmed, the producers sit in an editing room and cut together the footage in a way that tells the most compelling story possible… whether that story is completely true to life or not. Conflict and drama put asses in seats and renewal contracts on the table. I don't begrudge the producers for the story they created. I should have taken the time to educate myself on the whole process. I have a better understanding of what is needed now. The John Petrelli of today would play the game differently. The John Petrelli who's standing by the runway as the prop plane takes off, however, is in for a rude awakening.

Production starts immediately, and it doesn't stop. Everything is filmed, and when I say everything I mean *everything*. The producers shoot twenty-four hours a day. There is always a camera rolling... and there is always something to film. Things get serious quickly. My buddy Paul doesn't make it twenty-four hours in the wilderness. They have to helicopter him out for medical reasons. The strongman on the other team, a guy who's almost seven feet tall and weighs well over three hundred pounds, is forced to throw in the towel just a couple of days later. It turns out it's not how strong your body is, but how mentally tough you are that counts. I'm about to find out what I'm made of.

The first night sets the tone for what is to come. We arrive at our designated campsite just before dark. The producers have severely limited our gear, but each of us has been given a few primitive tools: I've been placed in charge of our team's axe, flint stick, and toothpaste. It's my job to cut wood, start fires, and make sure everyone has fresh breath. We're all soaking wet, having waded across an ice-cold river to the location, and with the sun now setting it's imperative that we get a fire built. *Great. Fire good. I'm on it.* Just as the sun fully sets behind the mountains, the producers throw their first curveball: for "safety reasons" we need to tear down our newly-constructed shelter and build a new one thirty yards away—thirty yards away, mind you, from the fire that I *finally just got started.*

Building a fire with a flint stick and wet tree branches and moss is no walk in the park: doing so all over again in the dark—walking through bear-infested woods with no flashlight to look for fuel—is a whole other can of worms. In fact, it's a literal nonstarter. Not that the team tasked with rebuilding the shelter fared much better: the dark makes it too dangerous to even gather materials to build with. Tonight we're sleeping rough.

The producers are fucking with our heads.

The temperature starts to drop. We're completely exposed. I can't stop shivering. I haven't even had a chance to take off my wet clothes yet. I strip down. For what feels like an eternity, but I'm sure now was only a few brief moments, I and my half-frozen dork stand exposed to the freezing Canadian night. I quickly get redressed with dry clothes from my daypack. Tonight these clothes and a single thin canvas tarp will be my only insulation. Twenty-four hours earlier I'd kissed my beautiful Cheyenne goodbye: now I'm snuggling up to some dude I met just a few hours earlier, trying to conserve body heat.

By the middle of the night I'm still wide awake, shivering like I've never shivered before. My teeth are knocking together and my body is shaking uncontrollably. I can't take it. I have to do something. I get up, go down to the first fire I built, pull hot rocks out of the ring I'd made, and stuff them into my pants.

Let me tell you: nothing has ever felt better. The trick is to find rocks that are hot, but not so hot that they burn through my gloves... or my frozen Johnson. That night we make foray after foray down to the fire ring to stuff hot rocks down our pants. We barely sleep, but we don't succumb to hypothermia. When the sun finally appears the next morning, we're all totally exhausted.

Fantastic. Only fourteen more days to go.

How best to describe the days that follow? Imagine you've been stranded in the wilderness with limited food and gear, throw in a heaping helping of that bully from school who knew *exactly* how to make your life absolute misery, and you're in the ballpark. Stress creates conflict, conflict makes for compelling TV, and the producers don't pass up any chance to milk the situation for all it's worth. Gains are erased, arbitrary limits are imposed and enforced, and effective workarounds are disallowed. And that's not to mention the fact that the premise and format of the show itself adds a layer of stress to what would be a stressful enough situation on its own. In a genuine survival situation, groups learn to work together and rely on each other. While we are technically working in teams, this show will only have one winner. This fact specifically disincentivizes group cohesion and trust. It's all for one and one for all when it serves individual needs; when it stops doing that, it's every man for himself.

With limited food, extremely limited rest, and constant physical demand, it doesn't take long for the human body to start breaking down. Competitors drop like flies. They're tapping out left and right, and I honestly don't blame them. Before long every inch of my body aches. Every muscle hurts. I develop huge blisters on my feet that plague me as we hike mile after mile between challenges. I'm hungry all the time. At one point my blood sugar drops so low that I nearly pass out right into the campfire. And it's always cold. A few times during the day the weather approaches what you'd call comfortable, but every night, as soon as the sun drops below the horizon, you can fucking forget it. It's as cold as anything I've experienced before or since. On a few occasions it actually rains on us all through the night. Do you have any idea what it's like to try to sleep with rain falling on your face? Few people I know have had the pleasure of that experience. I remember the optimist in me making a mental note that if it was raining that meant it wasn't cold enough to snow... but looking back on that now, it seems like I might have been blurring the line between optimism and psychosis.

Still, things are going about as well as can be hoped for. I've outlasted some of the other contestants. I'm holding on. On days four and five, though, I make a potentially catastrophic mistake. I leave my cold and water-logged boots on all day and all night. I'm just too exhausted to take them off. When I do take them off, late on day five, I'm greeted by a sickening sight: a weird fungus has started growing on my feet. For a second I'm too stunned to even react. I can't believe how fast it happened. What really signals the alarm bells, though, is what I discover next: either because of the fungus or because of the constant moisture, huge pits like open sores have opened in the bottoms of my feet. It looks like the flesh is rotting or being eaten away. *Fuck.* I'm too tired to freak out, but I start to freak out anyway. If my feet go, so do my chances of winning the show. For the next couple of nights I sleep barefoot by the fire, and during the day I make sure to always have on dry socks. Slowly, the things inside my boots start to resemble feet again.

We're running around all over the place doing challenges, but our base-camp remains the same. Accordingly, we're able to make steady, small improvements to our shelter. It helps us sleep a little better at night. We're still expending tons of energy, though. On day six—after basically not eating for five days straight—we're lucky enough to catch a few fish. As I'm cleaning one of the fish I find a small, partially-digested rainbow trout in its stomach. We divide it up and eat it without a second thought. We consider it an appetizer. After five days of gnawing hunger, those fish taste better than anything I've ever eaten.

I've come pretty close to dying several times in my life, and two of my personal top five happen in the days that follow. The first happens on day eight. Today we're plotting longitudinal and latitudinal coordinates to locate a bunch of items that the producers have hidden in the wilderness. Today, the challenge is going to take place on horseback.

As you now know, I've spent a lot of time around horses. However, you shouldn't confuse "spent time around" with "comfortable around," because I am not. One way to put it would be to say that I have a great deal of respect for horses. Another way to put it would be to say that horses freak me the fuck out.

Here's a statistic you may not know. In the wild, horses cause more major injuries than any other animal. They cause more major injuries than

226

snakes, bears, cougars, wolves, or any of the other animals that most people think of as dangerous. Here's something else you may not know. There is a difference between a packhorse and a saddle horse. A saddle horse doesn't mind being taken out on its own, just horse and rider. A packhorse *does* mind. In fact, depending on the animal, a packhorse can mind a lot. Today, the horse the producers want me to ride is A) a packhorse who B) does mind and C) is having no part of what the producers have planned. As soon as I mount him he starts bucking and trying to bite my arms. Fuck that. I'm off that horse faster than you can say the word "horse." I go over and I explain to the producers and the wrangler that this is a packhorse, that he wants to stay with his pack, and that when he sees his pack going off in the opposite direction he gets uncomfortable and he reacts. I also explain to them that, for this reason, there is absolutely no way in hell I'm riding this fucker.

Unsurprisingly, they're not happy. They send the horse wrangler over to try and shame me into getting back on this crazed stallion. No dice. I'm not budging. I may be crazy, but I ain't stupid. So, after a lengthy discussion, we settle on a compromise: I will *walk* the horse by his reins. This works for about a minute. Then the horse comes to his senses and reminds me who's boss. He turns, bucks, rears up on his hind legs. He does everything he can to kick me in the face with his two front hooves. When that doesn't work— when I don't release my grip on his reins—he goes back to biting.

That's the last straw. I've had enough, and apparently so has the horse wrangler. He comes over, grabs the reins, and shows me how to whip the horse back into submission. No thanks. I'll be walking on my own the rest of the way. With a snort of derision, the wrangler mounts the scared horse, calls me a pussy, and rides off.

Unfortunately for him, it doesn't take long for the wheel to come around, and for Mother Nature to remind him who's really in charge, no matter who's holding the reins. Just a little ways down the trail, in a dry creek bed, the horse rears up again. He kicks his front legs high in the air and then he topples over on his back, crushing the wrangler under his massive weight. The impact breaks the wrangler's back. An emergency medical helicopter is called in to take that wrangler to the nearest hospital. I don't know if he recovered, or to what extent. I never saw that man again. I feel bad for him... but I also know that it very easily could have been me.

I also know that he knew better: that as a professional wrangler he knew the difference between a packhorse and a saddle horse better than I did. For that reason, I feel confident saying that he wouldn't have done what he did—he wouldn't have pressed the issue—if not for the pressure of the TV show. He let what the producers were telling him override what the horse was telling him, and he paid for it dearly. To the rest of us, if it wasn't already, the message is now doubly clear: good TV is the order of the day, and that means at almost any cost. If we didn't know what we were getting into when we signed that waiver, we sure as shit know it now.

Twelve days into the competition there are only three contestants left on my team: me and two women. Now, with only a couple of days left, our task is to travel approximately eighteen miles downriver *via the river*. That's right: we've got to make a raft out of the only material we have available to us—driftwood and twine.

I have zero experience doing this sort of thing, and it shows in the finished product. Both of the ladies on my team are super competitive and eager to work, but the simple fact of the matter is that there's only so much power a ninety-pound woman can generate—especially after she's been damn-near starving for the past twelve days. It's looking like I'm going to be the one to build this raft... and the one to paddle it.

Oh, and maybe I should also mention: I have about as much experience paddling a raft as I do building one. I absolutely suck at paddling.

Not that it matters much, maybe. It's not like we've got oars here. Our paddles are more driftwood. It's going to be what it's going to be... and what it's going to be is fucking exhausting. We're not on the river for two minutes before my knees are bleeding from kneeling on the jagged deck. My hands and ass are riddled with splinters. The water that is splashing up from the sides and between the planks is absolutely freezing, and we've got to do this for *eighteen fucking miles.*

And where's the film crew, you ask? They're right behind us... in a fully-equipped Zodiac, complete with a four-stroke engine.

I should probably mention that at this point in the show, things are getting a bit tense between me and the crew. The snafu with the packhorse was just the beginning of it, and the last incident had occurred only that morning. One of the cameramen who was filming us build the raft had decided that here—right in front of us—was the perfect place to eat a fucking sandwich, and it wasn't appreciated. I told him that he'd better get his fucking sandwich the fuck out of my face, or as soon as I could muster the strength I was going to knock him over the head with some fucking driftwood. That did the trick—he scurried off—but a couple of minutes later one of the producers came over.

"Did you just threaten one of my cameramen?" he asked.

The thought crossed my mind that I was about to get kicked off the show.

"Maybe," I said, "but I think, if you were in our situation, you would have done the same damn thing."

I didn't hear another word about it... but it was certainly in the air as we set off down the river.

The first seven miles of river are flat, calm water, and it's almost impossible for our team to get up any speed. At around the seven-mile mark, though, things suddenly change. The current catches us and starts propelling us forward. At first, I'm glad. I'm finally able to put my paddle down. However, as we pick up speed, it quickly becomes evident that we are now at the mercy of the river's power. Our driftwood oars are going to be no match for the churning water. For the first time in our journey we actually need to slow down—and we can't.

The rapids increase, and steering becomes nearly impossible. It takes all of our collective effort just to avoid all of the boulders and downed trees that we're careening towards—efforts that we are more than happy to give. Before we'd launched on our raft adventure, the producers had briefed us on the extreme danger that these fallen trees pose to our safety: a fallen tree that partially blocks the flow of a river becomes a strainer for any and everything that is being carried downstream. Get caught by one of these "sweepers," they told us, and the force and weight of the flowing water will pin you there and drag you under.

"Sweepers will kill you," they told us. "Plain and simple."

Now, rocketing downstream at the absolute limit of our control, I'm doing my best not to imagine going out that way, pinned and helpless under the massive weight of all that flowing water. I'm doing my best not to imagine the call the producers will have to make to Cheyenne and my family, doing my best not to imagine my body shipped home in a box... and all for a stupid TV show.

The Zodiac has pulled around in front of us, now—I guess to get a better shot of our demise—and suddenly the camera crew starts yelling.

"Go to the right!" they yell. "Paddle to the right! Turn right!"

Right? Yeah, right. All the yelling in the world isn't going to improve my paddling skills; nor is it going to dampen the force of the class-four rapids you've just siphoned us into.

I look downstream and see the reason for all the commotion: up ahead and coming on fast, the river forks around a central island. Neither side of the split looks like particularly smooth sailing, but the lefthand side is an absolute nightmare. It's a labyrinth of sweepers and boulders: a gaping maw waiting to chew our little driftwood raft to bits and suck us down to a watery grave. The ladies see it, too. We paddle as hard as we can, but we can't gain an inch against the current. We're being pulled closer and closer to the left-hand fork. The Zodiac has already steered clear—a fact which does nothing for my state of mind. If they're not willing to go down this stretch of rapids in a motorized Zodiac—the same kind of boat used by the military to navigate some of the roughest waters on the planet—to catch all the coming craziness on camera, then we on our little driftwood raft are well and truly fucked.

The river's force is tremendous, and despite our best efforts the lefthand fork is pulling us in. Fighting it is futile, so at the last second I tell the ladies to start paddling *into* the fork. We can't escape: our only chance now is to try to gain some control by steering ourselves *with* the flow of the river. It's too little too late, though. No sooner have we made the switch than— *SMASH!*—we crash head-on into a boulder. Shards of wood spray everywhere. The damaged raft spins from the combined force of the impact and the water still pushing at us from behind. We clear the boulder but continue to spin. It's impossible to stop and impossible to steer. At this point, we can do little more than hang on and pray. We don't have time for anything else anyway. Immediately the next obstacle is barreling down on us: a big dead tree lying just above the surface of the water. We hit the deck and lay face down, clinging to the boards. Water rushes into my open mouth. I feel my jacket catch and snag on the tree's branches and I'm jerked backward toward the water. I grip the raft tighter and my jacket tears, releasing the tree's hold. We clear the sweeper, still spinning out of control. Another boulder looms up in our path and we meet it head-on. The impact splits our raft in two: the ladies are on one side and I'm on the other. We reach across and clasp hands, trying to pull the two halves back together. Whatever comes next, for the moment at least, it's all for one. And good thing, too, because here it comes: the mother of all sweepers, a spiny wall of jutting branch ends and crooked limbs waiting to grab us, skewer us, poke our eyes out, and pin us underwater. We don't have time to think, we only have time to act. Holding the raft together with our hands and sheer willpower we grab the deck and instantly we are in it. The sweeper has us in its grasp, and the force of the water starts to push us under. The raft begins to crackle as the driftwood buckles under the pressure. Once the raft goes, I know, we go with it. I'm anticipating the moment, the feeling of the floor disappearing beneath me and the water taking hold, when—*BOOM!*—there is a sound like a shotgun blast, and the branches of the sweeper *shatter* before us. Wood splinters explode everywhere and we break through. We're free.

Exhilaration, fear, and grateful disbelief flood my mind and body. At this point in my life I've jumped out of airplanes, saved a man's life, stared down a gun... but this is different. This is pure sensory overload: adrenaline, terror, triumph, physical and mental exhaustion, and so much more all rolled up in a super burrito of *life and living*. For a moment I am overcome with a kind of awe and wonder—at the savage beauty of nature in its most unfiltered form, at its elemental force, its power and its grace—and it is in that moment I understand with a shining certainty unlike anything I have ever known that I no longer want to go through the world experiencing all of this on my own: that I need to step up to the plate and ask Cheyenne—my girlfriend of ten years now—to marry me. I need to experience all that life has to offer with her by my side, to experience life's beauty and power together, to love and laugh and cry on this adventure with her, always and forever.

In that moment, my goal on the show shifts. I no longer need to win the hundred grand. Now, all I need to do is make it out alive. I have things I need to do back home. I need to ask for Cheyenne's hand in marriage.

Somehow we make it through the rest of our river challenge with no more near-death experiences, and three days later—after fifteen days of brutal, life-changing competition—I finish second by about five minutes. If I didn't have the map-reading abilities of Helen Keller, I think I actually would have won. I'd opted to follow one of my opponents, a Marine drill instructor, because I thought he could read a map better than I could, and it turned out to be a big mistake. My intuition was telling me to trust my own instincts, but I didn't listen. Lesson learned. I can promise you this: I will always trust my intuition in the future.

By the time I arrived back in LA, I could have passed for my own shadow. I'd lost twenty-five pounds, most of it muscle. I decided to address the problem by stupidly gorging myself on anything I could get my hands on: whole pizzas, a dozen doughnuts, a couple of Whoppers, you name it. And —and this may be hard for you to believe, but it's true—in less than thirty-six hours *I gained over twenty five-pounds back*. I have the pictures to prove it. I went from looking like a prisoner of war to a swollen hippo in just a day and a half.

The problem is, of course, that the human body is not designed to tolerate such massive bodyweight fluctuations. For fifteen days I'd hardly consumed enough calories to stay alive while expending massive amounts of energy. My system had been breaking down muscle tissue to stay alive, which was wreaking havoc on my liver. Once I started piling in all of this fatty food, my body basically shut down.

The doctor explained it to me this way: your liver is like a strainer, and when you break down muscle tissue for energy the muscle fibers clog the strainer. I'd broken down a lot of muscle tissue over the course of those two weeks, and my strainer was severely clogged.

What does that mean, you ask? I don't want to be gross... but I also made a promise that I would be honest. Therefore I feel compelled to tell you that I couldn't go to the bathroom for several days. No, not even pee. All of the food that I'd gorged myself on was stuck in my intestines, and that's where it stayed. My stomach protruded out like I was nine months pregnant. On top of that, my entire body was sore beyond anything I had ever experienced. All the delayed onset muscle soreness I'd experienced bodybuilding didn't come anywhere close.

I'd gone to the hospital when these symptoms first appeared—this was when I got the "clogged filter" explanation for what I was experiencing—but aside from telling me to wait it out, the doctor hadn't had much for me. After a few more days, though, I broke down and went back. I was miserable. I was so uncomfortable. I wanted to crawl out of my skin. My stomach had kept right on growing, and I was starting to get worried that my intestines were going to burst. The doctor ran several tests and, after seeing that many of my enzyme levels were still off the charts, he simply replied, "Look, there's really not much I can do for you. I could give you medication, but that would just put your liver under more stress. You're going to have to do this the old-fashioned way: lots of vegetables and plenty of water."

I hadn't peed in days, and this guy wanted me to drink *more water*?

"You want me to drink *more* water?" I said.

He nodded. "Yep," he said. "If that doesn't work, come back and see me."

That night, as I lay in bed, my stomach made sounds that no person should ever hear coming from their own body. I was too uncomfortable to sleep, but that didn't matter: I was up almost constantly trying to pee anyway. The memory of standing over the toilet waiting and hoping, staring down past the bowl at my honest-to-God cankles, will be with me forever. Then, finally, at around four in the morning, it happened. I felt it coming. I ran to the bathroom and I peed for what felt like ten minutes straight. I've never experienced anything like it in my life. I literally watched my body deflate. I was like an old above-ground swimming pool that somebody had punched a hole in. Every ounce of liquid I'd consumed for the past several days came rushing out of me in one brilliant, powerful stream. It was glorious.

I was disappointed by my loss on the show, but not as much as you might think. I'd gained so much from the experience. Those two weeks taught me a lot about myself. Perhaps most importantly, they taught me that I am—that we human beings are—always capable of so much more than we imagine. This lesson has served and, I'm sure, will continue to serve me well, and I am so grateful for it. Those weeks also gave me the gift of clarity and certainty about what I want my life to be and, most importantly, who I want to share it with, and that is a gift I value far more than any gold I might have won.

If you look around online, I'm sure you can still find the series somewhere. It's all there for you to see: all the highs and lows and the near misses, all filtered through the producers best shot at making "must-see" reality TV. Honestly, there's only one moment I cared about them getting right: the moment where, completely cashed out and overwhelmed by our experience on the river, I face the camera and, blubbering, ask for Cheyenne's hand in marriage.

PART IV

BEGINNINGS AND ENDINGS...
AND BEGINNINGS

MUST-SEE TV

About six months after *The Wild Rules* wrapped, the show finally started airing on ESPN. The only person I ever told the final outcome to was my father, so every week my family and friends were glued to the TV to see what would happen next.

At the time, to be perfectly honest, it would have been okay with me if they'd all skipped a few weeks. There were many, many scenes in the show where—to put it mildly—I was a total embarrassment to myself and everyone who knew me, and the week after any given episode aired brought a steady stream of jokes at my expense about whatever priceless moment the most recent episode had broadcast to the masses. It was all good-natured kidding, of course, but I'd be lying if I said there weren't moments when I wanted to crawl in a hole until the whole thing was over. Looking back on it now, though, and seeing it in context, I feel differently about it. My father had passed away recently, and within that sorrow the show provided us all with some much-needed laughter.

After thirteen weeks of episodes, we were down to the last three contestants: a Marine drill sergeant, a fisherman, and myself. My good friend, Mark Harris, offered to host a grand-finale party at his house for the final episode, and we invited all of our close friends to watch with us. I think everyone was certain that we were throwing the party because I'd won: who throws a party to celebrate losing, right? They didn't know that this final episode was going to show something even more important, something I wanted everyone to see.

My moment of clarity came on the river, but it was far from the whole story. There hadn't been a single moment on the show when Cheyenne was far from my thoughts, and as the challenge of the show progressed the voice in my heart telling me what I needed to do only grew louder and more certain. I remember one specific moment, eight days into the competition, when we were all set to rappel down a sheer mountain face: I was shaking in my boots as I clung to the safety ropes. The prospect of rappelling down this vertical cliff scared the shit out of me, but I couldn't let the other competitors know that I was frozen in fear. I needed to calm my mind, needed to relax, and looking down at the void beneath my feet wasn't helping. So instead, I looked up. I looked straight up at the sky, straight up to heaven. I started taking deep breaths. I watched wisps of white cloud sail across the clear blue sky like ships on a vast, calm ocean. A cool breeze blew over my sweaty face and swayed the tops of immense pines in the forest around us. A calmness washed over me. I felt my heart rate slow. My soul felt at ease. The immense beauty of nature was all around me, and I'd been so fixated on my fear that I hadn't noticed. The answers were all around me: all I had to do was look and listen.

Thoughts came into my mind, then, like they were being blown in by the wind. I thought of Cheyenne, of how she had stood by my side for over ten years, supporting me in everything I did, loving me no matter what. I could have thought of a million other things in that moment—of the other competitors, of the challenges ahead, of the prize at the end—but instead I thought of her. That's what God put in my conscious mind. And I knew in that moment that it would be far too selfish to experience all of the adventures to come without her.

You might think that knowing this in my heart would have helped me stay calm as I waited for the final episode's big moment. Nope.

The excitement in the room is at a fever pitch as the competition comes down to the wire between myself and one other competitor. In the end, as you now know, I make a critical error in judgment and I lose by a handful of minutes.

The show cuts to a commercial. I'm sitting next to Cheyenne. My heart is racing and I'm sweating profusely. I feel like I'm right back on that cliff face, about to step off into the unknown. My nervousness is compounded by my uncertainty about the show itself: two days earlier I'd had a phone conversation with the producers, and they'd promised me that my proposal to Cheyenne would come at the end of the final episode... but at another point they'd also told me that it might be cut for time. Fucking TV. You never know how these things are going to turn out until you actually see them. Sitting there on the couch, I know there's a chance that this has all been for nothing: that we'll come back from the commercial break to a final wrap-up and the credit roll.

Meanwhile, everyone in the room is disappointed that I finished second. They're all trying their best to console me. They don't know that I couldn't care less: I'm about to embark on the biggest adventure of my life.

I'm trying to keep everyone calm, to keep them focused on the TV. Our phones are ringing off the hook, but I can't talk to anyone yet. Cheyenne's family is calling both of our phones, and I can't give her a solid reason why we shouldn't talk to them. It's a crazy couple of minutes. Finally, the show returns from commercial. The lead-in shows me sitting on the river bank. I have no shirt on, and you can see how emaciated I've become from the immense output on limited food. My face is drawn from days with no sleep. I look into the camera, look through the camera to Cheyenne, now sitting on the couch beside me. My voice is cracking and tears are running down my face as I muster all my courage and ask Cheyenne to marry me.

Cheyenne turns to face me. I get down on one knee. She says yes. My life has been better ever since. I love you, babe.

Our wedding day, on the beach in Malibu, with friends and family.

MY FATHER

My relationship with my father got better as we both got older. Part of it certainly had to do with my move out to California: I know my father respected what I was doing and what I was trying to accomplish on my own. Another big part of it, though, was the fact that my father softened as he aged. Part of this was physical: his health began to deteriorate dramatically and he became very dependent on others, my mother in particular. Agent Orange and whatever else he'd been exposed to during his long military career were exacting their terrible price: diabetes wreaked havoc on his system, neuropathy in his feet pained him constantly, and macular degeneration robbed him of his eyesight. Eventually, it would do even more. Meanwhile, decades of unacknowledged and untreated PTSD seemed to exact an equally heavy toll on his mind and heart. He became vulnerable in a way I never could have imagined... and it opened the door to moments with him that I will cherish for the rest of my life.

I happened to be visiting my parents in New York when my father started having pain in his throat when he swallowed. It had been a great visit: for the first time in my life, my dad had started asking my opinion on important issues. He wanted to know how my business was doing, wanted to know what I thought about the stock market. We joked around and had some laughs. I felt like he had finally started accepting me as a man: that I had finally graduated from Private First Class Petrelli. Still, I was surprised when he asked me if I would accompany him to his doctor's appointment. Such a small display of vulnerability, but it meant so much to me. I was there with him when the doctor told him that the tests had come back positive for throat cancer, there when the doctor told him he would have to go through radiation. I remember my dad taking it well. I remember him joking with the doctor, but I don't remember what about. All I remember is him saying, "Okay, when do we start?"

During the radiation treatments my dad lost his appetite, and when he did eat the pain in his throat made it difficult for him to swallow. Pretty soon his diet consisted mainly of Ensure. I hated seeing him drink that stuff. In an Italian family, food is everything: food is family, connection, *life*. This thin, milky goop was no substitute, no matter what the nutrition label said. I tried to convince him to at least use some of the supplements I recommended, but he wouldn't do it. He had so much faith in his physicians that he didn't want to do anything they hadn't specifically advised. His weight loss was dramatic. Soon, this powerful man—the man I'd been deathly afraid of as a child—started looking small and frail.

In addition to the pain in his throat, my dad started having trouble breathing. One day it got bad enough that my mom wanted to call an ambulance—but my father wouldn't let her. He forbid her from calling 911. Undeterred, my mom threw him in the car and rushed him to the hospital herself. On the ride there, he asked her to call me. When we spoke I could immediately tell things were not good. His voice was panicked and his breathing was labored. I booked a ticket as soon as I hung up with him, and the next day I was on a plane home to New York.

At the hospital, they told me the news. The cancer had metastasized, and had now spread to his lungs. His oxygen level had fallen dangerously low, and the doctors and nurses were having a hard time getting it to come back up. Additionally, since my last visit, he'd kept on losing weight. He was now shockingly thin. When neither condition improved after several days in the hospital, the doctor performed a tracheostomy and inserted a feeding tube. My dad lay in the bed with tubes connecting him to machines. It was hard to see, but we knew it was what he needed to stay alive. Still, I don't think any of us had any illusions about what was happening. The cancer was very advanced, now, and there was little the hospital staff could do.

We didn't want to leave his side even for a minute, so my mom, my sisters, and I took rotating shifts in his hospital room. The nursing staff was kind enough to put a recliner in the room so we could try to get some sleep, but I don't think any of us slept very much. You couldn't. The whole place was filled with death. It smelled of death. Everywhere you looked, people were suffering. After a couple of weeks we were all exhausted.

My dad was still in the hospital when I had to return to California for work. In all I believe he spent three months in the hospital. In that time I made several trips back to see him. Each time, I felt helpless. I wanted so much to just break him out of the hospital, to get him away from all that death and suffering and just take him home, but I knew I couldn't. I knew it wouldn't make any difference. I knew in my heart that he wasn't making it out alive.

Cheyenne and my dad at my sister Gina's wedding.

At that time *The Wild Rules* was set to begin broadcasting on ESPN. My dad wanted dearly to know the outcome. I told him he would have to stay around long enough to watch the whole series. In my head it was something, a small incentive to keep him fighting. He insisted, though, and I understood. He couldn't hold out until the end. He was exhausted and in pain. He'd fought his whole life. He'd fought in three wars and then returned home to fight the demons in his mind through long, nightmare-filled nights. He'd fought hard and he'd fought as long as he could, until his body gave out. Now, he was ready to rest.

We sat in his hospital room, just the two of us, and we talked. He told me he was afraid to die. He told me that he loved me and that he was proud of me. Then he directed me on what to do when he passed.

245

I let him know that I'd made it to the end of the show but finished second. I could see the disappointment in his eyes. Then I told him that I was going to ask Cheyenne to marry me at the end of the last episode. I told him that if we were blessed with children, I was going to name our first son after him. The disappointment disappeared from his expression and was replaced with the biggest smile I'd seen on his face in months. He lay there, overcome, with tears rolling down his cheeks.

I came back to California exhausted. I went to bed and fell into a deep sleep, and in that sleep I had the one and only dream I've ever had of my father. In my dream we were all together—my dad, my mom, my sisters Gina and Rosanne, and me—all of us sitting around the dinner table at home in New York. My mom had made pasta, one of my dad's favorite meals. My dad looked healthy and whole. He had a small scar on his neck from the tracheostomy, but that was all. He had put all his weight back on. The frail, sick man I'd left lying in that hospital bed was gone.

I couldn't believe it. I asked my dad how he'd made it out of the hospital, asked him what had happened. He looked at all of us, then, and he said that everything was going to be all right. He said that he was no longer in pain. He told us that he was so happy that he could now finally eat mom's food again. He smiled as he twirled a big forkful of spaghetti.

At that moment I was pulled from the dream by a noise in our bedroom. In half-sleep it took me a second to orient myself, to figure out what it was. It was our bedroom telephone ringing. I looked at the clock and saw that it was three in the morning. I picked up the phone. In my mind I was still nearly in the dream. I could still see my father so clearly, could see him happy and whole and finally free from pain.

My mother was on the other end of the line. She was crying. Between sobs she told me what I somehow already knew: my dad had just passed away.

I hung up the phone in a daze. For a second I didn't know what was real and what was a dream. Cheyenne was beside me, asking what had happened, and I couldn't even tell her. I couldn't process it all. I couldn't speak.

You can believe whatever you want to believe about this life, what it is, and what comes after. For myself, I have no other explanation than that my father's spirit spoke to me in my dream: that in those few brief moments between his passing and my mother's call, he came to me to comfort me, to let me know that his suffering was over and that he was no longer in pain, that he was happy again, and that it was all going to be okay. I am so grateful that we were able to have this one last conversation.

No one gives you a manual on how to be a parent. You have to use the tools you've picked up along the way. My dad's tools were mainly acquired from his career in the military and the relationship he had—or, more accurately, didn't have—with his own absentee father, and understandably these tools were sometimes lacking. This is not to say that we didn't have some good moments, because we did. And this is not to say that he wasn't a great provider for all of us, because he was. I never went without. I never went hungry. But for a long time, I also never felt that my dad was proud of me. So many times he made me feel so small and insignificant. This is not to say that my father didn't love me, because I know he did. As a kid, though, I couldn't see it. I didn't feel it. And I know now that this is one of the main reasons I went into acting. I did it to make him proud, to prove that I could do anything. I did it because he couldn't ignore me if I was on TV. But acting forced me to learn about myself, to open up the dark rooms in my mind and bring to light my own reasons for being the way I am. It made me unpack the character I'd played for so many years back in New York: the tough guy who was too strong to be pushed around by anybody, too strong to be hurt by anyone's disapproval or rejection. I'd carried a lot of shame about that guy and his behavior during those years, but unpacking him allowed me to understand and forgive him: allowed me to understand and forgive myself. And it made me understand, too, that I could not extend this compassion to myself without extending it to everyone: that in the end we are all confused and misguided children doing the best we can with the tools we have, with what we understand about life in the world and who we need to be in it, my father included. There are so many parts of his life that are a mystery to me: so many dark areas that must have been so very painful for him to endure and carry with him. That hurt became anger, that anger hurt his son, whose hurt also became anger. I believe in our last moments together we finally stopped that cycle. I believe in our last moments together we were finally able to drop the shame associated with it, and that in those last moments we were both set free. My father shaped my life in so many ways. He is part of the fabric of who I am. If you like anything about me, you are seeing part of him. The road of our relationship wasn't always smooth, but it's a road I'm glad we traveled together. I will be forever grateful.

CURTAIN CALL

Even with the incredible experiences I had on *The Wild Rules* and the other amazing experiences I'd had working in TV, the thrill of acting eventually wore off. The auditioning process became a grind, and even the work itself felt less rewarding. No matter the project or the pay, it never gave me the same level of satisfaction that I got from personal training—the same level of satisfaction I got from helping people pursue and achieve their goals. This all came to a head when I found myself in a casting room, waiting to audition for a commercial... and dreading it. I wasn't inspired. What had started off as a fun and exciting adventure had become *work*. I was no longer the kid who was willing to drive all over town delivering head shots and hanging out on studio back lots. All I could think of now was how I could be at home, spending this time with my family, instead of sitting in this room waiting to read. I had an amazing wife and a newborn son that I'd left to be here. I made a decision right then and there: no matter the outcome, this audition would be my last. I was done.

Like a lot of people, I'd come out to Hollywood with the dream of being a star, and—like a lot of people—I'd come out with some pretty naive notions about what that meant. We see these beautiful, successful, and larger-than-life celebrities on TV and in movies and we imagine that they never feel bad, never feel lonely, never feel slighted or forgotten or insignificant. We imagine that all of that success and adulation has somehow made them whole in a way we feel we're not, and are secretly worried we'll never be. For me, I'd thought that being successful in Hollywood would finally make me a somebody in my dad's eyes: that it would finally make me somebody significant in his world, somebody worthy of his attention. And guess what? It worked. Whatever success I found, my father's attention followed. My family watched entire episodes of shows they didn't even like just to see me give my few lines as "Police Officer #2." My dad would set the VCR to record it, and make copies to show his friends. But despite this, or maybe even because of it, out in California my view on the whole thing was changing. Bit by bit, my mindset evolved. Part of this had to do with the fact that, as a trainer to some pretty high level celebrities, I came to fully realize the thing that should have been obvious to me from the very start: famous people are just people, and the mirror shows you the same face whether you're living in a Beverly Hills mansion or a studio apartment in West Hollywood. Whatever hurt you're carrying around inside has to be healed inside, and no amount of fame or success or admiration layered on top is going to change it one bit. Another big part of it, though, had to do with the undertaking itself. There's nothing remotely easy about acting, and really doing that work requires you to go into some very dark rooms and make friends with what's inside. In all honesty, I wasn't prepared going in. I was more than willing to put in the work, but I didn't have any real concept of what that work would be. I got my first taste in my very first acting class. The teacher had me sit down across the table from a very attractive girl to read a scene. I'd always been a terrible reader, but for many years I'd been able to hide this flaw. Now, though, there was nowhere to hide. I was exposed. I fumbled my way through the first page, lost in a fog of self-consciousness. My hands were so clammy they were sticking to the paper. I felt beads of sweat running down my back.

Then the girl across the table said she had been seeing another guy behind my back, and that she was leaving me. Her words, the way she said them, pulled me in. I forgot all about my anxiety, forgot all about myself, and for the first time I was listening—*really listening*—to what she was saying. Emotions bubbled to the surface. What she was saying made me furious. I looked back down at the script, but my anger made it even harder for me to read what was written there. I became so frustrated that I began to cry. Tears rolled down my face. I couldn't wipe them away fast enough. We finished the scene and I sat there in this pool of emotion and sweat, still disconnected from the real world. Then the teacher spoke, and his voice rocketed me back into the present. I was so embarrassed. I couldn't remember the last time I'd cried, let alone in front of people, let alone in front of strangers. In the world I came from crying meant weakness, and I'd worked long and hard to bury or avoid any thought or emotion that threatened to break down my tough guy facade. But as the teacher continued to speak, my embarrassment faded, and a new feeling took its place. I felt calmer, lighter. I felt cleansed. I felt as though a small part of the emotion I'd been bottling up and carrying around with me for years had been released. It was the beginning of a journey that would last many years and would strip me down to my bare elements, a journey that would involve me unpacking myself and my past in a way I'd never thought was possible, and rebuilding an identity that was finally in harmony with my soul. Now though, sitting in that last audition, I knew in my heart that that journey had come to its end. I no longer needed to prove to my father or to anyone that I—the *real* me—mattered: I knew deep in my soul that I did. I saw it in my son's eyes when he looked at me, in my clients' smiles when they crushed a new PR, and heard it in Cheyenne's voice when she said my name. I'd set out thinking I knew what I wanted to achieve, and instead I'd achieved something even better. I was happy.

Turns out, though, that God wasn't sure I really meant it. Seems He thought it would be worth checking twice.

I'd called my agents the day after that audition to let them know my decision. I thanked them for everything they'd done for me, sent the whole office lunch, and moved on with my life. Two weeks later, though, I received a call, an email, and a text all within two minutes of each other from my (now, former) agency. In all my years of acting, this had *never* happened. I stepped out into the backyard and called in. It turned out a director who had hired me on several different projects in the past had contacted them and asked for me specifically. He was casting a part—a lead in a miniseries he was directing—that he thought I was perfect for, and he wanted to *offer* it to me. I wouldn't even have to audition.

The miniseries was slated to film in San Diego. It would mean several weeks of work, a decent chunk of change in my pocket, and a ton of exposure. And what was this miniseries about, you ask? Only the life of Jesus Christ. Talk about a test from above.

I'd worked my ass off for a long time: dropping off pictures, going to classes, sucking at audition after audition, playing bit parts and building my résumé, praying that someone would just give me a chance... and now here I was being *offered* a lead role in a miniseries.

I was surprised. I was flattered. For a moment I wished that this offer had come in three weeks earlier. It hadn't, though, and that made my decision easy. The decision had already been made. I told my former agent that I really appreciated the offer, but I was officially retired. I said goodbye and I hung up with them for the last time. I looked up at the bright blue sky on that beautiful southern California day and smiled.

"Pretty slick of you to test me this way, God," I said aloud. "I get it. If anyone ever said you don't have a sense of humor, they have no fucking idea what they're talking about." Then, still smiling, I stepped back inside to be with my wife and son. Seeing their faces, any hint of doubt I may have had disappeared. My life was here, with them. It's the easiest decision I've ever made.

Ultimately, I had a decent amount of success in show business. I had the opportunity to do so many things I'd once only dreamed about. I got paid to play war, chase people in police cars, pull damsels in distress out of burning buildings. I played security guards, cops, paramedics, tough guys, military officers, and mobsters. I wouldn't trade these experiences for anything. Once I decided to walk away, though, the training I was able to offer my clients went to the next level. With my increased and renewed focus, my understanding of what it took to really help people increased exponentially. Hollywood was a great part of my life, and I'm very proud of what I accomplished there, but there's no question in my mind: today, in the gym with my clients, I am right where I belong.

OUR BOYS

For better or for worse, our family is where we come from. It's the soil from which our children grow and, if we do our job as parents well, it's the wellspring to which they feel they can return when they're in need of support and rest. If we do our job as parents well, family is a source of strength for them, and bolsters them with the knowledge that they always have a home to which they can return.

Cheyenne and I struggled to become parents. After we were married, we tried unsuccessfully for over three years. We visited a number of doctors, who all told us the same thing: there was no medical reason we shouldn't be getting pregnant. So we kept trying. We tried everything. We tried acupuncture. We tried hot yoga. Cheyenne did handstands in our bedroom. We flew out to Sedona, Arizona to do energy work. Still, no baby. The only thing we got out there was sunburned.

It was a challenging time, and we were both exhausted. The general stress of our lives and careers was already taking its toll, and this inability to conceive added an extra layer of tension to our lives. The fear that we would never conceive—that this thing we so desperately wanted would be denied forever—was always lurking in the background, and was compounded by a nagging sense of guilt, a feeling that this was somehow all our fault. Finally, it was all too much. We sat down and had a heart-to-heart. For the first time we acknowledged the possibility that maybe we just weren't meant to have kids. Maybe that was what God wanted for us. Still, we weren't ready to give up just yet. We agreed we'd give it one last, all-out effort. We'd try IVF.

In vitro fertilization, or IVF, is an incredibly involved series of hormone treatments, extractions, and injections. Basically the mother's eggs are fertilized with the father's sperm in a laboratory and placed back into the mother's womb... but that description does little to convey how long and disruptive the entire process is to whatever you call "life as you know it."

Also—and not for nothing—*it's fucking expensive.*

The doctor we visited at the IVF clinic at UCLA explained all of this to us. He explained that there could be no guarantee of success, and that many couples had to try several times before they became pregnant. I sat there listening to him, running the numbers in my head... and somewhere south of the border someone got the memo. I have no other explanation than that the doctor's words literally scared my sperm into swimming. Cheyenne was pregnant the next week, no laboratory required. I sent that doctor a very nice "Thank You" card.

Nine months later, Cheyenne and I were blessed to welcome our first son into the world. We named him John Hunter Petrelli, in honor of my dad. My wife is so selfless that once Hunter was born she was willing to give up her acting career to become a full-time mom. And even though they say lightning doesn't strike in the same place twice, a few years later Cheyenne surprised us with the news: Hunter was going to be a big brother. Nine months later, our second son, Rocco, was born.

The boys couldn't ask for a better mother than Cheyenne. As for me, I try to be a better father every day. I try to teach them by example to strive always for growth and improvement, to strive always to be the best version of themselves. It is my dearest hope that they grow up to be good men: that they are compassionate and grateful for what they have, no matter their circumstances. It is my hope that, whatever they choose to do in life, if it is what they love, that they give everything they have to it, and hold nothing back. Above all, though, I want them to know that in the absence of all of this we will love them just the same and just as much, always and unconditionally.

COLD WATER

Not long after Hunter was born, I accompanied my very close friends Mark Harris and Gary Harris, Jr. and a couple other guys on a fishing trip up to Alaska. The Harris family had been fishing Alaska for years, and I knew there was a lot I could learn from this crew. It was destined to be an unforgettable trip... though in my case, it was memorable for reasons that no one who was there would ever begin to suspect.

The following story is something I've never told anyone: not the guys who were there in Alaska when it happened, not my wife, not my family. On one level it's a somewhat embarrassing story, and I'm a bit worried what they'll all think when they read it. On the other hand it was an important experience in my life, and one I wouldn't trade for anything. Plus, as you'll recall, I made a promise to be truthful, no matter what. I'll let you decide if I made the right call.

If you've read this far then you know that I'm—one—fairly extreme in pretty much everything I do, and—two—a bit of a fishing nut, willing to risk life and limb and that of at least one Grammy-award-winning recording artist for some quality time on the water. You'll understand what I mean, then, when I tell you that if you go on a fishing trip with me, you *will* tap out first. You'll be cashed out, ready for beers back at the dock, while I'll just be getting started... which is exactly what happened on this trip.

We've been out all day fishing on the open ocean, but after about ten hours everyone is ready to head back to shore... everyone, that is, except me. If you've ever been to Alaska in the summertime you know that it can stay light out for twenty or more hours a day, and even though it is now well past dinnertime the day is still bright and clear. There is simply no way on God's green earth that I'm going to pack it in and sit on shore downing beers and bullshitting when I could be out making the most of the experience. So after dinner I tell the guys that I'm heading back out, and that anyone who wants to join me is welcome to come along. No one is in a hurry to take me up on my offer, though: they've all had their fill. To their credit, they try to convince me that I shouldn't go either: in any outdoor activity, it's always safer to have another person with you in case something goes wrong... and eventually, something always goes wrong. I *should* shut up and listen to what the seasoned pros are telling me... I *should* take their advice… but I don't. Instead, I assure them that I won't go out too far. I tell them what they want to hear. Then, against their protests, I head back down to the dock. I'm going out to sea alone.

We'd rented a pair of boats for the week: a twenty-footer that could fit all of us and that we used to fish the open ocean, and a sixteen-foot aluminum boat with an outboard motor that we used for in-shore fishing and checking crab pots. With just me onboard the twenty-footer feels like overkill, so I throw my gear into the smaller aluminum boat, start the motor, cast off the lines, and take off. I'm in such a hurry to get going, though, that I forget a few things. Specifically and most importantly, I forget to grab my ship-to-shore radio. If anything goes wrong—if shit goes sideways out on the water—I'll have no way of communicating that information back to my buddies on shore, or to anyone else who can help. Once I realize this, it's obvious to me that the smart thing to do—the only thing to do—is to turn around and grab the radio… but I'll give you two guesses what I do next. I'm already going. The shore is falling away behind me, and turning around, tying off, and running up to the cabin, all feel like a hassle. I'll take my chances.

If anything happens out on the water, I'll be completely on my own.

As I clear the bay and pilot out onto the open water, the wind picks up dramatically. This light little boat, which was already skimming along high in the water and being tossed around plenty by the chop, becomes even harder to control. This is where I should slow down, where I should think about turning back… but I don't. I keep the engine throttled full, and through the steady whine of the engine and the heavy drumming of the waves against the bow, a thought comes like a whisper in my brain: at this speed, if I catch a wave broadside, or if I cut the tiller too hard to the left or right, if I do anything other than barrel on straight ahead, disaster is sure to follow.

Fear is a funny thing. The right amount in the right circumstances can make you fight like hell, can make you run farther and faster than you'd ever imagined yourself capable. The wrong amount at the wrong time, though, can shut down your central nervous system and leave you frozen in the fetal position, unable to lift a finger in your own defense. If you've read this far, you know that I've had a long and varied relationship with fear. For many, many years, fear—of my father and his criticism, of the bullies at school, of the seemingly insurmountable challenges I faced academically and what they meant for my future, *of the future itself and all the unknowns in it*—overwhelmed me. These fears pressed in on me and pinned me to the ground. They made me feel small and powerless. This made me angry, and as I grew this anger grew with me. Slowly, this anger remade me in its image. It became the fuel I used to push harder than other people in the gym, to train harder in martial arts. It became the fuel I used to face down challenges, real or imagined, in a never-ending quest to defeat any and everything that made me feel the fear I hated. It made me rush headlong into fights with people twice my size, but it also made me get on a plane to California to face down that big unknown and show it that it couldn't scare me. It spurred me into action, for good or ill.

The high of overcoming these things—things that had once filled me with fear and doubt, that had once seemed insurmountable—was intoxicating. It was like a drug and, as with any drug, the use itself perpetuated the need. I'd become addicted to the cycle. Where I'd once run from danger and fear, now I ran toward it, chasing the high that lay on the other side. If I started getting too comfortable, I went out looking for it: the next obstacle, the next challenge, the next hit of the juice that made me feel so alive... to an extent that bordered on an addict's obsession. Now, with the midnight sun burning overhead, the engine running full bore, the wind blowing hard against me, and the boat shuddering with the waves' impact beneath me, I hear that old familiar voice whispering: *Cut the tiller. Find out what happens. Or are you too chickenshit? Are you too afraid?*

And it pisses me off.

Still, I try to shut it out. I try not to listen. All my higher instincts are screaming at me that I know better, that nothing good can come of this. It's no use, though. I'm already anticipating the great exhilaration that is waiting for me on the other side of that dark door... the exhilaration that will be mine, if I'm only man enough to handle what I'll face once that door is opened. My addiction is calling loud now, and for one brief, fateful moment—the space and span of an impulse, a muscle twitch—I can't think of a good reason not to answer.

I do it. I cut the tiller arm full right. Before I can react, before I can even think, my ass is launched from the boat and I'm sailing through the air. The grip I have on the throttle is no match for the centripetal force. I'm tossed into the freezing Alaskan water like I've been shot out of a cannon. I plunge in face-first and come up gasping and sputtering.

The boat speeds on.

The war that has been raging between my ears immediately surrenders its primary position on my list of priorities. I've got much bigger things to worry about, now. If I don't play my cards right, I realize, I'm not getting out of this.

But, hell—I might not have any cards to play. I'm in open water in the freezing North Pacific. The boat is long gone, and the shore is a distant memory. I have a life vest on, but I'm also wearing hip waders... which I suddenly realize are filling with water. I barely have time to recognize what's happening before the weight of the water in the waders overcomes the buoyancy of the life vest, and I'm pulled under. Suddenly I look up through water, inches and then feet and still gaining, at the sky, still bright and blue above the surface. I kick and paddle with my arms as hard as I can, struggling against this impossible weight. Whatever oxygen is in my system is quickly consumed by the effort, and my lungs start screaming for air. I manage to break the surface, cough up saltwater and gasp for breath.

There's a sound that I know, a sound that's growing louder, but with everything that's happening I'm not processing what it is or what it means. By the time I turn to look it's almost too late. The boat's tiller arm is still where I left it, cranked all the way to the right, and the boat that I thought had kept speeding away from me has actually traveled in a broad circle. Now it's come back around to its origin point and is bearing down on me, on a direct collision course with my head. I take the fastest inhalation I've ever taken in my life and I push myself back beneath the surface. The hip waders are actually helping now, but with the buoyancy of the life vest I barely get deep enough in time. The churning motor blades pass inches above my upturned face. I kick as hard as I can and I rise up through the bubble trail and wake. I gasp for more air. The boat's chopping wake slaps me in the face and fills my mouth with saltwater. I choke and cough.

My heart and my thoughts are racing. I need to calm down, assess and make a plan. If I don't... well, we all know what will happen if I don't.

The boat is rocketing through its high-speed loop again. For the time being, the tiller is holding in its far-right position. It's affording me an opportunity, but I don't know for how long: at any moment an errant wave may jostle it out of position and send the boat careening back toward the shore... or further out to sea. On top of that, my arms are already growing tired from the effort of staying afloat and my fingers and hands are almost completely numb. Between the effort and the cold, I don't know how much longer I can stay afloat. If I'm going to survive, I'm going to have to maneuver myself far enough out of the boat's path to keep from being cut to shreds by the propeller but close enough that I have a chance to grab the side of the boat and pull myself aboard. And I'm going to have to act fast, because the boat is coming back around and is heading straight for me.

I kick as hard as I can and I get into position. I get ready. Here it comes, and—*FUCK!*—there it goes. I've moved too far and I'm a second too late. In an instant the boat is gone again, out of reach, speeding off.

I'm running out of time. Soon my fingers will be too numb to grasp any-

259

thing. But I know what I need to do, now. I know where I need to be, know when I need to make my grab, and with this knowledge comes calm and clarity. And that's when I remember: *I have a knife attached to my belt.* Quickly I pull it out of its sheath and I cut my right wader free. I feel my body lighten as the wader slips off and sinks into the depths. I have no time to cut the second one, though: the boat is already coming around again. I have to position myself perfectly if I'm going to have any chance at this… and God knows how many more chances I'll get.

Possibilities gather at the edge of my awareness: I could miss and be struck by the propeller, miss and be struck by the hull, be knocked unconscious and pulled down… Fish food. I push those thoughts from my mind and I focus. Here it comes. I go for it with everything I've got. My right hand slips off the wet aluminum gunwale… but my left hand finds a hold. I hang on for all I'm worth. The boat is still running at top speed and my legs are being pulled underneath, back toward the spinning prop. With the right wader gone there's nothing to protect my foot from the spinning blades but a wet sock… and the other wader, while protecting my left, is also acting like an aquatic drag chute. I'm not out of the woods yet.

I manage to reestablish a hold with my right hand, and with both arms working now I manage to pull myself halfway up onto the gunwale of the speeding boat. The weight and pull of the remaining wader is tremendous, but I am able to position myself well enough to free my right hand. I reach out as far as I can. From where I'm laying across the gunwale I can barely get my fingertips on the tiller. I summon what feels like every ounce of energy I have left in my entire being and I reach even farther… and I reach… and I reach the throttle, and I turn that fucking thing down.

The boat slows. The whine of the engine calms to a low drone. I reach for my knife—I honestly have no idea or memory of when or how, but I've put it back in its sheath—and I cut the other wader free. It slides off and sinks. I heave myself fully into the boat and I hit the kill switch. The engine goes silent. I flop onto my back in the bottom of the boat and I stare up at the Alaskan sky. The whole world seems to slow. For a moment there is no sound but my panting breaths, the call of some distant birds, the slap of the water against the hull, and the blood thrumming in my ears.

All of my senses feel heightened, sharpened, and everything is so vivid that it's almost surreal. The wind beating on the side of the boat, the trickle of water dripping off my hair and down my face, the pale moon looking down on me out of the blue sky: in that moment it all seems impossibly beautiful. The magnitude of what could have just happened settles into my soul. It's not fear that I feel in that moment: not the knot in my stomach and the anger that is always so quick to follow. Instead, a calm washes over me— and with it comes a certainty. Cheyenne and Hunter deserve better. My decisions now have far-reaching consequences for the people I care about the most. It's time to sober up, time to get clean. It's time to get this monster under control. I have to end it before it ends me.

A lot has happened in the last few years. I got married. I turned forty. I became a father. My own father passed away, and in his final weeks we became close in a way we'd never been before. We finally moved past the distance and hurt that had defined so much of our lives together. I realized that my big Hollywood dream, which had been central to my life for nearly twenty years, was over. I have more life behind me and less life ahead of me than I once had. Still, I'm older, wiser, and stronger mentally and spiritually than I've ever been. I'm not the same person who'd been pinned down by fear all those years ago. I'm not the same person, either, who didn't know what to do with all of his fear and anger except rush in and fight any and every one or thing that stood in front of him. I think of my father, and the never-ending battle he fought in his own heart and mind, and what it cost him. I think of the battle I've fought in my own heart and mind, and what it has cost and almost cost me... and in that moment I finally feel ready to let it go.

"Truce," I tell my anger.

"Truce," I tell my fear.

Then, feeling old and young and a thousand pounds lighter, feeling washed clean by the frigid Alaskan waters, I stand and I strip off my sopping clothes. It's not by choice: hypothermia can set in fast and kill you just as dead as any out-of-control propeller. It's eleven o'clock at night, the sun will be down soon, and I'm in an open boat and soaked to the bone. For a moment I stand there naked as a newborn baby. Then I get dressed. I didn't bring my radio, but I had the foresight to pack a change of clothes in my dry bag. I start the motor and I pilot the boat back to shore. From a ways out my buddies hear me coming, and they come down to the dock to greet me. Seeing them standing there, I make a decision: there's no way in hell I'm going to tell them what happened. They'd ask me to explain myself, explain my reasons, and I don't know if I can. I don't know that I fully understand it all myself. But this plan presents its own challenges: I'm wearing different clothes, my hair is still wet, and I can't hide my hair because the hat I was wearing when I left is floating somewhere out in the big blue sea. This is going to take some doing.

...or maybe not. All I can say is, thank God for whiskey. It turns out that my buddies had a few too many drinks to notice that anything is amiss with my wardrobe. Talk about a lesson learned: now I know how Cheyenne feels when she comes home from the hair salon and I don't realize that anything is different. They give me shit about going out, about not catching anything, and then we all walk back up to the cabin together.

Even though it's late by the time we head to bed, I can't sleep. I feel awake and excited. I feel ready to face the next chapter, whatever it is and whatever it brings. As luck would have it, I don't have to wait very long to find out.

Mark Harris and me in Alaska... Twenty-four hours later those hip waders were at the bottom of the ocean.

CEDARS-SINAI

In 2015 my family and I were returning from a trip home to New York. Rocco was one, and on the flight he started acting very fussy. Cheyenne and I initially chalked it up to lack of sleep and the stress of flying, but as the journey continued he got worse. Our flight from New York to Los Angeles was delayed several times, and by the time we got home—nearly fifteen hours later—Rocco had been crying for so long that his eyes were nearly swollen shut.

It was two in the morning when we finally arrived, and we were all fried. I was hopeful that a good night's sleep in his own bed was all Rocco needed to feel better. Cheyenne had the intuition that something more serious was going on, but I convinced her to put Rocco to bed and see how things looked in the morning. Against her better judgment, she agreed.

The outcome of *The Wild Rules* had taught me to trust my intuition, no matter the circumstances. I was about to learn that—especially when it came to our boys—I needed to trust Cheyenne's.

Rocco woke up the next morning looking much worse. His eyes were still swollen, and now he'd developed small sores on his lips and body. We rushed him to the doctor. The doctor examined him and prescribed some antibiotics. He wasn't exactly sure what was going on, he said, but he hoped the antibiotics would take care of it. He told us to come back if Rocco's condition didn't improve within twenty-four hours. We took Rocco home, hopeful that the antibiotics would take care of it.

Rocco's condition did not improve in the next twenty-four hours. Instead, it got steadily worse. By the next morning nearly eighty percent of Rocco's body was covered in lesions. Our poor little man had open sores from head to toe. His skin was literally splitting open. New lesions were appearing right before our eyes. He looked like a burn victim.

We immediately rushed back to the doctor's office. The doctor took one look at Rocco and called the hospital. He told them to make a room available in the ICU.

In the ICU Rocco was diagnosed with SSSS, Staphylococcal Scalded Skin Syndrome, a rare and potentially deadly form of staph infection that manifests itself in burn-like wounds. For the next five days, while friends stayed with Hunter at the house, Cheyenne and I stayed with Rocco around the clock in isolation in the ICU. Cheyenne and I took turns sleeping on the couch and tending to our son—though there was frustratingly little we could do. He couldn't lay on his back because there were open sores across his entire back. He couldn't lay face down because his chest and stomach were also covered in oozing sores. His cheeks, nose, and lips were all split wide open from the sores. Watching him in so much pain broke our hearts. The nurses ended up administering morphine to try to give him some relief. Still, I don't think there was a single moment in those five days when he wasn't in agony.

On our first day in the ICU I took a walk down to the hospital cafeteria to get Cheyenne and me something to eat, and was shocked by what I saw there. The food looked like it had been sitting under a heat lamp for weeks. There was no health-building nourishment to be found, just empty calories and processed foods. Even the green beans looked like soggy balls of Play-Doh. There was no way in hell I was going to put this crap in my body. Our son needed us. He needed us to be healthy and alert, needed us to be firing on all cylinders so that we could do whatever we could do for him to the absolute best of our abilities.

I looked around the cafeteria at the doctors and nurses all eating this garbage. These caregivers were working their asses off to literally save lives; meanwhile the institution that was supposed to support them offered them nothing in the way of healthy, energy-giving, health-sustaining fuel. These poor people were running on potato chips and chocolate bars, for fuck's sake! I looked around at the patients eating the same stuff. How the hell were these people supposed to heal on a *hospital-provided* diet of sugary punch and french fries? Just what the fuck was going on here?

I was pissed off. I was incensed. I was angry for all the people who had no choice but to eat this crap every day. Standing there in the cafeteria, I decided that—in our little corner of the healthcare battlefield, at least—I was going to do something about it.

Luckily for us, we lived only a couple of miles from the hospital. Food became part of our regular routine. Every day one of us would go home, prepare healthy meals, and bring them back to the hospital. It wasn't long before Rocco's doctors and nurses noticed, it wasn't long before they started asking what we were eating... and it wasn't long before they were taking us up on our offer to share. Growing up in an Italian household, you learn the golden rule: always bring extra food. It actually makes me uncomfortable to eat anything without offering food to everyone else first. In this case, my natural inclination and my mission were in absolute accord: I *wanted* the doctors and nurses who were treating our son to eat the healthy foods we'd prepared rather than the junk they could get in the cafeteria. If we couldn't help Rocco directly, then we would do everything in our power to support those who could. We weren't going to escape the ICU without their help. We needed them to succeed. So every day we prepared food or bought a bunch of healthy meals from a local restaurant, enough to feed the staff that was helping Rocco.

Finally, eventually, through the love, care, and incredible skill of Rocco's doctors and nurses and the grace of God, our dear son started to recover. After five days in the ICU, we were finally able to take our baby home.

The whole experience humbled me in ways I never could have imagined. Everyone likes to believe that they are strong and capable: that they can handle anything that comes their way. In so many ways, modern life and the technologies we take for granted contribute to this sense. Cars and planes stand waiting to whisk us off to any destination we choose. Stores and shopping centers put anything we could ever want at our fingertips. Online ordering makes each of us king-like in our ability to demand and have the object of our desire brought and laid at our doorstep. Within so much ability, it is a far rarer experience to feel utterly at the mercy of powers greater than ourselves. Sitting in the ICU and unable to help my son, I thought about the things I'd taken for granted. I thought about how many times I'd felt inconvenienced when I had to pull over to let an ambulance pass—this, while in the back of that ambulance someone was fighting for their life. I thought of all the times I'd driven past this very hospital without a second thought, totally wrapped up in whatever seemed so important at that moment, while behind a few walls and just a few floors up, other couples were anxiously waiting at the bedsides of other sick children. Sitting there in the ICU, I'd made a deal with God: *God, if You help these doctors and nurses bring Rocco back to good health, I will never take these things for granted again. I will remember, and I will pay it forward for the rest of my life.*

After we were finally able to return home, I thought long and hard about what it meant to hold up my end of that bargain. I thought about that hospital cafeteria, and about the doctors and nurses saving lives while running on empty. Despite the decades and decades of collective medical knowledge walking those hospital halls and running things on an institutional level, a blind spot seemed to exist around the role that nutrition and fitness had to play in everything from job performance to patient outcomes. A plan began to form: I would give complimentary motivational and educational speeches on nutrition and fitness to hospital caregivers. I would share what I knew in the hope that, in doing so, I could help them help others. And I would hold myself to an even higher standard, practicing what I preached in every aspect of my life. I had my mission: all I needed now was an audience.

I figured I'd start off small and work my way up... and then I chucked that idea. It was time for Sho'nuff to take the dance floor. Los Angeles is the home of Cedars-Sinai, one of the nation's biggest and most prestigious hospitals, and I set them dead in my sights.

It wasn't easy convincing the people at Cedars-Sinai to meet with me, but I refused to take "no" for an answer. I made dozens of phone calls, left dozens of messages. When that didn't work, I started showing up without an appointment. Day after day I walked through those big front doors, and day after day I was told to call first, to come back later, told that I needed an appointment or that the person I needed to meet with was out. It didn't matter. I smiled and thanked them and came back the next day. They were going to meet with me, and when they did we were going to do great things together. I knew it in my bones.

Finally, I got a call. Honestly, at that point, I wouldn't have been surprised if it had been a police detective letting me know that a restraining order had been issued against me, and I wasn't allowed within five hundred feet of the hospital campus... but it wasn't. Someone at Cedars-Sinai's Employee Wellness Department was willing to meet with me. That was all I needed. I knew in my heart that they would have no choice but to work with me, once they understood how passionate I was about helping.

I had explained my vision to one of my colleagues, Marc Monroe, and we'd begun to develop the idea together. I brought him along to the meeting. We'd decided ahead of time that if Cedars gave us ten minutes of their time, we would consider the meeting a success. An hour later we were still in the room. They weren't fully convinced, but they wanted to bring us back for a second meeting. Fine by me. I would take fifty meetings if I had to. The second meeting went even better than the first, and we were invited to give an hour-long presentation as part of what is called "The Grand Rounds," an ongoing series of events in which experts share perspectives, experience, and knowledge on matters related to healthcare delivery and patient experience.

Standing up on stage and waiting to be introduced, I was nervous. I'd faced down guns, survived in the wilderness, rappelled down sheer cliffs... but this was something else. I was set to tell a room full of medical professionals with decades if not centuries of experience between them that they were missing the boat when it came to health. Still, I knew that what I had to tell them was the truth. More than that, I knew that what I had to say could potentially affect the lives and healthcare outcomes of innumerable patients going forward. I thought of them as the moderator introduced us. I took the microphone and I began.

Once I started talking, any trace of doubt I had disappeared. And the longer I spoke the more certain I became: not just that I was doing the right thing for these doctors and nurses, but that I was doing the right thing for *me*. I had helped scores of clients over the years, and been nourished in my soul to see them grow and thrive as people. Here, though, I was helping dozens who would go on to help hundreds, if not thousands of patients— patients like Rocco, like my dad in his last months. The thought of that filled my heart. I knew, then, with absolute certainty that this was supposed to be part of my life.

After our first presentation, the people at Cedars asked if we'd be willing to return. We gladly accepted the invitation, and our presentation was even better-received the second time around. From there, my public speaking career has only grown. I've spoken to doctors, nurses, hospital administrators, home healthcare workers, and paramedics.... and I'm just getting started. I will continue to pay it forward. I made a promise, and I fully intend to keep it.

And Rocco? Today, thanks to the incredible work done by his caregivers in the ICU, he is a healthy and happy boy. He's his own unique blend of fearless maniac and funny guy. And he's a huge fan of classic rock. Any of his caregivers who happen to read this will remember him as the one-year-old who demanded that Queen's "We Will Rock You" be played on a nearly continuous loop for the duration of his ICU stay. Seriously. The doctors were laughing their asses off. These days our little D. Rock still loves Queen, but he's also branched out into Aerosmith, Bon Jovi, and old-school East Coast rap. He and Hunter are the center of my world. For all the many incredible experiences I've had, there is no moment that brings me greater joy than the moment I arrive home every day. The moment when I place my key in the front door and I hear the sound of their feet running to meet me, the moment they scream "Daddy!" and jump into my arms. See this and you are seeing me at my happiest. I thank God every day that He has given us these moments to share… and I will never forget those five days in the ICU, when moments like these felt far from guaranteed.

MOVING ON

When I arrived in Southern California in 1993, I was almost overwhelmed. After rural Upstate New York, Southern California seemed like a magical land of natural beauty and opportunity. For a long time, I was very happy living there. I bought a house, built a business, and raised kids. Unfortunately, however, much of what made Southern California such a special place started to erode before our eyes somewhere around 2017. The homeless population exploded seemingly overnight, and property crimes skyrocketed. Cheyenne and I no longer felt safe raising our boys there. Twice we had our car windows smashed and everything inside stolen while the cars were parked in our own driveway. And when I say everything, I mean everything: they even took my boxing and Jiu-Jitsu gear. Somewhere in LA there is a criminal walking around in my Jiu-Jitsu gi.

There is no easy solution to the homeless situation, and I have tremendous sympathy for those who end up living under those circumstances. I cannot imagine how hard it must be to live on the street. Nor is there an easy solution to the public health crisis of mental illness that so profoundly contributes to this issue. I don't judge these people for their circumstances. However, I have to know that my wife and kids are safe. I have to feel confident, when we leave the house in the morning, that everything will be all right in our absence. For as much as we loved our home, Southern California was losing its ability to provide these basic assurances. We were left with no choice. So, in 2018, we packed up and headed east to the fabled weirdness of Austin, Texas.

Austin offered us a lot to love, compared to Los Angeles. There's easy access to the outdoors, clean air, a lot less traffic, and a significantly lower crime rate. I hadn't fully realized it, but LA was weighing on me: I'd been living on perpetual high alert, always on the lookout for the next potentially dangerous situation. Just being out of the city, I breathed easier.

Not that I had much time to enjoy it, at first: during this period I was still on tour with Sebastian, and I was traveling in excess of a hundred flights a year. State after state and city after city, time was flying by, and our boys were growing up fast. They were making new friends, starting at new schools, playing sports on new teams, and I was missing it. I was fully committed to my work with Sebastian, but once that commitment was fulfilled I eagerly returned home. I had a new life to build in Austin... and a new and exciting challenge to face.

Back in Los Angeles, I had a thriving personal training business. I was booked solid week after week, with new referral clients coming in all the time. I was constantly having to turn potential clients away because I just didn't have any time for them in my schedule. In Austin, I had none of that. I was starting over again from zero. After more than twenty-five years in the business, I had to reestablish my name. It was humbling... but it was also invigorating. I put my ego aside and put all of my focus on my clients. I started working out of a country club in my neighborhood, and quickly gained traction with the local clientele. Twenty-five years' worth of experience and knowledge went into helping them achieve their goals: from the eighty-two-year-old grandmother who wanted to be able to go dancing with her husband to the aspiring high school soccer player who needed more acceleration and endurance to make the team. I knew that once these people started seeing results, they would become my biggest advertisers... and they did. A couple of months in, and I was the guy to see for training. From there it continued to grow: soon, out of the hundreds of clubs owned by the corporation I worked for, I was on top of the national leaderboard.

Even in recent years, with all the challenges of the pandemic, my personal training business has thrived. It has been an incredible and incredibly rewarding experience, and I can only say "Thank You" to our Austin community for their support and their welcome. Even after so many years in Los Angeles, I can say without hesitation that Austin truly feels like home.

GBS

The sun was shining, my business was thriving, and we were all healthy. Then, in the fall of 2021, our whole family contracted COVID.

Our two boys picked it up at school. Mild symptoms, almost no down time. It barely registered a blip on the radar for them. Then Cheyenne and I tested positive. Cheyenne came through it okay. Me? Not so much.

I know I made things worse by not resting enough. I thought I didn't have to. I felt like I could handle it. I was healthy and strong, and besides: our kids had barely had any symptoms. I was so certain I wouldn't be affected by COVID, in fact, that as soon as I tested positive I immediately went and hopped on the Assault Bike for thirty minutes of intense intervals, and then cranked out a full body workout right after. I even posted my workout on Instagram. I thought I was Superman. Life was about to teach me that I was very, very wrong.

Shortly after I recovered from COVID, shit started to go sideways. It began with my feet. Suddenly, for no apparent reason, they went numb. I chalked it up to a pinched nerve. I figured it would resolve itself as the inflammation subsided. It didn't. Instead, it got worse. The numbness was accompanied by an endless dull pain, like frostbite. I would lay in bed at night unable to sleep from the pain. It started getting so bad that I would get up at two in the morning and take ice baths. It was the only thing that seemed to help.

Then, overnight, my vision became blurry. One morning I woke up and I wasn't able to read my computer. Again, I wrote it off. I figured it was just fatigue, that my being unable to sleep from the pain in my feet was making my eyes tired. But the next symptom that came along wasn't so easy to dismiss. I had a tremendous urge to pee... and I couldn't. It was like my "clogged filter" issue following my time on *The Wild Rules*, only this time there'd been nothing to precipitate it. I fessed up to Cheyenne, and she put her foot down. She took me to the emergency room.

Ever wonder where the band in *This Is Spinal Tap* got their name? On that trip to the ER I was lucky enough to find out. The doctor inserted a special needle into my spinal canal, withdrew some cerebrospinal fluid, and tested it for what he already suspected he'd find: high protein levels. I had Guillain-Barre Syndrome, a rare autoimmune and neurological disorder. My immune system was malfunctioning, sending antibodies to attack my nerve endings. No one knows what causes Guillain-Barre Syndrome, though it usually appears after a respiratory or digestive tract infection... like my recent bout with COVID. And, unlike my recent bout with COVID, this time I would have no illusions about powering through. They placed me in the ICU and there, more or less overnight, I became weak as a baby. I couldn't walk on my own. Gone was the guy who could lift five hundred pounds. I was as close to being paralyzed as you can be without actually being paralyzed. I struggled to hold up my own head. I couldn't open a water bottle. And the scariest thing was, there was no guarantee it would stop there: if the deterioration of motor control progressed to my respiratory muscles, the doctors told me, they would need to put me on a ventilator. I'd willed myself through countless repetitions in my lifetime—now I was facing the possibility that I would be unable to do the one rep that counts most: the simple, unconscious respiratory muscle contraction that makes life possible. I was humbled beyond belief.

In the ICU, I keep getting weaker. The combination of the GBS attacking my nerves, lack of sleep, and my inability to swallow solid foods are all starting to get the better of me. I'm exhausted. On my third day, when my symptoms still haven't improved, the doctors put me on a transfusion of intravenous immunoglobulin, or IVIG, to combat the GBS and try to stop it before it can shut down my heart and lungs. During the treatment, I completely lose control of my bladder. I'm embarrassed to say that I actually piss myself as I lay in bed, waiting for the nurse to help me get up to use the bathroom. Not my proudest moment, but it soon proves to be the least of my worries. Suddenly, I start having pain in the left side of my chest. It's hard to breathe without pain. The doctors hope that it's just a side effect of the IVIG and not the GBS attacking my heart and lungs, they tell me, but they need to send me down for an extensive CT scan to be sure.

They load me into a wheelchair and they wheel me down to the CT scan. As they help me up from the wheelchair, I go into full orthostatic hypotension—that sudden decrease in blood pressure that can happen when you stand up too fast from sitting or lying down, and that can make you dizzy or even cause you to black out. I'd blacked out from orthostatic hypotension three times since my bout with GBS started, so I know what's happening. I do my best to give the nurse a heads-up, but by then it's too late. All I remember is collapsing. I wake up with three nurses and a doctor pulling me up off the floor. Once I regain consciousness, I have this sudden urge to urinate. I'm in no condition to go to the bathroom on my own, though, so the nurse brings me a bedpan. I've been using one of those for days, and I'm too exhausted to be self-conscious. With everyone standing around, I try my best to relieve myself. It's no use. Slowly, two tiny drops of urine drip out of my penis. I have to sit in the wheelchair the whole time. I'm too weak to even stand. The head nurse on that night—a very fit, very stern, thirty-year-old man in Texas by way of Botswana—orders my nurse to schedule a catheter for me once the CT scan is complete. I plead with him to give me another shot before they catheter me. He isn't having it, though. I ask him if we can postpone the hour-long CT scan until I regain some strength. He isn't having that, either. At that moment, I do not like him. Over the coming days I have the chance to spend some time with him, to discover how much we have in common, and to develop a deep respect and appreciation for his knowledge and his firm stance on my medical treatment... but right now I feel so weak, so emasculated, and I just want him to leave me alone. I can't stand on my own, I can't pee on my own, and the last thing I want is a tube going up my dork. Of course I'm in no position to tell him or anybody else anything. Right now, he's the boss. The CT scan is going to proceed as scheduled. So is the catheterization. Luckily, as the doctors hoped, the scan shows that the chest pains are a false alarm. I'm wheeled back to the ICU, where the catheter goes in... and where I pass out from sheer exhaustion.

Some time later, the sound of a consistent low beep wakes me. I open my eyes. Through blurry vision I see wires extending out of the left sleeve of my yellow hospital gown. The wires snake their way around the metal rails of the bed and up to a monitor. I do my best to focus on the monitor, to read what it says, but it's all so blurry. I try to sit up so I can get a closer look, but I can't. It feels like I'm frozen in place, like someone has pulled the parking brake on my body. I'm even weaker than I was when they wheeled me back in. Now even moving my head a few inches seems impossible. At that moment I feel something warm running down the side of my right leg, and I realize what it is: a catheter line full of urine trailing from inside my hospital gown connects me to a plastic bag dangling from the side of my bed. I'm filled with shame.

My pity party is brought to an abrupt halt by a knock on the window leading out onto the hall. I shift my gaze over and I see the door swinging open. A very petite Hispanic doctor wearing scrubs, an N-95 mask, and oversized goggles comes in.

"Good morning, Mr. Petrelli," she says. "I'm your neurologist, Dr. Santiago. I hope you were able to get some rest last night." She walks over to my bedside. "I'm here to check your vitals and see if your body is responding positively to the transfusions." She takes hold of my hand. "Go ahead and squeeze my fingers," she says.

I muster up all the strength I have, but my tank is empty. It takes everything I've got just to hold the grip.

'Okay, Mr. Petrelli," she says, "let's try your lower extremities." She puts her hand on my right shin. "Can you push your leg against my hand?"

I don't even have the strength to tell her that I'm already trying my best to do just that.

For the next several days I lay in my hospital bed, trying to make sense of what is happening to me. For all of my adult life I've been able to rely on my strength and physicality. I've never even had to think about it: I've always known it was there. Now, suddenly, all of that is gone. GBS has weakened me to the point that I feel literally paralyzed. I feel like my entire world has been turned upside down.

As I lay there, though, it occurs to me again that this isn't the first time I've felt paralyzed. This isn't the first time I've felt pinned down, too weak to fight the forces holding me in a situation that I want desperately to escape. As I've said, in my youth I often felt this way: trapped by my circumstances, the victim of things beyond my control. Laying in my hospital bed in the ICU, I see clearly how my journey out of that paralysis began the day I started to truly believe that I could do more: that somewhere out ahead of me was a future John Petrelli who lived beyond the limitations of my present. I realize that now, as then, the battle will be fought—will be won or lost—in my mind and in my spirit, and realizing this, I make a decision. I make a promise to myself and to my family and to all of the doctors and nurses working so hard to help me get better that I will never once—not even for a fraction of a second—let my mentality slip into a negative place. I know they're all doing their part: now it's on me to do my part, even if for the moment that only means keeping my head in the fight. I know that if I give up and start feeling sorry for myself I'll be of no help to myself or to anyone. So instead, I choose to focus on being grateful. I choose to focus on my love for my family, my friends, and my life. I choose to focus on my gratitude for all the doctors and nurses who are working so hard to help me get better. I think about the future me, the one who's going to walk out of this hospital. I think about all of the challenges I've faced in my life, and about what each of them has taught me, and about how each one has helped me prepare for this exact moment. I think about how, together, they've given me all the tools I need to escape the ICU.

I talk to Cheyenne, and together we make a plan to fight this thing on every front. While the amazing doctors and nurses throw everything Western medicine has at it, we're going to do our part. Like with Rocco, Cheyenne brings in healthy, nourishing foods from home. I make sure my room is filled with positive vibrations. My favorite Ziggy and Bob Marley songs play on a continuous loop. I understand, then, Rocco's demand for Queen: sometimes the right tune feels like the only thing that can pull you through. And I meditate. I meditate a lot. I lay in bed and I visualize my antibodies. I visualize them attacking my nerves. It may sound crazy to you, but I start politely asking them to stop. I tell them that they don't need to be on the attack anymore, and I meditate. Then I tell them, firmly, to stop, and I meditate. Then I command them to stop, and I meditate. I know that, even if this is having no effect on my recovery, it's keeping my mind busy. It's keeping me engaged and fighting. It's filling all of the empty time and space where fear and doubt could creep in with belief and hope.

Slowly, I start to get better. Around day five I'm able to get off pureed foods. Up until then Cheyenne had been bringing me organic soups that she made at home; they were certainly delicious, but I'd be lying if I said I wasn't very glad to sink my teeth into something solid. My strength starts to return. After seven days in the ICU, I'm finally discharged to a general hospital bed. Not long after that, I'm discharged from the hospital. I walked into the hospital on my own and I walk out on my own. I need a walker to do it, but I fucking do it.

I start physical therapy immediately. I'm there every day, Monday through Friday. With Cheyenne's help, I do more rehab at home on Saturdays and Sundays. Seven days a week, we go after it. I've made it this far, and I'm not letting up. The doctors have told me what they expect my rate of recovery to be, and I intend to smash those projections and leave them in the dust. In a week's time I graduate from the walker to a cane. Two weeks earlier I'd been nearly paralyzed in a hospital bed—now I'm walking with a simple cane. Still, I'm not even close to satisfied. I keep pushing. While everyone else is asleep I sneak down into the living room and practice walking on my own, keeping close to the couch in case I fall... which I do plenty of times. But so what? I get back up and I try again. All of these efforts put me way ahead of schedule for recovery. By my second week out of the hospital, I'm able to kiss the cane goodbye.

As I lay there in that hospital bed, unable to get up and move on my own, I'd made a promise to myself. I promised myself that, no matter what happened, I would take Guillain-Barre as a teacher, and try to understand and be grateful for its lesson. And, crazy as it might sound, this turns out to be an easy promise to keep. In the weeks following my release from the hospital the lesson becomes very clear, and the gratitude follows easily. My family is and always has been at the center of my thoughts: they are the most important thing in my life, bar none. However, Guillain-Barre Syndrome made me realize that in the weeks and months and maybe even years leading up to my illness, I had been hyper-focused on work, and had been taking them for granted. Some of the most important things in my life—my sons' laughter, Cheyenne's beautiful smile—I'd taken for granted. Guillain-Barre reminded me of something I knew but had allowed myself to forget or ignore: that these things are not guaranteed, that life, time, and the moments we cherish with the ones we love are fragile and fleeting, and that we should be present and grateful every day for each and every one.

IT'S UP TO YOU

Over the past nearly thirty years, I've had the privilege of helping many, many people. My goal—my challenge—now is to help many, many more... and that starts with you.

The good news is: You've already done the homework. You've read this book. You've seen that it's possible to come from simple means and still succeed. That it's possible to come from a small town and have big dreams. That it's okay to have faults, as long as you don't let them define who you are—or who you're going to be. That you can screw up royally and still make good. Now it's up to you how—and whether—you want to apply what I've told you in these pages to your own life.

I don't know what would have happened if I'd grown up in a "perfect household." For me, the water had to boil to get me out of the bathtub. I'm grateful that it did—but that doesn't mean it has to for you. You don't have to be at your wits' end—don't have to hit your personal rock bottom—before you take action. You can do it right now. Whatever it is you want, whatever it is you're dreaming of, it's yours for the taking. That doesn't mean it won't be hard. It doesn't mean that you won't hit every obstacle imaginable along the way. It doesn't mean you won't experience failure. It's very likely that you'll fail many, many times. I certainly have. These failures taught me so much. They've made me a better trainer, a better husband, a better father, and a better man than I would have otherwise been, and for that reason I wouldn't trade them for anything.

Nor does it mean that it won't be scary. I can guarantee you that no matter who you are or what you're chasing, you will have moments where you doubt yourself—moments when fear rears its ugly head and threatens to swallow you whole. It certainly did for me. As you now know, for a long time my fear held me back. It imprisoned me and filled me with anger—anger that I pointed at everything except the fear itself. For a long time I thought I wasn't brave enough to face it down. I didn't know then what I understand now: that bravery—courage—is not the absence of fear; it is simply the act of deciding that what you want is much more important to you than your fear could ever be. Yes, I've been afraid. Yes, I've been angry, and yes, I've been violent. I rode that merry-go-round for a long time. It was only when I started looking out—when I started focusing on what I wanted to achieve, on growth and potential and the life I wanted—that I finally got off. Fear can be a powerful motivator, and anger can be a powerful tool, but I'm telling you because I know: love and inspiration, connection and compassion for each other and ourselves, is so much more powerful than fear and anger could ever be. It's a lightbulb against the sun. It ain't even close.

So risk it. Risk failure. Risk making a fool of yourself. Life is an opportunity, and seizing it will always mean leaving the comfortable and the familiar and venturing out into the unknown. I took a risk leaving my family and hopping on a plane to start a new life in California. I took a risk stepping out onto that dance floor and giving Sho'nuff everything I had. If I hadn't been willing to risk making a fool of myself, I would have missed out on the best thing that ever happened to me.

So do it. Take that leap of faith. You have to take a risk if you want to move ahead. And it's true that you'll have to hustle, have to grind, have to work your ass off. But I'm telling you because I know: if you're willing to put in the work, you too can make your dreams come true.

So dream, my friends. Dream big, dream loud, dream crazy, and then get to work. Surround yourself with people who believe in you, who want you to succeed, and who will always tell you the truth. Pay it forward when and how you can. And most importantly, be grateful. No matter where you are or what's happening in your life, if the sun can shine on your face then you're not in your grave, so be grateful.

I don't know how this story ends, but I'm excited to see what happens next. I'm excited to see what you do. I think you'll do incredible things. I truly believe you can. I hope you believe it, too. I wrote this book in part to tell you. What you do with it is now all up to you.

I will leave you with a prayer. It's a prayer that I started crafting in my mind during some of my darkest times. It is the first thing I've verbalized every day of my life for many, many years now:

I thank You, God, for another day. I am nothing without You. Please continue to send me Your love. Fill my life with Your light and Your happiness and allow me to use the talents You have given me at birth—including my passion, persistence, persuasion, creativity, love, compassion, understanding, sense of humor, and playfulness—to bring out the greatness that lies inside everyone by showing them the greatness that is us.

ABOUT
the
AUTHORS

JOHN PETRELLI is a certified professional fitness trainer. For nearly thirty years he has used his signature style of motivation and his unique program of physical exercise, nutrition, and martial arts training to positively impact the lives of countless people, from Grammy Award-winning recording artists to corporate executives to world-class athletes to film celebrities to busy moms and dads alike. He and his work have been featured in *Men's Health*, *Men's Fitness*, *Muscle & Fitness*, *GQ*, and *Vogue*, and shown on national television networks including NBC, CBS, The USA Network, and FOX TV. He continues to train clients out of Five Star Fitness in Austin, Texas, where he lives with his wife, Cheyenne, and their sons Hunter and Rocco. More information about John and the training he offers is available online at www.JohnPetrelli.com.

SCOTT BURR is a graduate of the creative writing program at the Colorado College. He is the author of the novels *Bummed Out City* and *We*

Will Rid the World of You, the short story collection *We Drove Out to the Desert*, the strength training manuals *Get a Grip* and *Suspend Your Disbelief*, and the martial arts, mindset, and health and fitness essay collection *Superhero Simplified*. He is the co-author of Richard Bresler's memoir of his over 40 years' involvement with Gracie Jiu-Jitsu and the Gracie family *Worth Defending: How Gracie Jiu-Jitsu Saved My Life*, which was an Amazon #1 New Release and an Amazon #1 Bestseller, and the co-author of *Blood in the Water: America's Assault on Innovation*, Kip Azzoni Doyle's genre-defying memoir / exposé about corruption in the US Patent System, which was also an Amazon #1 New Release and an Amazon Top-10 Bestseller. He was the editor and designer for Robert Drysdale's #1 Bestselling book *Opening Closed Guard: The Origins of Jiu-Jitsu in Brazil: The Story Behind the Film*. His work has appeared in *Metonym*, *Mildred*, the *Decades Review*, and elsewhere. He lives in Northeast Ohio. Connect with Scott online at www.ScottBurrAuthor.com.